QuickBooks®
Online

2025 Edition

by David H. Ringstrom, CPA

QuickBooks® Online For Dummies®, 2025 Edition

Published by: **John Wiley & Sons, Inc.**, 111 River Street, Hoboken, NJ 07030-5774, www.wiley.com

For general information on our other products and services, please contact our Customer Care Department within the U.S. at 877-762-2974, outside the U.S. at 317-572-3993, or fax 317-572-4002. For technical support, please visit https://hub.wiley.com/community/support/dummies.

Wiley publishes in a variety of print and electronic formats and by print-on-demand. Some material included with standard print versions of this book may not be included in e-books or in print-on-demand. If this book refers to media that is not included in the version you purchased, you may download this material at http://booksupport.wiley.com. For more information about Wiley products, visit www.wiley.com.

Library of Congress Control Number is available from the publisher.

ISBN 978-1-394-28202-9 (pbk); ISBN 978-1-394-28204-3 (ebk); ISBN 978-1-394-28203-6 (ebk)

SKY10087166_100824

Contents at a Glance

Table of Contents

Introduction

Welcome to *QuickBooks Online 2025 For Dummies*! If you're new to QuickBooks, my goal in this book is to help you get up and running quickly and then carry out tasks in the most efficient way possible. QuickBooks Online is known as *cloud-based accounting software*, whereas QuickBooks Desktop is typically installed locally on your computer. I only discuss QuickBooks Online in this book, so if you need help with QuickBooks Desktop, please refer to Stephen L. Nelson's *QuickBooks All-in-One For Dummies 2025* (John Wiley & Sons, Inc.).

TIP

QuickBooks Online has good intentions and is designed in a way that tries to take the pain out of accounting, but it sometimes falls short. I do my best to anticipate those areas for you and offer explanations, but if you have a question that this book doesn't answer, please feel free to email me at ask@davidringstrom.com.

Some of the tasks in QuickBooks are easy. For instance, you can jump-start entering transactions in QuickBooks by emailing receipts to a unique address for your company. You can automate other tasks after you complete an initial setup process, such as downloading activity from your bank accounts and credit cards into your accounting records. Other tasks, such as entering journal entries, may appear to be difficult, particularly if you don't have much of an accounting background, but I guide you through just about everything you may want to do inside QuickBooks (and sometimes outside of QuickBooks with Microsoft Excel).

About QuickBooks Online

In the past, QuickBooks Online was a fairly static platform, with new features being rolled out incrementally. We are now in uncharted waters. As I wrote this book, I noticed that QuickBooks Online features would sometimes appear and then disappear, only to reappear again, all without notice. My editors and I have done our best to describe what has in some cases been a moving target.

WARNING

Because updates occur so frequently in QuickBooks, by the time this book is published, some features and screens may have changed. (On second thought, make that *will* have changed.)

Then there's the matter of the six subscription levels:

>> **Solopreneur** ($25/month, $300/year): Previously known as QuickBooks Online Self-Employed, this is best suited to users who are operating a side business. This book has some feature overlap, but I don't cover QuickBooks Online Solopreneur specifically.

>> **Simple Start** ($35/month, $420/year): This most basic business version of QuickBooks has the lowest monthly cost, includes 59 reports, now offers the ability to enter bills to be paid later, and allows one full access and two accountant users.

>> **Essentials** ($65/month, $780/year): This version is a step up in price and functionality. The biggest differences are multiple currencies, time tracking, as well as three full access and two accountant users, and "track time only" users. QuickBooks' online help shows that Essentials users should be able to access up to 82 different reports; however, I only counted 63. Further, seven bill-related reports are inexplicably currently available to Simple Start users but not to Essentials users.

>> **Plus** ($99/month, $1,188/year): This version represents another step up in price but also a much greater depth of functionality, including inventory, budgeting, project tracking, customizable access for up to five business and two accountant users, unlimited "track time only" users, as well as unlimited "view company reports" users who can access up to 90 reports, versus the 120 reports listed in QuickBooks' online help documentation.

>> **Advanced** ($235/month, $2,820/year): This high-end version of QuickBooks offers built-in business analytics with Microsoft Excel via Spreadsheet Sync, employee expense tracking, customizable user roles for up to 25 business users, unlimited "reports only" users, a custom report writer, workflow automation, and data restoration. Such users are supposed to have access to all 120 reports purported available to Plus users, but by my count only 91 reports are actually available.

TIP

Opting for an annual subscription, instead of a monthly one, reduces your subscription fees by 10 percent.

>> **Accountant** (free for members of the QuickBooks Pro Advisor program, which is also free at https://quickbooks.intuit.com/accountants/proadvisor/): This version of QuickBooks offers one free Advanced subscription for accountants and bookkeepers to manage their own books. It also offers practice management features and allows seamless access to clients' QuickBooks companies.

As you can see, much of QuickBooks' best features are stratified into the higher price points. Accordingly, for this edition of the book I've gone with a "choose your adventure" approach for organizing the material. Every QuickBooks Online user will benefit from reading Part 1 of this book, which is where I cover all the core functionality that's available in QuickBooks versions from Simple Start through Advanced. Whether you keep reading is predicated upon your current subscription level or curiosity of what you would gain by opting for a higher subscription level.

About This Book

Before diving in, I have to get a few technical conventions out of the way:

>> Text that you're meant to type as it appears in the book is **bold**. The exception is when you're working through a list of steps. Because each step is bold, the text to type is *not* bold.

>> Web addresses and programming code appear in monofont. If you're reading a digital version of this book on a device connected to the Internet, note that you can tap or click a web address to visit that website, like this: www.dummies.com.

>> Everyone can use QuickBooks Online in a web browser or a mobile app. Intuit recommends any of the following browsers for desktop use:

- Google Chrome version 78 or higher
- Mozilla Firefox version 76 or higher
- Microsoft Edge version 79 or higher
- Safari version 12 or higher on your desktop computer

Mobile devices need to be running iOS 11.1 or higher or Android Nougat 7.1.1 or higher. Advanced and Accountant subscribers can download and install a desktop app that offers functionality unavailable within a web browser.

>> When I discuss a command to choose, I separate the elements of the sequence with a command arrow that looks like this: ⇨. For example, when you see Sales ⇨ Invoices, that command means that you should click Sales in the left bar and then click Invoices in the drop-down menu that appears.

Foolish Assumptions

I had to assume some things about you to write this book, so here are the educated guesses I made:

>> You know that you need to manage a set of accounting records for one or more businesses, and you might even have some sort of setup in place already. I *did not* assume that you know how to do all those things on a computer.

>> You may want to analyze some of your accounting data outside QuickBooks, which is why I include chapters on using Microsoft Excel. Some of that information translates to Google Sheets as well.

>> You have a personal computer running Windows 10 or 11 (I wrote this book in Windows 10) or a Mac running macOS 10.11 or later.

>> You have a copy of Microsoft Excel on your computer, or you plan to use Google Sheets at https://sheets.google.com.

Icons Used in This Book

Throughout the book, I use icons to draw your attention to various concepts that I want to make sure that you don't skip over in the main part of the text. Sometimes I share information to help you save time; in other cases, the goal is to keep your accounting records safe.

TIP

This icon points out time-saving tricks or quirks that you may encounter in QuickBooks.

REMEMBER

This icon points out tricky aspects of QuickBooks that you should keep in mind.

WARNING

This product can burn your eyes. Oh, sorry. Wrong type of warning! Your eyes are safe in this book. But do pay careful attention to warnings that you encounter so that you can avoid problems that could wreak havoc in your accounting records or more often simply cause you frustration.

TECHNICAL
STUFF

At some points, I may include some geeky stuff about QuickBooks, your web browser, or your computer. You can safely skip over the technical stuff if that's not your cup of tea.

Where to Go from Here

You can start where ever makes sense to you! Here's how the book is broken down:

» Part 1, "Core Functionality," describes the core functionality available to all QuickBooks users.

» Part 2, "QuickBooks Online Essentials Features," covers additional features that upgrading to an Essentials subscription adds, such as multicurrency functionality, product bundles, time tracking, applying billable time to invoices, and billable expenses to expense entries.

» Part 3, "QuickBooks Online Plus Features," describes capabilities that a Plus subscription adds, including inventory management, purchase orders, using classes and locations, tracking profitability by project, and creating budgets.

» Part 4, "QuickBooks Online Advanced Features," covers the additional features that an Advanced subscription provides, such as a desktop app, backups, customizable security, and enhanced reporting and charting features, including pivotable reports, tasks, work flows, revenue recognition and depreciation. Advanced users can also use the Spreadsheet Sync feature to create self-updating reports, consolidated reports, adding and updating list records, initiating or editing transactions, and working with budgets, all within Excel.

» Part 5, "QuickBooks Online Accountant Features," walks through accountant-specific features, such as client and team management, accountant tools and screens, and practice management screens.

» Part 6, "Microsoft Excel Analysis," discusses ways that you can analyze your data in Microsoft Excel, including disabling the Protected View feature, filtering your data, and creating summary reports with PivotTables. You also see how automate repetitive analytical tasks with Power Query.

» Part 7, "The Part of Tens," covers ten common journal entries and ten shortcuts for the Chrome browser to help you optimize your use of QuickBooks.

Beyond the Book

In addition to the book content, this product comes with a free, access-anywhere Cheat Sheet that lists keyboard shortcuts and toolbar buttons. The Cheat Sheet also covers how to use the multicurrency feature, convert a company from QuickBooks Desktop or Sage 50 to QuickBooks Online, and enter payroll history.

To get this Cheat Sheet, go to www.dummies.com and search for **QuickBooks Online For Dummies Cheat Sheet.**

TIP

You can keep the learning going with the most up-to-date information and tutorials from School of Bookkeeping (https://schoolofbookkeeping.com/). The folks there (one of whom is the technical editor of this book) have broken down every version of QuickBooks Online, QuickBooks services (Payments and Payroll), and other tasks into bite-sized lessons that you can watch and get back to business. Use promo code QBO4DUMMIES to save 20 percent on any membership. If you're looking for video-based Excel training, please visit my site at www.professionalsexcel.com. The same QBO4DUMMIES promo code enables you to save 20 percent on any individual videos or subscriptions here as well.

1

Core Functionality

IN THIS CHAPTER

» Getting to know QuickBooks Online

» Pricing for subscriptions, payroll, and other add-ons

» Exploring features by subscription level and reviewing usage limits

» Customizing QuickBooks menu and account listing

» Attaching external documents to list records and transactions

Chapter **1**

Beginning Your Journey with QuickBooks

Welcome to QuickBooks Online! In this book, you'll discover all the ins and outs of your accounting platform so that you can handle your clients' or your own accounting records (colloquially referred to as books) more effectively. I've organized this book by subscription level so you can easily determine the capabilities of each version — from Simple Start, Essentials, and Plus to Advanced and Accountant.

I first explain QuickBooks Online and give you a sense of the annual costs to expect. After that I discuss reviewing your chart of accounts to ensure that you can categorize your assets, liabilities, equity, revenue, and expenses correctly.

QuickBooks Online Overview

QuickBooks Online is a cloud-based accounting software for computers and mobile devices. The software and your data are housed securely in remote data centers and accessed via the Internet. Conversely, QuickBooks Desktop is a traditional accounting software installed locally, alongside your data, on your office computer or network. Intuit has been implementing a low motion discontinuation of their desktop platform, and as of this writing, QuickBooks Desktop Enterprise is the only remaining version.

REMEMBER

Some folks see the "anywhere, anytime" aspect of the cloud as a potential disadvantage because it makes information too readily available — and therefore a target for hackers. Rest assured that Intuit, the maker of QuickBooks, stores your data on servers using bank-level security that creates encrypted backups of your data automatically.

With QuickBooks Online, your accountant or bookkeeper also has access from anywhere. The Accountant version empowers accounting professionals to quickly toggle between multiple clients' accounting records and keep up with deadlines and tasks using a centralized communication hub. Conversely, QuickBooks Desktop requires you to send an electronic Accountant's Copy to your accountant and specify a dividing date, before which you can't make changes until your accountant returns the Accountant's Copy to you. QuickBooks Desktop also requires you to install periodic software updates, which are a thing of the past with QuickBooks Online.

REMEMBER

It can be confusing any time a software platform uses the same term, such as *accountant*, in multiple contexts. For example, you may run across the term Accountant View, which previously reconfigured the sidebar menu. This is separate from inviting your accountant or bookkeeper to oversee your books. This is also separate from the QuickBooks Online Accountant subscription that your accountant or bookkeeper probably uses to manage your books and their own.

Most modern computers should easily exceed the minimum requirements for QuickBooks Online, but you can get the nitty-gritty computer specification details here: https://intuit.me/3yEaSJL.

TIP

My technical editor extraordinaire, Dan DeLong, has created a free QuickBooks Chooser chatbot that can help you choose the right version of QuickBooks Online based on your specific business needs. Check it out at https://chat.school ofbookkeeping.com/QBChooser.

Considering QuickBooks Pricing

You can cancel QuickBooks subscriptions at any time, although the service is billed in monthly or annual increments with no refunds or prorations. You can no longer create new transactions once your subscription expires, but you can view your accounting records and run reports for up to one year. As you will see in the next three sections, your "drive-out" price for using QuickBooks may mushroom far beyond the base subscription price. You've likely experienced how the base price of a car is far from what the bottom-line price ends up being. Similarly, depending upon your needs, you may end up paying more than you expected for QuickBooks Online. In Chapter 7, I discuss apps that you can install, which often come with additional subscription fees.

REMEMBER

QuickBooks Online subscriptions and the various add-ons are priced on a per-company basis. If you maintain the books for two or more entities, you have to pay for two or more subscriptions plus fees for ancillary add-ons.

QuickBooks Online base pricing

As shown in Table 1-1, QuickBooks Online is available in six different versions and price points. The Solopreneur and Simple Start versions are best suited to fledging businesses, whereas QuickBooks Online Accountant is a free portal that accountants and bookkeepers can use to support their clients. You can get more details and start a QuickBooks Online subscription at https://quickbooks.intuit.com/pricing/ or start using QuickBooks Online Accountant at https://quickbooks.intuit.com/accountants/products-solutions/accounting/online.

TABLE 1-1   **QuickBooks Online Subscription Pricing per Company**

Version	Monthly	Annually	Users
Solopreneur	$25	$270	1 billable user
Simple Start	$35	$378	1 billable user + 2 accountant users
Essentials	$65	$702	3 billable users + 2 accountant users + unlimited time tracking users
Plus	$99	$1,069	5 billable users + 2 accountant users + unlimited time tracking users + unlimited reports only users
Advanced	$235	$2,538	Up to 25 billable users + 3 accountant users + unlimited time tracking users + unlimited reports-only users
Accountant	$0	$0	No limit

TIP

QuickBooks allows you to choose between a 50 percent discount for the first three months of your subscription or a free 30-day trial. You may also be offered a 70 percent discount for the first three months during the 30-day trial. Take the deal immediately if you plan to move forward with QuickBooks because it's unlikely to be offered again during your trial period. The annual prices shown reflect a 10 percent prepayment discount.

PROADVISOR DISCOUNT

Accounting professionals can arrange an ongoing 30 percent discount on QuickBooks Online (excluding QuickBooks Solopreneur), QuickBooks Payroll, and QuickBooks Time in exchange for being billed directly by Intuit. Accountants can pass all or part of the savings on to their clients if they want. Alternatively, accountants who prefer that their clients pay for QuickBooks directly can arrange a 30 percent discount for 12 months for charges billed directly to their clients. I discuss the ProAdvisor Discount in more detail in Chapter 17.

REMEMBER

You must cancel your subscription if you opt for the discount and decide Quick-Books isn't right for you. Conversely, the 30-day trial simply expires, and no further action is required on your part.

REMEMBER

A QuickBooks company is a set of accounting records for a single business entity. Each QuickBooks company entails separate subscription fees, and you need to establish a QuickBooks company for each company you own or maintain accounting records for.

Payroll and time tracking pricing

You will incur additional subscription costs if you need to process payroll or enable employees to track their time. As shown in Table 1-2, QuickBooks offers three different payroll options. I've calculated the associated costs for a hypothetical team of five employees to give you a frame of reference. The Premium and Elite plans offer time tracking, which you can also purchase on an à la carte basis.

TABLE 1-2   **QuickBooks Payroll Subscription Pricing for Five Employees**

Version	Monthly	Annually
Core	$75 ($50/month + $6/employee × 5 employees)	$900
Premium	$120 ($85/month + $9/employee × 5 employees)	$1,458
Elite	$175 ($130/month + $11/employee × 5 employees)	$2,064

TIP

You can test-drive the QuickBooks payroll service for free for up to 30 days. This annual pricing reflects a 10 percent prepayment discount on the monthly fees. Intuit does not offer a discount on the per-employee charges.

All QuickBooks Payroll plans include the following features:

>> Paying employees with printed checks or by direct deposit.

>> Calculating tax payments automatically and paying them electronically.

>> Processing federal and state quarterly and annual reports and preparing W-2 and 1099 forms.

>> Processing payroll for employees and filing for one state. Core and Premium subscribers incur a $12/month charge for any additional state filings.

>> Keeping payroll tax tables up to date without having to install updates (as you do with the QuickBooks Enterprise Desktop product).

>> Using the QuickBooks Workforce mobile app to enable employees to view paychecks, see time off, and log their time.

The Core tier offers next-day direct deposit, and the Premium tier enables same-day direct deposit and adds time tracking. The Elite tier adds project tracking, tax penalty protection, a personal human resources advisor, mileage tracking estimated vs. actual hours worked, and geosensing GPS logging through the Workforce app. You can get more details and start a payroll subscription at https://quickbooks.intuit.com/payroll/pricing/, or you can choose Payroll from the sidebar menu.

WARNING

Make sure that you're ready to start processing payroll immediately before you embark on a QuickBooks Payroll subscription because you must connect your bank account and provide your tax identification numbers. If you want to try before you buy, use the online test drives I mention later in this chapter in the "QuickBooks Online Plus" and "QuickBooks Online Advanced" sections.

Table 1-3 shows the additional annual cost of adding a standalone QuickBooks Time subscription if you want time and attendance tracking but not necessarily payroll processing. It's worth running the numbers for the various offerings because QuickBooks Core Payroll for five employees at $80 per month plus QuickBooks Premium Time at $60 per month is $140 per month versus paying $130 per month for QuickBooks Payroll Premium, which also offers time tracking. With that said, an Elite time subscription does include project tracking.

REMEMBER

Although you can add time tracking on an á la carte basis, it typically makes more financial sense to use the time tracking bundled into the upgraded payroll service tiers. This also ensures that you avoid the complications that can arise if you start out with QuickBooks Time and then switch to a QuickBooks Payroll tier that offers time tracking.

TABLE 1-3 **QuickBooks Time Subscription Pricing for Five Employees**

Version	Monthly	Annually
Premium	$60 ($20/month + $8/employee × 5 employees)	$720
Elite	$90 ($40/month + $10/employee × 5 employees)	$1,080
ProAdvisor	Free for accounting professionals	$0

QuickBooks Payments

QuickBooks Payments enables you to accept electronic payments from customers and entails per-transaction fees instead of a monthly subscription. Table 1-4 shows the current rates as of this writing.

TABLE 1-4 **QuickBooks Payments per Transaction Fees**

Payment Type	Rate per Transaction
ACH Bank payments	1% (customer enters bank information online). Note: The maximum fee is $20 for customers who created accounts prior to September 5, 2023; otherwise, there is no maximum.
Swiped credit card	2.5%; you swipe the card via the available mobile reader.
Invoiced credit card	2.99%; your customer enters credit card online.
Keyed credit card	3.5%; you enter your customer's credit card information online.

TIP

QuickBooks Payments deposits money from qualifying credit or debit card transactions into your bank account the next business day. Your payments and deposit transactions are recorded in your books automatically, based on the funding date.

Comparing QuickBooks Features

As you can see, the ongoing expenses for QuickBooks can add up fast. You can upgrade or downgrade your subscription at any time, although downgrading can entail disabling inventory or removing users. Use the search term **downgrade** at https://quickbooks.intuit.com/learn-support/en-us for more details. Read on for information on the various tiers so that you can find the right fit for your needs.

QuickBooks Online Solopreneur

This version of QuickBooks is aimed at freelancers and self-employed people who file Schedule C of IRS Form 1040 (www.irs.gov/forms-pubs/about-schedule-c-form-1040). Unlike the higher-level offerings, QuickBooks Solopreneur allows you to mix business with pleasure, meaning that you can track personal and business expenses, as well as mileage. It's best suited to someone with a side hustle who wants to keep track of their business and simplify income tax filing. As of this writing, Solopreneur users cannot invite accountants to access their books. Intuit has indicated that this capability is in the works.

WARNING

I don't discuss QuickBooks Online Solopreneur any further in this book, although some of the features may mirror what you see in the higher subscription levels.

QuickBooks Simple Start

A QuickBooks Simple Start subscription is ideal for a new business with basic bookkeeping needs. With Simple Start, you accomplish the following tasks, broken down by chapter in Part 1:

» Chapter 2 covers all things customer related, including:

- Creating an unlimited number of customers.

- Sending estimates and invoices.

- Tracking and paying sales taxes.

» Chapter 3 discusses money going out the door to vendors, including:

- Printing checks and recording transactions to track expenses.

- Using accounts payable functions, including scheduling payment of vendor bills and online bill payment.

» Chapter 4 is all about making sure that your team gets paid:

- Processing payroll.

- Paying contractors and sending 1099 forms.

» Chapter 5 helps you keep tabs on your financial activity:

- Recording bank deposits.

- Reconciling bank statements.

- Downloading transactions from your bank and credit card accounts.

>> Chapter 6 helps you view your business activity multiple ways. You can by view and customize more than 50 reports.

>> Chapter 7 is all about app and automation:

- Connecting one online sales channel, such as Amazon, eBay, or Shopify.
- Tracking mileage manually or from the QuickBooks Online mobile app.
- Categorizing expenses by taking pictures of receipts.
- Importing bank data, customers, products and services, and invoices from comma-separated value (CSV) files.
- Adding functionality with free and paid apps.

Although the Simple Start version supports accounts-receivable functions, you can't invoice customers on a recurring basis, and you'll have to dig to find the details of your unpaid invoices — the Reports screen makes it appear as if only a summary report is available. If you're on the fence between Solopreneur and Simple Start, you'll have more options in the future with Simple Start.

QuickBooks Online Essentials

Established businesses that don't have inventory may be able to use QuickBooks Essentials, which includes all the Simple Start functionality, plus a total of three sales channels, a total of 85 reports, and the following, broken down by chapter in Part 2:

>> Chapter 8 is all about apps and automation:

- Controlling the areas of QuickBooks your users can access.
- Utilizing multiple currencies.
- Adding up to three custom fields.

>> Chapter 9 streamlines repetitive tasks:

- Creating and using recurring transactions.
- Establishing bundles of products and services.
- Tracking time for unlimited users.

QuickBooks Online Plus

A Plus subscription offers all of the functionality of an Essentials subscription, plus unlimited sales channels, 124 reports, and the following, by chapter in Part 3:

>> Chapter 10 is all about tracking and procuring physical goods:

- Tracking inventory using the first in, first out (FIFO) inventory valuation method.

- Creating, sending, and tracking purchase orders.

REMEMBER

If you need to assemble finished goods for sale, QuickBooks Online alone won't meet your needs. However, you can explore apps to supplement your inventory and work-in-progress tracking needs. I discuss apps that integrate with QuickBooks Online in Chapter 7.

>> Chapter 11 gives you new levels of transaction tracking:

- Categorizing income and expenses by using class tracking.

- Tracking sales and profitability by department or location.

- Creating and monitoring projects.

>> Chapter 12 lets you plan ahead:

- Creating budgets to estimate future income and expenses.

- Planning out your cash flow.

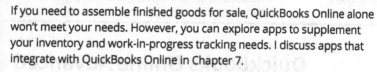

TIP

You can test-drive the QuickBooks Online Plus sample company at https://qbo.intuit.com/redir/testdrive.

Usage limits for QuickBooks Simple Start, Essentials, and Plus

Simple Start, Essentials, and Plus subscriptions are subject to the limits shown in Table 1-5. Long-term users may be allowed higher limits but can't add any element that exceeds the use limit without upgrading to a higher-level plan or deactivating current elements. As detailed in the next section, you can work without limits in QuickBooks with an Advanced subscription.

TABLE 1-5   **Usage Limits for Simple Start, Essentials, and Plus Subscriptions**

QuickBooks Element	Usage Limit
Annual transactions	350,000
Chart of accounts	250
Classes and locations	40 combined; further, you can't track your balance sheet by class.
Billed users	1 for Simple Start, 3 for Essentials, 5 for Plus
Unbilled users	2 Accountant users; unlimited time tracking for Essentials and Plus; unlimited reports-only users for Plus

QuickBooks Online Advanced

QuickBooks Online Advanced incorporates all of the features of a Plus subscription and eliminates many of the use restrictions imposed on Simple Start, Essentials, and Plus subscribers. It is the flagship subscription for companies that have outgrown QuickBooks Online Plus. Advanced companies are allowed unlimited accounts, transactions, and classes, plus additional user types, plus Access to Intuit's Priority Circle, which provides elevated customer support and self-paced online training courses. Some of the additional functionality, broken down by chapter in Part 4, includes:

>> Chapter 13 is about user empowerment and disaster recovery:

- Installing a desktop app for more efficient company access.

- Establishing custom permissions for users.

- Backing up and restoring your QuickBooks Online data.

- Exporting certain lists and transactions to comma-separated value (CSV) files by way of the Local Backup feature.

>> Chapter 14 discusses custom reporting and charting:

- Using the Custom Report Builder.

- Building charts within QuickBooks Online.

- Summarizing reports by using the Pivot feature.

- Chapter 15 covers tasks workflows and other functionality:

- Assigning and tracking user tasks.

- Enabling workflows to trigger reminders for customers and team members.

- Defining and tailoring up to 48 custom fields.

- Automating employee expense management.

- Entering, editing, or deleting multiple transactions by way of the Batch Transactions feature.

- Complying with the Accounting Standards Codification (ASC) 606 revenue recognition regulation issued by the Financial Accounting Standards Board (FASB).

- Tracking fixed assets and compute depreciation.

» Chapter 16 documents how to synchronize QuickBooks Online with Microsoft Excel:

- Creating refreshable reports in Microsoft Excel.

- Importing and editing lists and transactions directly from Excel.

- Synchronizing Excel-based budgets with QuickBooks Online.

TIP

You can test-drive the QuickBooks Online Advanced sample company at https://qbo.intuit.com/redir/testdrive_us_advanced.

QuickBooks Online Accountant

The Accountant version enables accounting professionals to manage their practice and their clients' books. This free subscription includes a single QuickBooks Online Advanced subscription so that accountants can manage their own books as well.

TIP

Subscribe to QuickBooks Online Accountant at https://quickbooks.intuit.com/accountants/products-solutions/accounting/online.

Accountants are limited to subscription-based feature sets when accessing a client's books, but Part 5 breaks down the additional functionality by chapter:

» Chapter 17 introduces the Accountant version:

- Adding companies to the client list.

- Accessing a client's books.

- Managing team members access.

- Leveraging QuickBooks Online Ledger.

QuickBooks Online Ledger is a low-cost, streamlined version of QuickBooks Online designed specifically for accounting professionals. It offers essential bookkeeping features, such as bank reconciliation and journal entry management.

>> Chapter 18 discusses accountant-specific tools:

- Establishing chart of account templates.

- Reviewing a client's books.

- Employing a suite of accountant tools, including undoing bank reconciliations.

- Charting clients' financial performance.

>> Chapter 19 covers the nitty-gritty of practice management:

- Assigning and tracking work assigned to team members.

- Utilizing the free QuickBooks Online Advanced subscription.

If you're curious about the rest of the book, here's a quick overview:

>> Chapter 20 empowers you to analyze your data in Excel.

>> Chapter 21 helps you automate repetitive analytical tasks.

>> Chapter 22 deconstructs several common journal entries.

>> Chapter 23 offers ways to use the Chrome browser more effectively.

Now that you have a sense of what the various subscription levels and this book offer, let's explore how to tailor QuickBooks to suit your preferences.

Customizing Your Chart of Accounts

When you create a new company, QuickBooks creates a chart of accounts tailored to your industry. You can keep this list intact, edit it manually as I describe, or replace it with what you import from Excel, a CSV file, or Google Sheets, which I discuss in the later section titled "Importing accounts."

Your chart of accounts is limited to 250 active accounts unless you have an Advanced subscription.

I encourage you to review the chart of accounts that QuickBooks establishes for your company. To do so, choose the Gear icon ⇨ Chart of Accounts or Transactions ⇨ Chart of Accounts. The screen shown in Figure 1-1 displays your chart of accounts and lets you carry out a variety of actions:

>> Click Run Report to generate a report that lists your chart of accounts.

>> Click New to create a new account.

>> Choose New ⇨ Import to import a new chart of accounts, which I discuss later in more detail in the "Importing accounts" section.

>> Click Edit below New to turn on the Batch Edit feature, which enables you to edit multiple account names at once.

>> Click the Print to generate a printout of the Chart of Accounts screen.

WARNING

>> You're better off clicking Run Report versus clicking Print because the Print command generates a rather unaesthetic-looking report.

>> Click the Gear icon to control which columns appear on the screen and whether inactive accounts are displayed.

>> Click the checkbox for one or more accounts, and then choose Batch Actions ⇨ Make Inactive to deactivate unnecessary accounts.

>> Click View Register adjacent to balance sheet accounts or Run Report adjacent to income and expense accounts to view a register or report showing all activity.

>> Click the arrow next to an account to reveal the following choices, depending on the account type:

- **Connect Bank:** Starts the process of syncing checking and credit card accounts with a financial institution.

- **Edit:** Allows you to change the account type, detail type, name, description, or subaccount status of an account.

- **Make Inactive:** Deactivates an account so that it can no longer be used for new transactions.

WARNING

QuickBooks zeroes out accounts that you make inactive, so make sure that you move the account balances by way of a journal entry or other transaction. I discuss journal entries in Chapter 22. You can mark multiple accounts inactive by clicking the checkbox for one or more accounts and then choosing Batch Actions ⇨ Make Inactive.

- **Run Report:** Enables you to run a report showing the activity for a given account.

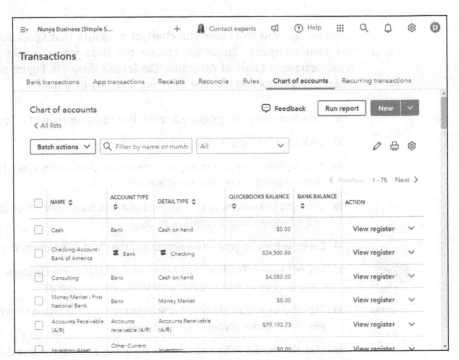

FIGURE 1-1:
The Chart of
Accounts screen.

Adding new accounts

Here's how to add an account to your chart of accounts:

1. **Click New on the Chart of Accounts screen to open the New Account task pane, shown in Figure 1-2.**

2. **Fill in the Account Name field.**

    Only enter words in this field. Later in the chapter, I show you how to enable account numbers for your chart of accounts. Don't be fooled by the relatively small size of the field; it accepts up to 100 characters.

3. **Make a selection from the Account Type field.**

    This list contains the major categories that typically appear on the balance sheet and profit-and-loss reports for a business.

4. **Make a selection from the Detail Type field.**

    Depending upon the Account Type you chose, you may only have one choice here, or you may have many.

5. **Optional: Click the Make This a subaccount checkbox under the Account Type field if you want to have this account roll up into a higher-level account on your reports.**

   You must specify a parent account for each subaccount that you create.

6. **Optional: Specify an Opening Balance and an As Of date if you are creating an account that will appear on your balance sheet.**

   Balance sheet accounts include assets, liabilities, and equities. Always defer to your accountant or bookkeeper if you're unclear as to if and when to start tracking an account.

7. **Optional: Enter a description for your account.**

   Enter up to 100 characters, providing additional documentation as to the purpose of the account.

8. **Click Save to record the new addition to your chart of accounts.**

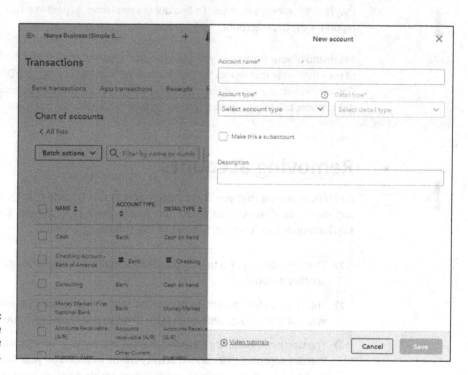

FIGURE 1-2:
The task pane you use to create an account.

A FEW NOTES ON PAYING OWNERS

Many small-business owners wonder about the accounts they should use to pay themselves. Owners and partners typically aren't considered to be employees and therefore aren't paid through payroll. To pay an owner or partner, use the Chart of Accounts screen to set up a Draw account (Owner's Draw, Partner's Draw, or whatever is appropriate; if you have multiple partners, set up Draw accounts for each partner) and use it to pay owners. The Draw account is an equity account. Similarly, owners and partners sometimes put their own money into the business. To account for these contributions, set up equity accounts (again, one for each owner or partner) called Owner's Contribution, Partner's Contribution, or whatever is appropriate.

Note that you use the Draw account not only to pay the owner, but also to account for personal items an owner might buy with the business's money. You record the withdrawals by using the appropriate bank account and the appropriate Draw account. Note that these transactions don't show up on your profit-and-loss report because they're not business expenses. To find out the total amount paid to an owner, run a report for the Draw account.

At the end of your fiscal year, you need to enter a journal entry, dated the last day of your fiscal year that moves the dollar amounts from the appropriate Draw or Contribution account to Retained Earnings, which is another equity account. If I've just lost you, talk to your accountant about how to handle closing the year.

Removing accounts

A common theme that you'll encounter across this book is that QuickBooks generally does not allow you to delete list items, such as accounts. You must instead mark accounts as inactive, subject to the following caveats:

>> The only way to permanently delete an account is to merge it into another account.

>> You cannot mark parent accounts that contain subaccounts as inactive until you edit the subaccounts and assign them to a new parent account.

>> Transactions remain intact within inactive accounts — which means that inactive accounts that contain activity will be included on your financial reports. You must, however, reactivate an account before you can edit any transactions within it.

>> Balance sheet accounts that you mark as inactive are automatically adjusted to zero with an offset to the Opening Balance Equity account.

Deactivating a balance sheet account that has a non-zero balance increases the risk that your income tax return may be filed incorrectly.

Here's how to mark an account as inactive:

1. **Choose the Gear icon ⇨ Chart of Accounts or Transactions ⇨ Chart of Accounts.**

   The Chart of Accounts screen opens.

2. **Choose Mark Inactive (Reduces Usage) from the drop-down menu in the Active column.**

   In Advanced companies, this command is labeled Mark Inactive because there is no limit on the number of accounts.

3. **Choose Yes, Make Inactive.**

   Conversely, here's how to merge two accounts:

4. **Choose the Gear icon ⇨ Chart of Accounts or Transactions ⇨ Chart of Accounts.**

   The Chart of Accounts screen opens.

5. **Choose Edit from the drop-down menu in the Active column for the account that you want to keep.**

6. **Make note of the account name and detail type, and then click Cancel.**

7. **Choose Edit from the drop-down menu in the Active column for the account that you want to remove from your chart of accounts.**

8. **Edit the Account Name and Detail Type accounts to exactly match the account that you want to keep.**

   Ensure that any parent accounts you are merging do not contain any subaccounts, and that any subaccounts that you are merging share the same parent account.

9. **Click Save and then Yes, Merge Accounts.**

   Any transactions in the account that you have chosen to remove are automatically recategorized into the account that you kept.

Implementing account numbers

By default, QuickBooks doesn't use or display account numbers; however, you can enable this feature by following these steps:

1. **Choose the Gear icon ⇨ Account & Settings ⇨ Advanced.**

2. **Click Edit in the Chart of Accounts section.**

3. **Toggle on the Enable Account Numbers option.**

4. **Click Show Account Numbers checkbox if you want to display the account numbers in QuickBooks.**

5. **Click Save and then click Done.**

You can enable or disable these settings as needed at any time. Use the Batch Edit method I discuss in the "Customizing Your Chart of Accounts" section earlier in this chapter. After you add account numbers, you can sort the chart of accounts in account-number order by clicking the Number heading of the Chart of Accounts screen.

REMEMBER

Click Save periodically as you enter account numbers in case you get pulled away unexpectedly. This prevents QuickBooks from signing you out and causing you to lose your work.

Importing accounts

You can replace the default chart of accounts provided by QuickBooks with one you've set up in Microsoft Excel, as a CSV file, or as a Google Sheet spreadsheet. The import file can include subaccounts and parent accounts.

REMEMBER

Use the convention *Account: Subaccount* when establishing subaccounts, with *Account* representing the parent account.

Here's how to import a chart of accounts:

1. **Choose the Gear icon ⇨ Chart of Accounts or Transactions ⇨ Chart of Accounts.**

2. **Choose New ⇨ Import to display the Import Accounts screen.**

3. **Use the links to download a sample CSV or Excel file or to preview a sample Google Sheet.**

4. **After you set up your Chart of Accounts file, choose New ⇨ Import again on the Chart of Accounts screen.**

5. Click Browse or Connect, as appropriate, to select your import file.

6. Click Next to display the Map Data screen.

7. Map the headings in your import file to the fields in QuickBooks by making selections from the drop-down lists in the Your Field column.

8. Click Next to display a preview of the accounts to be imported.

9. Click Import if everything looks to be in order.

TECHNICAL
STUFF

QuickBooks Online Accountant users can establish and apply chart of accounts templates to their clients' companies. This feature streamlines the setup process, ensuring consistency across multiple clients' accounts by quickly implementing standardized account structures tailored to specific industries or client needs. I dig into the details in Chapter 18.

Tailoring Your QuickBooks Environment

Once you choose a subscription, a comprehensive wizard walks you through the set-up process. I don't regurgitate the steps here, but I do share some customizations you may want to make. For instance, the navigation menu along the left side of the screen is called the *sidebar menu*, which I sometimes refer to as the *sidebar*. I also explain customizing the chart of accounts, which you use to categorize every transaction you make, but let's first see how to prevent QuickBooks from logging you out of a work session prematurely.

Extending the default length of a QuickBooks session

By default, QuickBooks signs you out of your company after 60 minutes of inactivity. You can extend this to as much as three hours like so:

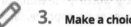

1. Choose the Gear icon ⇨ Account & Settings ⇨ Advanced.

2. Click Edit in the Other Preferences section.

3. Make a choice from the Sign Me Out If Inactive For field.

4. Click Save and then Done.

TIP

Advanced and Accountant users can use the QuickBooks Online desktop app, which I discuss in Chapter 13, instead of working in a browser window. The desktop app requires you to log in to your Intuit account only once every six months, unless you manually log out of the app.

Customizing the sidebar menu

The sidebar menu is on the left side of your QuickBooks company and is the primary navigation aid for working with QuickBooks. You can customize this menu to hide commands you don't use and bookmark commands you do use. For instance, you're not going to need the Commerce choice on the menu if you don't sell products online. Here's how to customize the sidebar:

1. **Click Edit next to the Menu or Bookmarks sections of the sidebar menu.**

   A Customize Your Menu dialog box opens with Menu and Bookmarks tabs.

2. **Optional: Toggle checkmarks on or off to enable or disable menu groupings or bookmarks by clicking on Menu or Bookmarks to switch between the lists.**

3. **Click Save to preserve your changes or Cancel if you change your mind.**

REMEMBER

Turning commands off doesn't remove any functionality from QuickBooks but instead moves those commands into a More section at the bottom of the Menu portion of the sidebar menu.

You can also use a second approach to add bookmarks:

1. **Hover your mouse over a grouping from the sidebar, such as Payroll, to reveal a submenu.**

2. **Hover your mouse over a command, such as Employees, and then click Bookmark.**

Reviewing company settings

Now that your chart of accounts is set up, it's worth your while to review the default settings for QuickBooks and make changes as appropriate. Choose the Gear icon ⇨ Account and Settings to display the Account and Setting screen, and then select a category and make any changes needed. Some setting changes require you to click Save, and you need to click Done to close the Account and Settings screen. Here's a rundown of the settings you can change:

>> **Company:** You can add your company logo and edit your company name, company type, address, and contact information, as well as your marketing preferences for Intuit.

Click Edit within any section to make updates, and then click Save to record your changes.

>> **Billing & Subscription:** You can view the current status of your subscription and change your payment method. You can convert a QuickBooks or QuickBooks Payroll trial to a regular subscription, but doing so terminates the trial period. You can also scroll down to order checks and supplies. As of this writing, you can choose to opt for annual billing — instead of monthly — and reduce your QuickBooks subscription fees by roughly 10 percent.

The Billing & Subscription section isn't shown if your QuickBooks company is being managed by an accountant who participates in the ProAdvisor Discount program, which I discuss in Chapter 17.

>> **Usage:** This section shows any usage limits based on your subscription. Click the link showing the count of users, accounts, and so on to display the corresponding screen.

>> **QuickBooks Checking:** This section offers a QuickBooks Checking bank account that integrates directly with your accounting records.

>> **Sales:** This section enables you to customize certain fields within your sales forms, including determining whether to show Product/Service or SKU fields. You can add a default charge to overdue invoices, utilize progress invoicing, customize default email messages, and include an aging table at the bottom of account statements.

>> **Expenses:** You can opt to display a table of expense and purchase forms so that you can itemize and categorize the products and services you buy, as well as show a Tags field on these forms. You can also choose to add a column for identifying the customer a purchase relates to, as well as a column where you can mark items and expenses as billable to your customers. You can opt to use purchase orders and create a default email message to be sent with them.

>> **Payments:** Use this section to establish a new QuickBooks Payments account here or connect an existing account so that you can accept credit cards payments or bank transfers from your customers. This feature also enables you to include a Pay Now button on invoices that you email to customers. This service entails per-transaction fees that I discuss in the "QuickBooks Payments" section earlier in this chapter.

>> **Time:** Your options here vary, based upon your subscription level, but at a minimum, you can set the first day of the work week and determine if a service field should appear on timesheets, and if time should be billable.

>> **Advanced:** Here, you'll mostly find nitty-gritty accounting settings that you'll probably want to hand off to your accountant. They include specifying the first month of your fiscal and tax years; choosing Cash or Accrual for your accounting method; picking a tax form; and, as mentioned earlier, determining if you want to use account numbers in your chart of accounts.

I discuss how to customize payroll settings in Chapter 4.

Customizing Sales Forms

QuickBooks enables you to customize invoices, estimates, and sales receipts. The default format is now known as Modern, which previously distinguished it from the Classic sales form designs. Sales forms have four different views:

>> **Edit:** Use to record the transaction.

>> **Email View:** Use to preview what your customer will see when they open the transaction email.

>> **PDF View:** Use to review the PDF version of the transaction.

>> **Payor View:** Use get review what clicking the View Details button will display within the transaction email.

Tailoring sales forms

To modify a sales form, follow these steps:

1. **Choose + New ➪ Invoice, Estimate, or Sales Receipt.**

   The corresponding form opens onscreen.

2. **Click Manage to display a design task pane that contains four sections:**

   - **Customization:** Use this section to turn fields and columns on or off, as well as modify column headings in the body of the transaction form.

   - **Payment Options:** Enable online payments via the QuickBooks Payment service, as well as fields to handle deposits, discounts, and shipping fees.

   - **Design:** Choose from existing templates, including the default Modern format, or click Add/Edit to display the Custom Forms Style screen, which enables you to add or edit sales form templates.

- **Scheduling:** Activate the Recurring Invoice setting to schedule an invoice to generate automatically, mark an invoice as Print Later or Send Later, and manage invoice reminders.

Simplifying your invoicing process

Invoicing your customers generally involves a lot of rote work. QuickBooks offers a couple of features that can speed things up for you:

>> **Bundles:** In Chapter 9, I discuss how bundles allow you to add a collection of two or more items to an invoice by selecting a single item.

>> **Pricing rules:** In Chapter 10, I discuss how Plus and Advanced users can enable *pricing rules* that automatically discount or increase the price of items for some or all customers, either permanently or for some period.

>> **Subtotals:** QuickBooks offers a limited ability to add subtotals to invoices for time activities only.

To add a subtotal, follow these steps:

1. **Choose the Gear icon ⇨ Custom Form Styles.** The Custom Form Styles screen displays any form styles you've set up.

2. **Select a form to customize, and then click Edit in the Action column.**

   The Customize Form Style screen contains three buttons in the top-left corner: Design, Content, and Emails.

3. **Click Content.**

   The Content screen opens, with all sections disabled.

4. **Click Edit within the Table section.**

   The Table section is where you see column titles such as Date, Product/Service, and Description.

5. **Scroll down the screen and click Show More Activity Options in the bottom-left corner.**

   Additional options for the Table section are displayed.

6. **Click the Group Activity By checkbox and make a choice from the drop-down menu.**

   You can group items by day, week, month, or type. For this example, choose **type**.

7. **Click Subtotal Groups.**

8. **Click Done in the bottom-right corner of the window to save the settings.**

   Although you can click Preview PDF, there's not much point in this context because QuickBooks doesn't show you the subtotals in use until you actually create an invoice.

REMEMBER

You must repeat the preceding steps to include subtotals for estimates and sales receipts if you want to have a consistent look and feel across all the forms you use.

Getting Attached

Most list and transaction records offer an Attachments field that allows you to upload an unlimited number of files as long as each attachment is 20MB or smaller and is one of the following file types:

» **CSV (Comma-Separated Values):** A simple file format used to store tabular data, such as a spreadsheet or database. Each line in a CSV file represents a row, and columns are separated by commas.

» **DOC (Document) or DOCX (Document Open XML):** The DOC file format is used by Microsoft Word for text documents and was the default file format for Word documents until the introduction of the DOCX file format in Word 2007. Word 2007 DOCX files are based on the Open XML standard and are more efficient in terms of file size and data recovery than the older DOC format.

» **GIF (Graphics Interchange Format):** A bitmap image format that supports up to 256 colors and is commonly used for simple graphics and short animations on the web. GIFs can include multiple frames, allowing for simple animations.

» **JPEG or JPG (Joint Photographic Experts Group):** A commonly used method of lossy compression for digital images, particularly for those images produced by digital photography. You can use the JPEG or JPG file extension interchangeably — the shorter extension was created to comply with the three letter file extension limitation in early versions of Windows.

» **PDF (Portable Document Format):** A file format developed by Adobe that captures all elements of a printed document as an electronic image. PDF files are widely used for sharing documents because they preserve the formatting and can be viewed on any device.

>> **TIFF (Tagged Image File Format):** A file format for storing high-quality raster graphics images, popular among graphic artists, photographers, and the publishing industry. TIFF files can be either uncompressed or compressed using lossless compression.

>> **XML (eXtensible Markup Language):** A markup language used to encode documents in a format that is both human-readable and machine-readable. XML is commonly used for data transfer between systems and for structuring data within various applications.

>> **XLS (Excel Spreadsheet) and XLSX (Excel Spreadsheet Open XML):** The XLS file format is used by Microsoft Excel for storing spreadsheet data in workbooks. XLS files were the default format for Excel until the introduction of XLSX in Excel 2007. The XLSX format is based on the Open XML standard and is more efficient in terms of file size and data handling than the older XLS format. XLSX files have 1,048,576 rows and 16,376 columns per worksheet, while XLS files only have 65,536 rows and 256 columns.

The message "We were unable to upload this type of file" is displayed beneath the Attachments field when you attempt to upload an unacceptable file type — such as compressed ZIP files or Excel binary workbooks (XLSB files).

Some transactions, such as invoices, give you the option to include the attachment when emailing the transaction form. Attachments appear in uploaded order within the Attachments dialog box of a list or transaction record, as well as on the Attachments list, which you can access by choosing Settings ⇨ Attachments.

The Attachments list is composed of the following columns:

>> **Thumbnail:** Displays a small preview image of GIF, JPG, JPEG, and TIFF files.

>> **Type:** A one-word description of the file, such as Document, Image, PDF, Spreadsheet, and so on.

>> **Name:** Shows the uploaded file's name, but you can assign a new one by selecting Edit from the Action column drop-down menu.

>> **Size:** Displays the size of the file.

>> **Uploaded:** Shows the date/time that the file was uploaded.

>> **Links:** Typically identifies the transactions and/or list records that the upload is attached to, but is blank if the upload is not attached to any records.

>> **Note:** Remains blank, but you can assign a note by selecting Edit from the Action column drop-down menu.

The Actions column drop-down menu includes the following commands:

>> **Download:** Enables you to save a copy of the attachment to your computer.

>> **Edit:** As noted, displays a dialog box from which you can change the file name for an upload as well as optionally add a note describing the file.

>> **Delete:** A prompt asks to confirm that you want to delete the upload, which removes the attachment from your QuickBooks company. The link to the upload will also be removed from any corresponding list or record pages. You can delete attachments only at a time. QuickBooks Online does support batch deletion.

REMEMBER

>> **Create Invoice:** Attaches the upload to a blank invoice and displays the corresponding transaction screen.

>> **Create Expense:** Attaches the upload to a blank expense and displays the corresponding transaction screen.

The Batch Actions commands are disabled until you turn on the Selection checkbox for two or more individual transactions, or the Select All checkbox at the top of the column. It contains the following commands:

>> **Download:** Creates a compressed file named Archive.ZIP that contains copies of the selected uploads.

>> **Create Invoice:** Attaches the selected uploads to a blank invoice and displays the corresponding transaction screen.

>> **Create Expense:** Attaches the selected uploads to a blank expense and displays the corresponding transaction screen.

IN THIS CHAPTER

» **Managing customer records**

» **Enabling sales tax**

» **Creating non-inventory products and services**

» **Creating sales transactions**

» **Writing off bad debt**

» **Utilizing estimates**

Chapter **2**

Tracking Sales and Accounts Receivable

The first three sections of this chapter cover groundwork that you need to complete before you can start recording sales transactions. I first show you how to create new customers in QuickBooks and then move onto enabling sales tax — skip this section if it doesn't apply to you. Be sure to read the section on creating non-inventory items and services; guidance for creating and tracking inventory items is in Chapter 10. I conclude this chapter with the nuts and bolts of recording your sales in QuickBooks, writing off bad debt, and working with estimates.

Managing Customers

Customers are the lifeblood of any business, so you need to be thoroughly familiar with the ins-and-outs of managing your customer records. I begin by explaining how to add customers.

Creating customer records

You can't create a new customer-related transaction without first setting up a customer record. Don't worry about getting it perfect right away — Customer Display Name is the only required field, as you'll see here:

1. Open the Customer screen by using one of these techniques:

- Choose + New ⇨ Add Customer.
- Choose Sales or Customers & Leads ⇨ Customers ⇨ New Customer.
- Choose Sales ⇨ Invoices ⇨ Create Invoice ⇨ select Add New from the Customer drop-down menu.

2. If you want to store contact information for your customer, fill in any combination of Title, First Name, Middle Name, Last Name, and Suffix.

3. Enter the customer name in one of two ways:

- Use the Company Name field to search for your customer in the QuickBooks Business Network. If you find a match, click Save and Send to populate the Customer Display Name field and send a connection request to your customer. If your customer accepts the invitation, invoices that you send post directly to their books as accounts payable bills. If you change your mind or select the wrong customer, you can click the Reset Link in the field.

- Complete the Customer Display Name field.

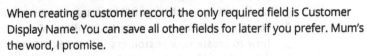

When creating a customer record, the only required field is Customer Display Name. You can save all other fields for later if you prefer. Mum's the word, I promise.

4. Consider completing the other sections of the customer record.

The Customer task pane includes the following sections:

- **Name and Contact:** Stores the name and contact information for your customer.

- **Addresses:** Records the billing and shipping addresses.

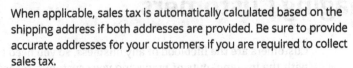

When applicable, sales tax is automatically calculated based on the shipping address if both addresses are provided. Be sure to provide accurate addresses for your customers if you are required to collect sales tax.

- **Notes and Attachments:** The Notes field stores up to 4,000 characters of free-form text, while the Attachments field enables you to upload files such as contracts, approvals, or other documents. Each file can be up to 20MB in size and in any of the following formats: PDF, JPEG, PNG, DOC, XLSX, CSV, TIFF, GIF, and XML.

REMEMBER

You can also store attachments with transactions. Any documents that you've attached appear in sequential order within the Attachments dialog box. QuickBooks alerts you to unacceptable file types, such as compressed ZIP files and Excel Binary workbooks (XLSB files).

WARNING

Any files that you upload as attachments become a permanent part of your QuickBooks Online company and cannot be removed. You can unlink an attachment from a record by clicking the X to the right of the filename, but the document will still appear in the Attachments list for your company as a whole. Click Show Existing beneath any Attachments field to see all attachments, and choose Unlinked to view attachments that aren't tied to a specific transaction or record.

- **Payments:** Stores details such as a customer's primary payment method, terms, sales form delivery options, and the preferred language for sending invoices.

- **Additional Info:** Captures sales tax preferences, such as whether a customer is tax exempt, if their sales tax should be calculated based upon their location, or a manual override is needed. You can also set an opening balance amount and date if you're just getting started with QuickBooks.

TIP

A Reason for Exemption drop-down list and 16 character Exemption Details field appear if you indicate that a customer is tax-exempt.

5. **Click the Save button to close the Customer task pane and return to the page you started from.**

Accessing and editing customer records

The Customers screen is sorted alphabetically by contact name, but you can also sort by the Company Name or Open Balance fields by clicking on the corresponding column heading. To display a customer record, click anywhere in a customer's row, except the Action column. Enter as little as a single character in the Search field to generate a list of matching records, then choose any customer from the resulting list to view their record. As shown in Figure 2-1, a customer page appears and may have multiple tabs:

>> **Transaction List:** Displays all transactions associated with a customer.

>> **Statements:** Lists statements generated for a customer.

>> **Recurring Transactions:** Presents a list of all automatically generated and scheduled sales transactions associated with a customer, such as invoices or sales receipts that repeat on a regular basis.

TIP

I dig into the details of recurring transactions in Chapter 9.

>> **Customer Details:** Summarizes a customer record and includes an Attachments section where you can add files, as described in the "Creating customer records" section.

>> **Late Fees:** Lists any late fees assessed to a customer.

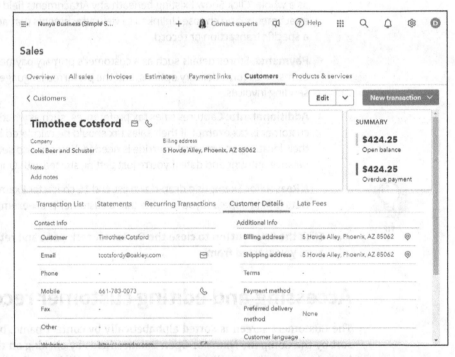

FIGURE 2-1:
A typical customer record page.

The Edit button, visible on every tab of the customer's page, allows three actions:

>> Click Edit to return to the Customer task pane, as discussed in the "Creating customer records" section of this chapter.

>> Click Edit ⇨ Make Inactive to mark a customer as inactive.

REMEMBER

You can't delete customers from QuickBooks Online, but you can mark them as inactive if their balance is zero.

WARNING

>> Click Edit ⇨ Merge Contacts to combine transactions from two different customer records.

All customer-specific details from the first customer, such as addresses and phone numbers, are discarded during the merge. Be sure to read the instructions in the Merge Contacts dialog box carefully to avoid unexpected data loss.

The New Transaction button, visible on each tab, enables you to create a variety of customer-related transactions as well as statements. Each transaction type is discussed later in this chapter.

Switching from record to record

The Split View pane shown in Figure 2-1 defaults to displaying recently viewed customers and includes a Search field that you can use to find the next customer record. Or you can click the Name field to display an alphabetical listing. Click Split View to hide or display the pane as needed.

To add a new record to the list, click the plus (+) symbol at the top of the Split View pane. To return to the Customers list page, click < Customers above the pane.

Batching activities for customers

A hidden Batch Actions button appears on the Customers screen when you click the checkboxes for one or more customers. You can also click the checkbox to the left of the Name caption at the top of the customer list to select all customers at once. The Batch Actions menu offers three options:

>> **Create Statements:** Use this command to generate the following types of statements:

- *Balance Forward:* Shows an open balance as of the start date of your choice and reflects activity through the specified end date.

- *Open Item:* Lists only unpaid invoices and unapplied credits for a selected time period.

- *Transaction Statement:* Reflects all transactions for a specified time period.

>> **Email:** Creates a blank message in your email software or platform, with the selected customers listed in the BCC field.

>> **Make Inactive:** Marks one or more customers without an open balance as inactive.

Customizing list columns

You can control the appearance of QuickBooks lists by hiding or displaying columns and choosing whether to include or hide inactive records:

1.   **Click the List Settings button above the Action column.**

2.   **Toggle checkboxes as needed to show or hide columns in the list, include inactive records, or determine the number of records shown per page.**

3.   **Click the List Settings button again to close the menu.**

Setting Up Sales Tax

Sales tax calculations in new QuickBooks companies are automated. After you complete a short setup wizard, QuickBooks automatically calculates sales tax based upon your customers' shipping addresses or billing addresses. However, existing QuickBooks Online companies, or those converted from QuickBooks Desktop, may still be using the old manual system, which required setting up sales tax rates by hand and then assigning them to each customer.

In this section, I guide you through switching to the Automated Sales Tax feature if you're currently using the manual system. Additionally, I cover how the Economic Nexus feature can help you identify when you might legally be required to collect sales tax, even if you're not currently doing so. Since taxes can vary, I show how to create custom sales tax rates for special circumstances, such as tariffs or excise taxes. It's important to review your sales tax settings periodically because government agencies will hold you accountable for any taxes that you fail to collect. Finally, I explain how to report and pay sales taxes to the appropriate taxing authorities.

REMEMBER

QuickBooks can calculate your sales tax liability and walk you through recording the payment, but it doesn't file your sales tax return for you. You or your accountant must file your return by mailing in a paper copy or by filling out the return online by way of the taxing authority's website.

Understanding sales tax liability

Depending on your volume of taxable transactions, you may be required to remit sales tax to tax authorities monthly, quarterly, or annually. When you enable the Sales Tax feature, you'll be asked to specify the accounting method QuickBooks uses calculate your sales tax liability:

- **» Accrual:** QuickBooks considers sales tax due in the period that you create the invoice, regardless of whether your customer has paid the invoice. If you later write off the invoice, you receive a credit for the sales taxes you previously paid.

- **» Cash:** QuickBooks considers sales tax due in the period that your customer pays the invoice. This method is easiest to track when customers pay invoices in full. Partial payments, non-taxable items, and discounts or credits that you apply can complicate sales tax calculations.

REMEMBER

You must provide accurate mailing addresses for your company and your customers once you enable the Sales Tax feature. QuickBooks verifies the addresses in real time and rejects any illegitimate addresses. Your home state and any local tax authorities are determined based on your physical address, while sales taxes are automatically calculated based on your customers' shipping addresses. If no shipping address is provided, the billing address is used instead.

Enabling the Automated Sales Tax feature

You're prompted to set up sales tax the first time you click the Taxes command in the sidebar menu in a newly created QuickBooks company:

1. Choose Taxes ➪ Sales Tax and then click the Use Automated Sales Tax button.

The wizard asks you to verify or enter your company's physical address, after which you click Next.

TIP

As is the case throughout QuickBooks, the State drop-down list is a little tricky. You can type the two-letter abbreviation for your state, but you then have to choose it from the list with your mouse. If I had my way, you'd be able to type in an abbreviation and press Enter.

2. The next screen asks if you need to collect tax outside of your state.

If you choose No, you can click Next to advance to the next screen. If you click Yes, you're prompted to specify the additional tax agencies. If you're not sure, check out the section titled "Exploring the Economic Nexus feature" later in this chapter.

WARNING

You can't edit or delete tax agencies that you set up in your company.

3. Click Next once you've answered the Yes or No question to display an Automated Sales Tax Is All Set Up screen.

You can either click Create Invoice or close the page, but — spoiler alert — sales tax isn't completely set up at this point. You have one more screen at a minimum, and you may need to mark certain customers as tax-exempt.

4. **When the How Often Do You File Sales Tax screen appears, specify your filing frequency for each agency and then click Save.**

   This step marks the true end of the sales tax wizard, so your next step is to indicate any tax-exempt customers.

QuickBooks assumes that all customers are subject to sales tax, so you need to edit any tax–exempt customers (such as government agencies, schools, and charities) by following these steps:

1. **Choose Customers or Customers & Leads ⇨ Customers.**

2. **Click the name of a tax-exempt customer and then click Edit on the customer record page that appears.**

3. **Scroll down to the Additional Info section and click This Customer Is Tax Exempt, as shown in Figure 2-2.**

4. **Specify a choice from the Reason for Exemption, which is a required field.**

5. **Enter up to 16 characters in the Exemption Details field if desired.**

   You can record a customer's exemption certificate ID in this field, or optionally upload a copy of the exemption certificate in the Notes and Attachments section, as described in the "Creating customer records" section.

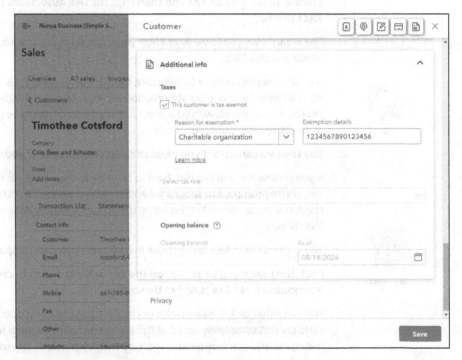

FIGURE 2-2:
Marking a customer as tax exempt.

Converting sales tax from QuickBooks Desktop

Setting up sales tax is a little different if you've imported your books from QuickBooks Desktop:

1. **Choose Taxes ⇨ Sales Tax and then click the Get Started button.**

   This screen gives you the option to Do It Later, but seize the moment and click Get Started.

2. **Confirm your business address on the first screen of the wizard and then click Next.**

3. **A Bulk Matching screen asks you to link your tax rates from QuickBooks Desktop to the tax agencies that QuickBooks Online recognizes.**

   Click the checkbox to the left of the Tax Rate Name column heading if all your tax rates relate to a single tax agency. You can make a choice from the Official Agency drop-down list, and then click Apply.

4. **Click Next to display a Review Your Rates screen.**

   Click Change next to any tax rates you want to modify.

5. **Click Save to finalize your changes.**

6. **Click Continue when prompted.**

   A two-screen help wizard appears to give you background about the Sales Tax Center. You can click through this wizard or close it without reviewing it.

7. **Specify your filing frequency for each agency when the How Often Do You File Sales Tax screen appears, and then click Save.**

   You can continue forward with your custom sales tax rates from QuickBooks Desktop, or you can enable automated sales tax.

Switching from manual to automated sales tax

You can easily switch to the Automated Sales Tax feature, whether you've just converted from QuickBooks Desktop or you've been continuing with the traditional manual sales tax method as a long-term QuickBooks Online user:

1. **Choose Taxes and then click the Sales Tax Settings button to display the Edit Settings screen.**

2. **Click Turn Off Sales Tax, and then click Yes when prompted to confirm.**

   In effect, this puts all your sales tax in a deep freeze, meaning the sales tax fields and settings vanish from QuickBooks, but you're just a few clicks away from restoring them again.

3. **Carry out the techniques listed in the "Enabling the Automated Sales Tax feature" section earlier in this chapter.**

REMEMBER

You can control whether QuickBooks automatically calculates sales tax for your customers or uses a custom tax rate that you establish. Click once on any customer in your customer list, and then click Edit. Scroll down to the Additional Info section and choose a custom tax rate from the Select Tax Rate field. Alternatively, choose Automated Based On Location to instruct QuickBooks to automatically calculate sales tax.

Exploring the Economic Nexus feature

As your business grows, you may draw in customers from other states and start wondering whether you're subject to sales or use tax in those states. The Economic Nexus feature removes all doubt by analyzing your sales for a time period of your choosing from January 2022 onward. You can run a report that informs you where you should be collecting and paying sales tax:

1. **Choose Taxes ⇨ Sales Tax.**

2. **Click the Economic Nexus button.**

3. **Review your activity by state.**

   States where you have a tax liability are marked with a green checkmark.

Customizing sales tax rates

You can establish custom tax rates if you have a tariff, excise tax, or other amount that you must collect on behalf of a governmental agency that QuickBooks doesn't automatically compute. Or you may be a free spirit who prefers to handle sales tax calculations on your own. Either way, just follow these steps:

1. **Choose Taxes ⇨ Sales Tax.**

2. **Click the Sales Tax Settings button to display the Edit Settings screen.**

   This screen enables you to add agencies.

3. Click Add Agency if you want to add a new tax agency.

A task pane prompts you to select an agency, specify your filing frequency, indicate your start date for collecting sales tax, and specify accrual or cash for your reporting method.

TIP

Your sales tax reporting method can be the same as the reporting basis for your books, or you can make it different.

4. Click Save to close the task pane.

Your new agency appears in the Tax Agencies list.

5. Optional: Click Add Rate to display the Add a Custom Sales Tax Rate task pane.

Choose Single if you have a single tax rate paid to a single agency or Combined if you have multiple tax rates that are paid to one or more agencies.

6. Click Save to close the task pane.

The next step is to apply the custom rate to your customers as needed.

7. Choose Customers or Customers & Leads ⇨ Customers.

8. Select a taxable customer from your customer list and then click Edit within their record.

9. Scroll down to the Additional Info section and choose the custom tax rate from the Select Tax Rate drop-down menu.

10. Click Save to close the task pane.

Repeat Steps 8 to 10 as needed to apply your custom tax rates to your customers.

Auditing your customers' sales tax settings

As I discuss earlier in this chapter, the Company Name and Customer Display Name fields are the only required fields when you create a new customer. Filling in the Company Name field isn't an issue because that feature fills in the address fields automatically. However, you can't charge sales tax to a customer if you've only completed their Customer Display Name field. Further, you may also want to review the tax rates assigned to each customer. Here's how to audit your sales tax settings by customer:

1. Choose Taxes ⇨ Sales Tax.

2. Choose Reports ⇨ Taxable Customer Report.

3. **A modified version of the Customer Contact List report includes the following columns:**

- **Customer:** As you might expect, this field displays the customer name.

- **Billing Address:** If this field is blank and sales tax is based on the billing address, you need to fill in this information.

- **Shipping Address:** Sales tax in QuickBooks is based on the shipping address, but it defaults to the billing address if no shipping address has been provided.

- **Taxable:** Yes appears in this column if the customer is subject to sales tax. No indication appears if you marked a customer as exempt or the customer is located out of state or out of the country.

- **Tax Rate:** This column shows the tax rate applicable to the customer, even if they've been marked as exempt.

TIP

Click any customer name or address to drill down into their customer record to make changes or to carry out a more detailed review.

4. **Optional: Click the Export button and choose Export to Excel if you want to view the report in Excel.**

In Chapter 20, I discuss how to use the Filter feature in Excel, which can make it easy to view all customers who have the same tax rate or to display customers where the billing or shipping addresses are blank.

Paying and filing sales taxes

Either you or your accountant can handle the sales tax filing process in this fashion:

1. **Choose Taxes ⇨ Sales Tax.**

2. **Scroll down to where you see all sales tax returns that are due and any that are overdue.**

3. **Click View Tax Return for the return you want to file.**

4. **Optional: Click + Add an Adjustment beneath Total Tax on the Review Your Sales Taxes screen to display the Add an Adjustment task pane.**

Provide a reason for the adjustment and the adjustment date, along with an account and an amount for the adjustment. Click Add to post the adjustment, or click the X at the top-right corner to close the task pane.

5. **Use the information onscreen to complete a paper return or electronic return by way of the taxing authority's website.**

6. **You can also click the report link on the next page of the sales tax wizard to get a report that you can use to file the sales tax return later.**

7. **Click Record Payment to display the Record Payment screen.**

8. **Enter a payment date, select a bank account, optionally enter a memo, and optionally click Print Check.**

WARNING

You can override the tax amount on the Record Payment screen, but doing so creates a discrepancy in your accounting records. The Add an Adjustment command discussed in Step 4 is the safest approach for altering your sales tax liability.

9. **Click Record Payment and, if needed, print the check that was generated.**

Working with Non-Inventory Products and Services

QuickBooks expects you to create items for each product or service that you offer. If you leave the Product/Service field blank on a sales transaction form, QuickBooks fills the field with a default item named Service. You can create the following items in any QuickBooks company:

>> **Inventory:** These include items that you buy/sell and track the quantity of. I discuss these items in detail in Chapter 10.

>> **Non-inventory:** These include items that you don't physically own, such as drop-ship items, or consumable items that are of immaterial value, such as nuts and bolts, where it's not feasible to charge for each nut or bolt.

>> **Services:** These items can streamline the invoicing process by giving you a way to standardize descriptions and pricing.

>> **Bundle:** These include collections of products and/or services that you might sell separately, but also sell bundled together, like a tablet and stylus set. I discuss creating bundles in Chapter 9.

Creating non-inventory and services items

Here's how to create a new item:

1. **Choose Settings ⇨ Products and Services to display the Products & Services screen.**

   Alternatively, choose Sales ⇨ Products & Services.

2. **Click New (or Add an Item if this is the first time you're adding a product or service) to open the Add a New Product task pane shown in Figure 2-3.**

3. **In the Item Type field, choose Non-Inventory Item or Service.**

4. **Supply a name for the item.**

   This is the only required field for non-inventory and service items.

5. **Optional: Enter a SKU.**

   SKU is short for *stock-keeping unit*. It's another way of referring to a part number or other identifier for your products and services.

6. **To upload a picture of the item, click Add an Image, select a .JPEG, .JPG, or .PNG file, and then click Open.**

TIP

   Hover over the picture to display the Replace and Delete buttons, which allow you to choose another image or remove the picture, respectively.

7. **If you want to assign a category, make a selection or click Add New in the Category field.**

   Categories are used to group similar transactions or items together, making it easier to organize financial data and generate more specific reports.

REMEMBER

   You can add new categories by way of the Categories field, but to create a sub-category, refer to the technique discussed in the "Managing categories" section later in this chapter.

8. **Fill in the Description field for how the item should be described on sales forms.**

9. **Fill in the Price/Rate field.**

   This is the amount you want to choose for a non-inventory item or the rate that you want to charge for a service.

10. **Select another account from the Income Account field if necessary, or click Add New to create a new income account.**

11. **A Sales Tax section will appear if you've enabled the sales tax feature, and you can optionally click Edit Sales Tax to override the default location-based sales tax calculations for this product.**

A Describe This Product or Service task pane appears, prompting you to choose a sales tax category. Alternatively, you can choose Taxable or Non-Taxable beneath the category list. Click Done to confirm your selection.

12. **If you procure this product or service from a vendor, click I Purchase This From a Vendor.**

You can fill in the description of the item, its cost, which expense account you use to pay for it, and select your preferred vendor.

13. **Click Save and Close.**

The Products and Services list appears, displaying your new item.

FIGURE 2-3:
A blank Add a New Product task pane.

TAKING ADVANTAGE OF SKUS

You can control whether SKU information appears in the Products and Services list and on transaction forms from the Account and Settings task pane. Choose Settings ⇨ Account and Settings ⇨ Sales. In the Products and Services section, toggle the Show SKU option on, and then click Save and Done. If you like, you can add the SKU to custom invoice forms, which I discuss in Chapter 1.

At any point, you can click Edit in the Action column of the Products and Services screen to edit an existing inventory item. The arrow in the Action column displays a menu with up to six choices, depending on your subscription level and the item type. I discuss the three options available to all QuickBooks users here:

>> **Make Inactive:** Choose this command to make an item inactive. To view items that you've marked inactive, click the funnel icon just above your list of products and services, change the Status to Inactive, and then click Apply. The Action contains a link that enables you to make an item active again.

>> **Run Report:** Choose this command to run a Quick Report for the past 90 days of transactions for this item.

>> **Duplicate:** Choose this command to display the Add a New Product task pane that you used earlier in the chapter to create a new item. In this case, some fields are prefilled to ease the process of setting up similar items.

You use the Products and Services list pretty much the same way you use the Customer and Vendor lists. For example, you can search for an item by its name, SKU, or sales description. You can identify the columns you can use to sort the list by sliding your mouse over the column heading; if the mouse pointer changes to a hand, you can click that column to sort the list using the information in that column.

Managing categories

Categories can help you organize what you sell and group related items on your inventory and sales reports. Categories don't affect your accounting or your financial reports, and you can't assign categories to transactions. That's what classes and locations are for; I discuss them in Chapter 11. The Category field in the Add a New Product task pane that you use to create an item enables you to create new categories on the fly, or you can use the Product Categories screen:

1. **Click Settings ➪ All Lists to display the All Lists screen.**

2. **Choose Product Categories.**

3. **Click Create New Category to display the Create Category Information task pane.**

4. **Enter a category name, optionally choose Is a Sub-Category, and then select a parent category.**

REMEMBER

You can't use existing item names as a category name. For instance, if you have a product called Skyhook, you can't use the word Skyhook as a category name, but you can be clever and use the plural *Skyhooks*.

5. **Click Save to create your new category, or click the Close button at the top right to cancel this action.**

TIP

You can create subcategories up to four levels deep, such as Clothing ⇨ Shoes ⇨ Women's Shoes ⇨ Sneakers. You can't create a sub-category for Sneakers because it's four levels down, but you can create another sub-category for Women's Shoes, which is three levels down, called *Dress Shoes*.

6. **To modify or delete a category name, click Edit from the Action column of the Product Categories screen if you want to modify or delete a category name.**

The resulting Create Category task pane includes a Remove button that you can use to delete the category. The Remove command also appears on the Action drop-down menu for each category. If you remove a sub-category, any items assigned move one level up. Any items assigned to a top-level category that you remove become uncategorized.

WARNING

Categories are an exception to the normal QuickBooks convention of keeping deleted items in an inactive state. When you remove a category, it is permanently deleted with no option to undo the change. To restore it, you must re-create the category and reassociate it with your items as needed.

7. **You must manually assign categories to your products and services by editing each record.**

As of this writing, Intuit has inexplicably removed the Batch Actions menu that is available on most list pages in QuickBooks, so you can no longer assign two or more items to a category at once.

Creating Sales Transactions

And now, the moment you've been waiting for: how do I create a dang invoice in this software? If you jumped to this page from the index, flip back a few pages, where I discuss how to set up customers, enable sales tax, and create non-inventory and service items. Customers and items are critical to the invoicing process, and for many users sales tax is critical as well.

WARNING

If your company is subject to sales tax, make sure to carry out the steps listed in the "Setting Up Sales Tax" section so that you don't inadvertently create transactions without sales tax. You'll be responsible for any sales tax that you don't collect should a revenue agent decide they want a look at your books.

MANAGING PRODUCT OR SERVICE ROWS

You can rearrange the rows within the Product or Service section by dragging a rows handle, identified as six dots at the start of a row, into a different position. You can click the Options button, identified as three dots on the right, to remove a line from an invoice. You can add rows in two ways: click Add Product or Service to add a new row to the bottom of the invoice, or click within the Product/Service field of any row to display an Add Row button represented by a plus sign within a circle. Click Add Row to add a blank row above the current line within the invoice. Finally, click the drop-down menu on the Add Product or Service button to reveal the Add Subtotal command.

Creating invoices

Invoices are written requests for payment for any goods or services that you've provided to your customers. An effective invoice makes it clear what value was provided. If you try to save a minute up front by creating a summary invoice with little detail, it could cost you time and frustration later in the form of delayed payment until you provide more detail about what the invoice covers.

Follow these steps to create an invoice:

1. **Choose + New ⇨ Invoice from the sidebar menu.**

    A new invoice window opens.

2. **Choose a customer from the Add Customer list.**

    The customer's mailing address, payment terms, invoice date, and due date appear.

    TIP

    Any pending estimates or billable time entries appear in a Suggested Transactions pane on the right side of the screen. I talk about estimates in the "Generating Estimates" section later in this chapter and discuss time entries in Chapter 9.

3. **Confirm the Invoice Number, Terms, Invoice Date, and Due Date.**

4. **To assign one or more custom labels to this transaction, fill in the Tags field and then choose Add, or select an existing tag.**

    Tags help categorize and track your transactions for more detailed reporting. I discuss the Tags feature in more detail in Chapter 6.

5. **Populate at least one row of the Products or Service section.**

    Enter an item name in the Product/Service field for each row of your invoice. If you skip this field, QuickBooks will automatically add a generic item such as Services for You.

a. *Click the Product/Service column and select an item for the invoice you're creating, or choose Add New to create a new item.*

A list of matching items appears as you type a few characters in this field.

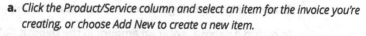

Refer to the "Working with Non-Inventory Products and Services" section earlier in this chapter if you need clarification on adding non-inventory items and services, to Chapter 9 for adding bundles, and to Chapter 10 for creating inventory items.

TIP

b. *The Description field prefills based upon the selection you made in the Product/ Service column, but you can always overwrite or edit the existing text.*

c. *Enter amounts in at least two of these fields: Quantity, Rate, and Amount.*

The amount in the third field will automatically calculate based up on the inputs you provide for the other two fields.

d. *If the Sale Tax feature is enabled, a checkbox will appear in the Tax column if an item is marked as taxable, but you can clear it to override this setting if needed.*

Click the three-dot More Actions menu to the right of the Tax checkbox to access the Delete command if you want to remove a row from an invoice.

e. *Repeat Steps a to d as needed to add more items to the invoice.*

Click Add Lines as needed to add rows to the invoice. You can also add rows by clicking on an empty cell in the row above — starting with row 2.

6. **To apply a discount, click the % or $ button to display the corresponding fields, allowing you to enter a percentage or dollar amount.**

ENABLING DISCOUNTS, SHIPPING, AND DEPOSITS

You can apply discounts to invoices on a pre-tax or after-tax basis, add shipping fees, and collect deposits. The Discount and Shipping fees are typically disabled by default, but you can enable them via the Customization Pane, which is typically displayed on the right side of the invoice screen, but click Manage if necessary. From there, you can toggle the Discount option on, and then click the Apply Discount atter Sales Tax checkbox if applicable. The Deposit option is typically enabled, but you can toggle it off if you do not collect deposits from customers.

7. **To add a shipping charge, enter an amount in the Shipping field.**

8. **To record a deposit, enter an amount in the Deposit field.**

   The Customization task pane appears and displays a Deposit section where you can optionally fill in the following fields: Payment Method, Reference Number, and Deposit To.

9. **To provide payment instructions to your customer, fill in the Tell Your Customer How You Want to Get Paid field.**

   You can use this space to provide a link to a payment page on your website, provide your PayPal, Venmo, or Zelle handles, along with any other relevant information.

10. **To write a note to your customer, fill in the Note to Customer field.**

    This field displays Thank You for Your Business unless you overwrite the default text.

11. **To draft a note to that will appear on your customer's statement, but not this invoice, fill in the Memo on Statement field.**

    The Statement Note field allows you to add a custom message or additional information that will appear on the customer's statement.

12. **To attach an electronic document to the invoice, click the Attachments box, and then navigate to the document or drag the document into the Attachments box, as described in the "Creating customer records" section.**

13. **At the bottom of the window, you can choose from the following options:**

    - **Cancel** to discard the invoice and close the window.

    - **Clear** the invoice form.

    - **Print or Preview**, enable the Print Later option, view a print preview of the invoice, generate a PDF version of the invoice from the Print or Preview screen, or print a packing slip.

TIP

      Packing slips are basically invoices that don't show prices — similar to menus in some upscale restaurants.

    - **Make Recurring** to schedule the transaction as a recurring invoice.

    - **Customize** to choose or create a customized invoice form.

- **Save** to assign an invoice number and save the transaction. The Save drop-down menu offers two other options:
  - Save and New creates a new invoice.
  - Save and Close saves the invoice and closes out the form.
- **Review and Send** to assign an invoice number, save the invoice, edit the default email message, preview the invoice, and then send a copy to the customer. The Review and Send drop-down menu enables you to share a link and then copy a unique URL for the invoice for inclusion in an email you want send outside of QuickBooks.

TIP

The email time- and date-stamp information appears in the header of invoices you send. Invoice emails are mobile-friendly and include invoice details so that customers see everything at a glance. The option you choose becomes the default behavior for invoices until you make a different selection in the future.

ENABLING CUSTOMER TIPS

You can enable a Tips field if your customers sometimes offer gratuities. To do so, choose Settings ⇨ Account and Settings ⇨ Sales. Click Edit for the Sales Form Content section and then toggle the Accept Tips option on. A prompt will ask you to indicate if you're the only one receiving tips, or your team. A second prompt will ask if you want to update the Sales Receipt template to include the Tips field. Click Save and Done. You can now record tips when applicable during your invoicing process.

ACCESSING RECENT TRANSACTIONS

Every transaction screen in QuickBooks has a Recent Transaction button that displays a list of recent transactions. Alternatively, click Search at the top of every page in QuickBooks to view a list of recent transactions. You can also view recent transactions on the corresponding page for a customer, vendor, and so on. Finally, you can also view all sales transactions by choosing Sales ⇨ All Sales.

Recording invoice payments

Oh happy day, your customer has paid your invoice, and it's time to record it to your books. Payments can come in from several avenues: paper checks, ACH transactions, credit cards, PayPal, Venmo, Zelle, CashApp — the list truly goes on and on. And now — the moment you've been waiting for — instructions for how to post a customer payment:

1. **Display the Receive Payment screen by using one of the following methods:**

   - Choose + New ⇨ Receive Payment.
   - On the Customer screen, click Receive Payment in the Action column of a customer.
   - On a customer's page, choose New Transaction ⇨ Payment.

2. **Make a selection from the Customer field if necessary.**

3. **If you want to search for a specific invoice, click Find By Invoice No., enter an invoice number in the resulting dialog box, and then click Find.**

   If the invoice number exists and hasn't been paid, the Outstanding Transactions list will be filtered for the invoice number and the invoice will be selected for payment.

4. **Confirm the payment date if you're posting the deposit directly to your bank account.**

   Doing so will make reconciling your bank account easier later. The Payment Date isn't as critical if you are posting the deposit to your Undeposited Funds account because you'll be assigning a date when you create a Bank Deposit transaction.

5. **Make a selection from the Payment Method field or click Add New to create a new method.**

   Default methods include cash, check, and credit card, but you can add others as needed. I discuss how to maintain other lists such as this in Chapter 1.

6. **Fill in the Reference Number field if applicable.**

   This is the check number if your customer paid by check. You can leave the Reference field blank for cash or electronic deposits or repurpose it as a note field.

7. **Make a selection from the Deposit To Account.**

   If you're posting a single check or payment for which no fees are deducted, you can choose your bank account from the drop-down list. If you're depositing two or more checks in your bank on the same day or making an electronic payment that incurs a processing fee, choose Payments to Deposit or Undeposited Funds.

TIP

Intuit has a tendency to rename long-standing features in QuickBooks, such as the Undeposited Funds account, now called Payments to Deposit. Regardless of the name, this account serves as a holding place for checks or transactions that you plan to batch together into a single amount, ensuring it matches what posts to your bank account and appears on your bank statement.

8. **Select the invoice(s) being paid by clicking the checkbox for individual invoices or the checkbox at the top of the column to select all invoices.**

   If your customer makes a partial payment, you can adjust the Payment field as needed for each invoice.

REMEMBER

You can't record payment-processing fees, such as those assessed by Stripe or PayPal, on the Receive Payment screen if your customer has paid you electronically. You must enter such fees on the Bank Deposit screen, which I discuss in the upcoming section titled "Recording bank deposits."

9. **Click Save and Close, Save and New, or Save and Send.**

   The Save button is a sticky preference, meaning that you can click it and change the default behavior for future transactions. Use Save and Send to email a copy of the payment receipt to your customer.

THE PAYMENTS TO DEPOSIT ACCOUNT

Older QuickBooks companies may still have an Undeposited Funds account, which might sound like an oxymoron. You're going to deposit those funds pronto, of course! This account is now named Payments to Deposit. If your bank deposits are always composed of a single check or ACH payment that doesn't incur a processing fee, you can skip this section. But if you make bank deposits with multiple checks or receive electronic payments that have deducted processing fees, using the Payments to Deposit account simplifies bank reconciliation.

The Payments to Deposit account mirrors what posts to your bank statement. For example, if you deposit five checks on a single deposit ticket, your bank posts one lump sum to your account. You want your bank account in QuickBooks to reflect that lump sum as well, not five individual deposits, which is what the Payments to Deposit account accomplishes. Think of this account as a holding area where you can accumulate customer payments and then batch them into amounts that match what the bank posts to your account. This way, your bank-reconciliation process runs smoothly, without the hassle of trying to match individual payments to the lump sum on your bank statement.

Handling overpayments

Occasionally, a customer might pay you more than expected. You can either credit the customer for the overpayment or treat the excess as a gratuity. Before doing so, ensure that QuickBooks is set to apply credits automatically. To enable this:

1. **Go to Settings ⇨ Account and Settings ⇨ Advanced.**

2. **In the Automation section, toggle on Automatically Apply Credits, then click Save and Done.**

    Once this setting is enabled, QuickBooks will automatically create credit transactions for overpayments. When you receive a payment with an overpayment, enter the full amount in the Amount Received field. You can then choose from the following scenarios:

    - **Apply the Overpayment to an Existing Invoice:** Select the invoice(s) to apply the payment against in the Outstanding Transactions section of the Receive Payment screen. This option might result in partial payment for one invoice and possibly full payment for others.

    - **Apply the Overpayment to a New Invoice:** Select an invoice in the Outstanding Transactions section of the Receive Payment screen. For example, if the invoice is $100 but you received $120, enter $120 as the amount paid. QuickBooks will create a $20 credit transaction when you click Save and Close. This credit will automatically apply to the next invoice you create for the customer.

    - **Keep the Overpayment as Income:** To do this, add a Gratuity income account to your chart of accounts and create a Gratuity service item assigned to this income account. Then, create a new invoice for the customer using the Gratuity item for the overpayment amount. QuickBooks will automatically mark the invoice as paid using the credit it created from the overpaid invoice.

Recording bank deposits

It's crucial to remember to record bank deposit transactions to prevent customer payments from getting stuck in your Payments to Deposit or Undeposited Funds account. Your holding account should always have a zero balance after you've recorded any current bank deposits. Here's how to post a bank deposit:

1. **Choose + New ⇨ Bank Deposit.**

    The Bank Deposit screen appears.

2. **Select a bank account from the Account field if needed.**

3. **Override the Date field if applicable.**

4. **To assign one or more custom labels to this transaction, fill in the Tags field and then choose Add, or select an existing tag.**

   Tags help categorize and track your transactions for more detailed reporting. I discuss the Tags feature in more detail in Chapter 6.

5. **The Select the Payments Included in This Deposit section will appear when you have one or more customer payments being held in the Payments to Deposit Account, from which you can choose what you want to include in the deposit.**

   Turn on the checkbox next to each payment that you're including in this deposit, or click Select All.

6. **If you have additional checks or deposits to record, or bank or processing charges to record, add rows to the Add Funds to this Deposit section as needed.**

   a. *Choose a customer or vendor from the Received From field.*

   b. *Make a selection from the Account field.*

   c. *Use the Description field to document the transaction.*

   d. *Make a selection from the Payment Method field, or click Add New to create a new method.*

   e. *Complete the Ref No. field if applicable.*

   f. *Enter an amount greater than zero for amounts that you are adding to your bank account, or less than zero for charges that you are recording.*

   g. *Turn on the Track Returns for Customers checkbox to display a Customer column from which you can associate additional checks or deposits with a customer.*

WARNING

   Make sure to enter a negative amount in the Add Funds to This Deposit section for charges; otherwise, you overstate your deposit by *adding* the transaction fees to the deposit amount instead of *deducting* the fees.

7. **Enter up to 4,000 characters in the memo field if applicable.**

8. **If you are taking cash back from the bank deposit, fill in three additional fields:**

   a. *Select an account from the Cash Back Goes To field if you are taking cash from the bank deposit.*

   b. *Document the withdrawal in the Cash Back Memo field.*

   c. *Record the cash withdrawal in the Cash Back Amount field.*

9. To attach an electronic document to the deposit, use the procedure described in the "Creating customer records" section of this chapter.

10. Confirm that the deposit total matches the net amount that posts to your bank account.

If you deposit $12,075.00 and post –$350.18 in the Add Funds to this Account section, the net deposit is $11,724.82. Conversely, if you're simply depositing paper checks that you take to your bank, you likely don't need to enter anything in the Add Funds to This Deposit section, so the Total should match the sum of the checks that you're about to deposit.

11. Click Save and Close or click Save and New.

Click the arrow on the Save button to toggle between those two settings. Your choice then becomes the default for future transactions.

Entering sales receipts

Sometimes you may get paid right when you provide goods or render services. Rather than entering an invoice and then immediately receiving a payment against it, you can create a sales receipt instead. Sales receipts are also ideal for receiving ad hoc payments via an electronic payment platform such as Stripe or PayPal.

To create a sales receipt, choose + New ⇨ Sales Receipt, or choose New Transaction ⇨ Sales Receipt on the Sales Transactions screen. The sales receipt form is similar to the invoice form, but in this case, your saved transaction is recorded to your bank account or the Payments to Deposit account, instead of your Accounts Receivable account. Fill out the form in much the same way that you do an invoice: provide the payment-specific details, such as payment method and reference number, and select the account where the funds should go. See the sidebar "The Payments to Deposit Account" earlier in this chapter for information on selecting an account from the Deposit To list.

TIP

When using a platform like PayPal, you may need to account for payment processing fees. To do this, create a Service or Non-Inventory item labeled something like Payment Processing Fee. When recording the fee, enter it as a negative amount. Although QuickBooks might display a This value is out of range warning when you type the minus sign, you can safely disregard this prompt. The net amount on the sales receipt should then match the net deposit that posts to your bank account.

TIP

You can generate packing slips from sales receipts in the same fashion as I described in the "Creating invoices" section earlier in this chapter.

Generating credit memos and refund receipts

Occasionally, you need to return money you've received from a customer. It's not ideal, but it happens. You have two options for returning money to customers — credit memos and refund receipts.

CREDIT MEMOS

Credit memos allow you to reduce the outstanding or future balance for your customer when warranted. To create a credit memo, follow these steps:

1. **Choose + New ⇨ Credit Memo or Sales ⇨ Transactions ⇨ New Transaction ⇨ Credit Memo.**

2. **Complete the Credit Memo screen in the same fashion as I discussed in the "Creating invoices" section earlier in this chapter.**

REMEMBER

Enter credit memo amounts as a positive number. It can get confusing because you're trying to offset an invoice, so you might think that the credit memo needs to reflect a negative amount, but you want both transactions to reflect positive amounts, and then you can match them against each other.

TIP

By default, credit memos are applied automatically to outstanding or future invoices. If you want to change that behavior, choose Settings ⇨ Account ⇨ Advanced ⇨ Automation, toggle off the Automatically Apply Credits option, click Save, and Done.

REFUND RECEIPTS

Refund Receipts record the return of money to a customer, typically when you've already received payment for goods or services but need to refund the amount, either partially or in full. To create a refund receipt, follow these steps:

1. **Choose + New ⇨ Refund Receipt.**

2. **Complete the Refund Receipt screen in the same fashion as I discussed in the "Creating invoices" section earlier in this chapter,** with the additional steps of choosing a payment method, selecting a bank account from the Refund From field, and filling out the Check Number field if applicable.

3. **You can either mark the transaction as Print Later, or click Print or Preview and then choose Print Check if you are issuing payment in that fashion.**

WARNING

Credit memos and refund receipts should never be used to record overpayments because doing so can result in confusion. See the "Handling overpayments" section earlier in this chapter if you need to post an overpayment.

TIP

To account for refunds that you issue when a customer doesn't return an item, add an Income account called Returns and Allowances to your chart of accounts and choose Discounts/Refunds Given in the Detail Type field. I discuss adding accounts to your chart of accounts in more detail in Chapter 1. Next, set up a service item on the Products and Services list called Customer Refunds or Returns & Allowances, but *don't* select Is Taxable for the service. Assign the service to the Returns & Allowances account, and leave the Price/Rate empty. I cover the process of creating a service in more detail in the "Working with Non-Inventory Products and Services" section earlier in this chapter.

REMEMBER

If you're using QuickBooks Payments, you can only refund credit card charges processed through your payment account. You can't refund ACH payments electronically. You have to kick it old school and print a paper check or facilitate an electronic transaction outside of QuickBooks.

Batching activities for sales forms

Sometimes, you may choose to print a sales document later. Additionally, instances may arise where a customer asks for copies of all their invoices or other forms from a specific period of time. You can handle both of these situations by following these steps:

1. **Choose Sales ⇨ All Sales.**

   A listing of all sales transactions appears.

2. **Use the Type, Date, and Customer fields to select the transactions.**

   You have the option to display a list of all transaction types at once, or you can filter by a single transaction type. However, it's not possible to select multiple transaction types simultaneously, such as viewing Invoices and Sales Receipts together. Similarly, you can view transactions for all customers or focus on a single customer, but you cannot display transactions for two or more customers at the same time.

3. **Select one or more transactions, or click the Select All checkbox to the left of the Date heading.**

4. **Click the Batch Actions button and then choose a command:**

   - **Convert to Invoice:** Converts estimates to invoices.

   - **Send:** Emails the form to the customer.

- **Send Reminder:** Emails reminders for unpaid invoices.

- **Print:** Prints multiple sales forms at once.

- **Print Packing Slip:** Generates packing slips for the invoices or sales receipts that you select.

- **Delete:** Physically deletes transactions from your books, which you can't undo.

Writing Off Bad Debt

An unfortunate reality of running a business is that, at some point, you may not get paid for products delivered or services rendered. It's a frustrating aspect of being a business owner or manager, but it's part of the hard-earned knowledge that comes with experience.

Before you can write off an invoice, some initial setup is required. However, once these one-time tasks are completed, writing off bad debt becomes straightforward: simply create a credit memo and apply it as a payment against the unpaid invoices.

Setting up a bad debt account and item

You must create a Bad Debt account and a Bad Debt item before you can write off an unpaid invoice. First add a Bad Debt account to your chart of accounts:

1. Choose Settings ⇨ Chart of Accounts ⇨ New.
2. Enter a name such as Bad Debt in the Account Name field.
3. Choose Expenses from the Account Type drop-down list.
4. Choose Other Business Expense from the Detail Type drop-down list.
5. Use the Description field to describe the account if you want.
6. Click Save.

Now create a Bad Debt item:

1. Choose Settings ⇨ Products and Services or Sales ⇨ Products & Services ⇨ New ⇨ Non-Inventory.
2. Enter Bad Debt in the Name field.

3. **If you want to assign a category, make a selection or click Add New in the Category field.**

   Categories are used to group similar transactions or items together, making it easier to organize financial data and generate more specific reports.

   I skipped over the SKU field in this context because a stock-keeping unit isn't typically assigned to an administrative item like Bad Debt.

4. **Turn on the I Sell This Product/Service to Customers checkbox.**

5. **Enter a description, such as $*#@_% (which stands in for curse words in comic strips), or be more reserved and enter** Bad Debt Write-Off.

6. **Leave the Sales Price/Rate field blank.**

7. **Choose Bad Debt from the Income Account list.**

8. **Clear the I Purchase This Product/Service from a Vendor if needed.**

9. **Click Save and Close.**

Creating bad debt write-off transactions

Once you've created the Bad Debt account on your chart of accounts and created a Bad Debt non-inventory item, you're ready to grit your teeth and start writing off some uncollectible invoices.

1. **Choose +New ⇨ Credit Memo.**

2. **Select your nemesis, er, I mean customer.**

3. **Choose Bad Debt in the first line of the Products/Service section.**

4. **Enter the amount that you're writing off in the Amount column.**

   In the particularly unfortunate event that you're writing off two or more invoices, the amount you enter here can be the sum of all invoices that you're writing off.

5. **Enter a missive such as** Write Off Bad Debt **in the Message Displayed on Statement field.**

6. **Click Save and Close, or click Save and New if you have other non-paying customers to dispatch as well.**

7. **Choose New ⇨ Receive Payment.**

8. **Choose a customer.**

9. **Select one or more invoices from the Outstanding Transactions section.**

10. **Select the credit memo you created from the Credits section.**

11. **Click Save and Close.**

REMEMBER

A bit of cold comfort: If you file your taxes on the accrual basis, you'll most likely get a deduction for the bad debt. There's no deduction if you file your taxes using a cash basis because you don't count invoices as taxable income until you receive payment.

Generating Estimates

Estimates, also referred to as quotes or bids, are essential tools for preparing documents that forecast the charges a client might incur for completing a project. These are nonposting transactions, meaning they don't affect your general ledger or financial statements, but they do allow you to effectively track the proposals you make to customers.

As I discuss in Chapter 10, if you're a Plus or Advanced subscriber, you can convert an estimate to a purchase order to streamline the process of ordering the necessary items for the job. Additionally, in this chapter, I demonstrate how you can also convert an estimate to an invoice when it's time to bill your customer, which not only saves time but also eliminates redundant typing.

WARNING

Only Pending or Accepted estimates can be converted to purchase orders or invoices. Converting to an invoice closes the estimate, so always convert to a purchase order first if both are needed.

Preparing an estimate

Creating an estimate is identical to creating an invoice, which I cover in the "Creating invoices" section earlier in this chapter. To get started, choose + New ➪ Estimate or Sales ➪ Estimates.

REMEMBER

Estimates are nonposting transactions, so they don't impact your financial reports. For example, if you enter a $10,000 estimate, it won't appear in your Profit & Loss report until you convert the estimate to an invoice. The status of an invoice is either Paid or Unpaid, while estimates can be assigned any of these statuses:

>> Pending indicates that the estimate is awaiting customer approval and has not been accepted or rejected yet.

>> Accepted shows that the customer has reviewed the estimate and agreed to its terms. Such estimates are ready to be converted to purchase orders if applicable, and invoices once the goods or services have been provided.

>> Rejected shows that the customer declined the opportunity.

>> Closed signals that the work has been invoiced and no further action is required.

TIP

You can open existing estimates in several ways. For instance, you can click the clock icon at the top-left corner of the Estimate screen to view recent transactions, choose the estimate from a customer's Sales Transactions list, or use the Search command on the QuickBooks dashboard.

Sales taxes, discounts, and shipping fees only appear on your estimates if you've enabled these fields for your invoices. See the "Creating invoices" and "Setting Up Sales Tax" sections that appear earlier in this chapter.

At the bottom of the Estimate screen, you can do the following:

>> Click Cancel to discard the estimate before you've saved it or to cancel any changes after you've saved it and close the Estimate screen.

>> Click Print or Preview to print the document now or mark it to print later.

>> Click Make Recurring to schedule the transaction as a recurring estimate.

>> Click Customize to choose or create a customized estimate form.

>> Click More to copy or delete the estimate or to view its audit trail. This button appears only after you've saved the estimate.

>> Click Save to assign a number to the estimate and save the transaction.

>> Click Save and Send from the Save drop-down list to assign a number to the estimate, save it, and email a copy to the customer. After you send your estimate, the email time- and date-stamp information appears in the header.

>> Click Save and New to assign a number to the estimate, save it, and open a new estimate form.

>> Click Save and Close to save the estimate and close out the form.

TIP

The Estimates by Customer report enables you to filter a list of estimates by status.

Converting an estimate to an invoice

You've completed the project and delivered the goods, so now it's time to send your customer an invoice. Since you already have an estimate, you're nearly done — just convert the estimate to an invoice after you change its status from Pending to Accepted:

1. **Choose +New ⇨ Estimate.**

   The Estimates screen opens.

2. **Click Recent Transactions and select the estimate that you wish to accept.**

3. **Click Manage to open the Estimate task pane.**

4. **Choose Pending to Accepted, and then click Convert to Invoice.**

   You can adjust the invoice by adding or removing lines as necessary. Other methods for converting accepted estimates into invoices include:

   - Open the Invoice screen and select a customer with the open estimate. Then choose an estimate and click Add to transfer the line items to your invoice.

   - Filter a customer's Sales Transactions screen to display only open estimates and click the Create Invoice link in the Action column to create a new invoice based on the estimate.

   - On a customer's Sales Transactions screen, open the estimate, and click the Create Invoice button. This button is available when the estimate status is Pending or Accepted. You can't create invoices from Closed or Rejected estimates.

REMEMBER

Converting an estimate to an invoice changes the status to Closed, which means you can no longer convert the estimate to a purchase order. If you need to generate a purchase order from an estimate, make sure to do that *before* you create the invoice.

TIP

No matter which route you take, creating an invoice from an estimate changes the status of the estimate to Closed, even if you don't invoice the customer for all lines on the estimate. You can change an estimate's status from Closed to Pending or Accepted (or even Rejected), but doing so makes *all* lines on the estimate available for invoicing, which means that you could accidentally invoice your customer twice for the same items. If you need to create a partial invoice, it's best to first make a copy of the invoice that includes only the pending items and then close the original estimate.

TIP

If you frequently need to send an invoice for only a portion of an estimate, progress billing may be a better fit for you. Read more in the upcoming section, "Creating a progress invoice for an estimate."

Copying an existing estimate

Copying an estimate enables you to make an exact duplicate, which is helpful if you want to send a partial invoice or another customer wants the same set of items. Open an existing estimate from a customer's Sales Transactions list or choose New ⇨ Estimates and click the Recent Transactions icon to the left of the estimate number.

Click More ⇨ Copy at the bottom of the screen to display a copy of the estimate. From there, you can modify the estimate as you want, including selecting a different customer. Click Save or Save and Send in the bottom-right corner of the window, as appropriate.

Creating a progress invoice for an estimate

If your business involves projects that extend over a long period — like six months, a year, or more — waiting until the end to collect payment can strain your cash flow, making it hard to cover your expenses. To avoid this, you can arrange for *progress invoicing*, where you receive payments at various stages of the project. This approach helps ensure a steady cash flow, allowing you to manage your bills while continuing the work.

TIP

Progress invoicing often goes hand in hand with project work, which I discuss in Chapter 11. You don't have to use the Projects feature to generate progress invoices, but if you plan to use projects, make sure to set up the project before you create an estimate.

Progress invoicing lets you send invoices to your customers at periodic milestones that you and your customer agree on. In short, you can create as many invoices as you need for a given estimate until the work is completed in full or all goods have been provided. Here's how to enable the Progress Invoicing feature:

1. **Choose Settings ⇨ Account and Settings ⇨ Sales.**

2. **Click Edit in the Progress Invoicing section.**

3. **Toggle the Create Multiple Partial Invoices From a Single Estimate option on, and then click "Yeah, man," I mean Update to confirm that it's groovy with you to update your invoice template to accommodate progress invoicing.**

4. **Click Save and then Done.**

Next, create an estimate in the usual fashion, as described earlier in this chapter. When you're ready to invoice a portion of the estimate, create an invoice as described in the "Converting an estimate to an invoice" section to display the window shown in Figure 2-4.

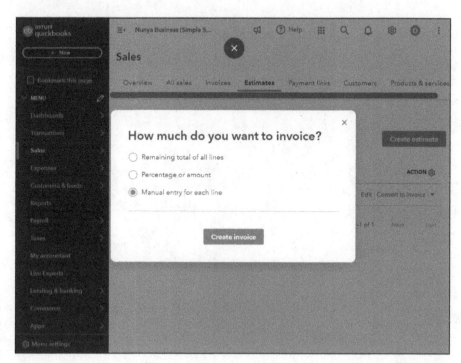

FIGURE 2-4:
Use this window
to establish the
amount of a
progress invoice.

Based on the choice you make in this window, an invoice is generated with the relevant values pre-filled. If you choose to create an invoice with custom amounts for each line, the invoice will be blank, allowing you to enter the amounts manually. You can continue to create additional progress invoices for the estimate as needed until the estimate is fully billed and closed out.

Chapter **3**

Logging Expenses, Checks, and Credit Card Charges

t's always more enjoyable to record money coming in than going out, but incurring expenses is a necessary part of business, and that's the focus of this chapter. You'll explore various transactions in QuickBooks to record money going out, such as checks, expense transactions, and credit card transactions. When you record expenses, they can be posted to either a bank account or a credit card account, affecting the respective account immediately. Checks will reduce your bank balance, and credit card transactions will increase your credit card balance accordingly. Additionally, you can enter Bill transactions, which allow you to post expenses and charges to your books as soon as they are incurred, allowing you to pay them later — a process known as accounts payable (A/P).

Working with Vendors

John Donne famously said, "No man is an island," and the same holds true for businesses — no business can be completely self-sufficient. For example, you'll incur charges for using QuickBooks Online, for Internet access, electricity to power your computer, and more. To manage these expenses, you need to set up each provider of goods and services as a vendor. An exception applies to individuals who are quasi-employees; you can set them up as a vendor or, as discussed in Chapter 4, as a contractor.

Initiating vendor records

You can't pay anyone or record an expense without first creating a vendor record. Well, if you're super stubborn you can use journal entries, which I discuss in Chapter 22, but that's a brute force approach. Ostensibly, there's only one required field, Vendor Display Name, but if you plan on printing and mailing checks or using an online bill payment service, you also should fill in the vendor address at a minimum. Follow these steps to create a vendor:

1. **Choose + New ⇨ Add Vendor or Expenses ⇨ Vendors ⇨ New Vendor to open the Vendor screen.**

2. **You can use either the Company Name or Vendor Display Name fields to fill in the vendor's name.**

   - Type the vendor's name in the Company Name field and select a match from the list. Click Save and Send to request for their invoices to post automatically to your books as bill transactions — your vendor must approve the request.

   TIP

   If you select the wrong vendor name or feel uncomfortable about the vendor's invoices posting directly to your accounting records, click Reset in the Company Name field to clear your selection and cancel the pending request, if applicable.

   - Fill out the Vendor Display Name field.

   The Company Name or Vendor Display Name fields are the only required fields when creating a new vendor record.

3. **If you want to store contact information for this vendor, fill in any combination of Title, First Name, Middle Name, Last Name, and Suffix, Email, Phone Number, Mobile Number, Other, and Website.**

   The Other field allows up to 30 characters, which can be used for any additional details you want to include about this vendor.

4. **If you will be paying this vendor by check from QuickBooks, make sure to properly complete the Name to Print on Checks field.**

5. **Complete the Address section if applicable.**

   The Preview Address link displays this vendor's location on Google Maps.

6. Use the Notes field to enter free-form text of up to 4,000 characters related to this vendor.

7. Use the Attachments field to attach an unlimited number of supporting files related to this vendor.

I discuss the Attachments feature in detail in Chapter 1.

8. If you plan to pay this vendor electronically via automated clearinghouse (ACH) transactions, fill in the Bank Account Number and Routing Number fields.

An optional QuickBooks Payment subscription enables you to automate paying vendors electronically, or you can store the ACH information here for use with an external service.

9. If available, enter a company's Employer Identification number or an individual's Social Security Number in the Business ID No./Social Security No. field.

10. If applicable, select the Track Payments for 1099 checkbox.

I discuss the Form 1099 in more detail in Chapter 4.

11. If you want to set payment terms for this vendor, make a selection from the Terms list or click Add New.

Payment terms define the conditions under which a buyer is required to make payment to a seller, including the due date and any discounts for early payment.

12. If you have the account number that this vendor has assigned to you, enter up to 100 characters in the Account field.

The contents of the Account field will appear in the Memo field of the Bill Payment transactions for this vendor.

13. Choose an account from your chart of accounts in the Category field or click Add New to add a new account.

In short, you'll typically use this field to specify the default expense account that you want to appear onscreen when you record a bill or expense transaction for this vendor.

14. If you're just getting started with QuickBooks, enter an amount in the Opening Balance field and then specify a date in the As Of field.

Opening balance refers to the amount of due to a vendor when the vendor record is first created. Always consult your accountant or bookkeeper if you have any questions about recording opening balances, as accurate entry is crucial for maintaining correct financial records, avoiding discrepancies, and heading off income tax implications.

15. Click Save to record your changes and close the Vendor task pane.

The Vendors screen or the corresponding transaction screen you started from opens.

Maintaining vendor records

The Vendors list is a tab within the Expenses screen, and it is sorted alphabetically by Vendor Display Name. Click the Company Name or Open Balance field headings to sort on either of those columns as well. Click in any vendor's row except the Action column to open the Vendors screen (shown in Figure 3-1), which contains two tabs:

» **Transaction List:** A list of all transactions associated with this vendor.

» **Vendor Details:** A summary of the vendor record, including an Attachments section. I discuss adding attachments to lists and transactions in detail in Chapter 1.

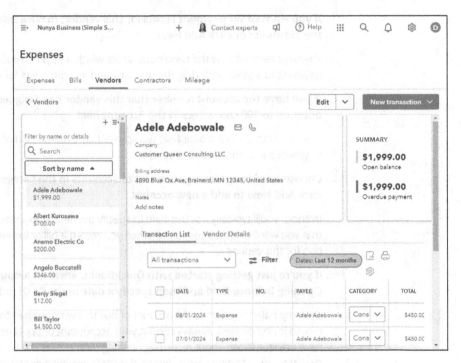

FIGURE 3-1:
A typical
Vendors screen.

Edit, visible on every screen within the Vendors tab of Expenses screen, allows three actions:

- Click Edit to return to the Vendors task pane, as discussed in the "Initiating vendor records" section of this chapter.

- Click Edit ➪ Make Inactive to mark a vendor as inactive.

  You can't delete vendors from QuickBooks Online, but you can mark them as inactive if their balance is zero.

REMEMBER

- Click Edit ➪ Merge Contacts to combine transactions from two different customer records.

  All vendor-specific details from the first vendor, such as addresses and phone numbers, are discarded during the merge. Be sure to read the instructions in the Merge Contacts screen carefully to avoid unexpected data loss.

WARNING

The New Transactions button, visible on each screen of the Vendors tab within the Expenses screen, enables you to create a variety of vendor-related transactions as well as statements. Each transaction type is discussed later in this chapter.

Switching from record to record

The Split View pane shown in Figure 3-1 defaults to displaying recently viewed vendors, and includes a Search field that you can use to find the next vendor record that you're seeking. Or you can click the Name field to display an alphabetical listing. Click Split View to hide or display the pane as needed.

To add a new record to the list, click the plus (+) symbol at the top of the Split View pane. To return to the Vendors tab of the Expenses screen, click < Vendors above the pane.

Batching activities for vendors

The Batch Actions button enables you to carry out two different activities. This button appears on the Vendors screen when you click the checkboxes for one or more vendors. You can also click the checkbox to the left of the Name caption at the top of the vendor list to select all vendors at once. The Batch Actions menu offers two options:

>> **Email:** This command creates a blank message in your email software or platform and lists the email addresses for the vendor(s) that you selected in the BCC field.

>> **Make Inactive:** Choose this option to mark as inactive one or more vendors that don't have an open balance.

TIP

The Transactions List tab of the Vendors screen in the Expenses screen used to contain a Batch Actions button that would enable you to print or recategorize multiple transactions at once, but this functionality has been replaced with a Categorize button as of this writing. The Categorize dialog box allows you to choose a single account that will then be applied to all of the selected transactions when you click Apply.

REMEMBER

I discuss how to customize lists such as vendors in Chapter 1.

Understanding Accounts Payable

As our society moves at an ever more frenetic pace, you may be expected to pay immediately for goods and services. This means you might use a credit card or an online payment service, such as Venmo or PayPal, or even print or write paper checks, although the recipient may look askance at you if you do. If you're looking to create a record for money that's already gone out the door, skip ahead to the "Recording Checks, Expenses, and Credit Card Charges" section later in this chapter. Otherwise, sit and stay a spell while I tell you about the accounts payable process, which involves entering bills that you plan to pay later, such as a rent bill, a car insurance bill, or a social media expert's invoice.

The accounts payable process works as follows:

1. **A bill arrives or is implied.**

   The vendor might send you a paper or electronic bill, or perhaps you're contractually obligated to pay a certain amount periodically, such as for office or car lease payments.

2. **You determine when you're going to pay the obligation and then enter the corresponding transaction.**

   If you're planning to pay the amount due within a couple of days, you can save time by not entering a bill, and instead record the transaction by using one of the methods covered in the "Recording Checks, Expenses, and Credit Card Charges" section later in this chapter. It doubles your work to enter a bill and then immediately pay it. Further, you clog up your financial records and reports with twice as many transactions. On the other hand, if the vendor expects payment, say within 30 days, you may decide to enter a bill.

3. **You pay the bill by the appointed due date.**

TIP

If you have a Plus or Advanced subscription you can create a purchase order transaction that you convert to a bill when the goods or services have been received. I discuss purchase orders in detail in Chapter 10.

Entering a bill

QuickBooks makes a distinction between invoices, which you send to customers and bills, which vendors send to you. It all depends on which side of the buyer/seller equation you happen to be on at any moment. Here I explain how to enter a bill, which is similar to entering an invoice:

1. **Choose + New ⇨ Bill.**

   Alternatively, choose Expenses ⇨ Bills ⇨ Add Bill ⇨ Create Bill.

2. **Choose a name from the Vendor list or click Add New to create a new vendor.**

3. **If necessary, enter the vendor's mailing address if you plan to mail the vendor a check or you're planning to use the QuickBooks Bill Pay service.**

WARNING

Address changes that you make on the Bill screen aren't saved back to the vendor record. If a vendor's address is missing or has changed, choose Expenses ⇨ Vendors, select the vendor, and edit the address. This can save you untold time in the future, from not having to enter the address again, to having checks sent to the wrong address or getting lost in the postal system.

4. **Make a selection from the Payment Terms list if the field is blank, or if you want to override the payment terms you established for this vendor.**

   Typical terms include Due on Receipt, Net 15, and Net 30. You can also choose Add New to create a new type of payment term. The Due Date field will recalculate automatically based upon the terms that you specify and the Bill Date field.

   The Terms list in QuickBooks applies to both customers and vendors. Choose the Gear Icon ⇨ All Lists ⇨ Terms to view your existing terms. Choose Make Inactive from the Action column if you want to disable a particular payment term.

5. **Enter the bill date.**

   Be sure to enter the actual bill date, as opposed to today's date, so that the bill's age is reflected properly on your accounts payable aging reports, and especially in your books if you use the accrual basis financial report.

6. **If you didn't make a selection from the Payment Terms field, or you want to override the calculated due date, enter a date in the Due Date field.**

You can either use the due date from the bill, if one is shown, or enter the date that you plan to pay the bill.

The Due Date field defaults to the same date as the Payment Date field if the Payment Terms field is left blank.

7. Enter the bill number.

This is the equivalent of the Ref. No field on the Expense screen and the Check No. field on the Checks screen, both of which I discuss in the "Recording Checks, Expenses, and Credit Card Charges" section. You enter your vendor's invoice number in this space.

8. If you are recording an expense, fill in at least one row of the Category Details section.

If you need to receive inventory, refer to Chapter 10 for detailed instructions and guidance on the process.

The Category Details section is composed of the following columns:

- **Category:** If you want to make a CPA's blood boil, label a column where one should choose an account from the chart of accounts as Category. Yes, I'm looking at you, Intuit. Okay, with that off my chest, let me elaborate and say that in Intuit's mind, you're choosing a tax category, or a line from your tax return where the expense will flow. No matter what, it's counterintuitive if you have any accounting experience at all, so just know that you'll pick an account from your chart of accounts in the Category column.

- **Description:** You can use up to 4,000 characters to describe what you exchanged for the money that you're about to send out the door.

- **Amount:** Enter the amount of money that will soon leave your hands.

Click Add Lines as needed to expand the Category Details section.

Be cautious when clicking Clear All Lines because you won't receive a confirmation prompt, and the entire Category Details section will be erased immediately. This action is irreversible, so double-check before proceeding.

You can avoid frustration by clicking Save periodically at the bottom of the screen when entering complex transactions. If something goes wrong with a saved transaction, simply close it without saving, then reopen and edit the transaction to restore the most recently saved version. This practice helps safeguard your work and reduces the risk of losing important details.

Plus and Advanced users may also see Customer and Class columns in the Category Details section. You can enter a customer's name if the charge being recorded is reimbursable, and you can use the Class field to associate the expense with a particular class, which I discuss in more detail in Chapter 11.

9. **If you want to document this transaction further, enter up to 4,000 characters in the Memo field.**

10. **Use the Attachments field if you want to upload one or more supporting files.**

    I discuss the Attachments feature in detail in Chapter 1.

11. **Choose a method from the Save And . . . button.**

    Save And . . . offers three choices. The most recent option that you choose becomes the default for that button — a behavior known as a "sticky" setting — until you make another selection from the drop-down menu on the button:

    - **Save and Schedule Payment:** Saves the transaction and then sneakily displays the QuickBooks Online Bill Pay service, which enables you to pay five bills for free each month, plus $0.50 per ACH payment and $1.50 per check thereafter. A 2.9 percent fee applies to bills that you want to pay via credit card.

      The QuickBooks Bill Pay service can't combine two or more bills for a given vendor into a single check, which means your fees can mount fast if you need to pay multiple bills for a single vendor.

      Bill.com also offers an online bill payment service to QuickBooks users that has a different pricing approach. I discuss apps that can enhance QuickBooks in Chapter 7.

    - **Save and New:** Saves the transaction and keeps the Bill screen active so that you can record another bill.

    - **Save and Close:** Saves the transaction and closes the Bill screen.

    The following commands also appear along the bottom of the Bill screen:

    - **Cancel:** Discards the transaction and closes the Bill screen if you confirm yes, you would like to leave without saving.

    - **Clear:** Discards the transaction and leaves the Bill screen active if you confirm yes, you would like to clear the transaction.

    - **Make Recurring:** Sets up a recurring bill on a schedule that you choose, such as for an annual property tax bill. See the section "Establishing Recurring Transactions" in Chapter 9 for more information.

Paying one bill at a time

As you sit at your desk, you can almost hear the crack of the bat and the roar of the crowd, daydreaming about a sunny afternoon at the ballpark. You're ready to step up to the plate, the anticipation building . . . Oh, wait — I meant "pay bills," not "play ball!" Time to get back to work!

The Save and Schedule Payment option that I discussed in the previous section frees you up from having to interact with a bill again. Conversely, if you chose Save and Close or Save and New when you recorded the bill, at some point you'll need to carry out the following steps to pay it:

1. Choose + New ⇨ Check or + New ⇨ Expense.

Create a Check transaction to record a handwritten check or to print a check, or an Expense transaction to record online payments you've made online via your bank account or a payment service like Venmo or PayPal.

2. Select a payee from the list.

Any outstanding bills appear in the Add to Check task pane. You only see this task pane when a vendor has unpaid amounts due.

3. Click Add All if you want to pay all open bills for the vendor, or click Add below specific bills.

The ground may feel like it has shifted on you, because the Write Check screen transmogrifies into a Bill Payment screen. The bill or bills that you've chosen to pay appear in an Outstanding Transactions section, in place of the Category Details section (and Item Details section that Plus or Advanced users may see).

4. Adjust payment amounts as needed or click Clear Payment if you change your mind about paying the bills.

Clear Payment returns you to the Check or Expense screen you were on sans the Add to Check task pane. You have to close and then reopen the Check or Expense screen at this point to access the Add to Check task pane again.

5. Choose Save and Print if you want to print a check. Conversely, you can choose Save and Close or Save and New to exit the screen or to enter another transaction.

Paying two or more bills at once

Given that bills seem to appear out of nowhere, you can thankfully pay multiple bills at once, streamlining the payment process and saving time. This feature allows you to manage and settle several obligations in a single transaction, reducing the hassle of handling each bill individually. Follow these steps to pay more than one bill simultaneously:

1. **Open the Pay Bills screen shown in Figure 3-2 by way of one of these choices:**

   - Choose + New ⇨ Pay Bills from the Vendor column.

   - Choose Transactions ⇨ Expenses ⇨ Print Checks drop-down menu ⇨ Pay Bills.

REMEMBER

The button to the left of the New Transaction button on the Expenses screen remembers the last choice you made. This menu enables you to print checks, order checks, and pay bills. Your most recent choice becomes the default state for this button until you make another choice, which means if you choose Pay Bills once, you then have one-click access to the command until you make another selection from the menu.

2. **Choose a payment account.**

   An Add New command enables you to add a new payment account on the fly if necessary.

3. **Select a payment date.**

   This date applies to all bills that you choose as part of this Pay Bills transaction.

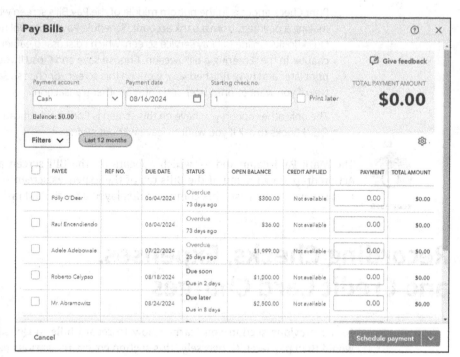

FIGURE 3-2:
The Pay Bills screen.

4. **Confirm the starting check number.**

   Typically, this automatically increments for you, but you can override the check number shown if needed.

5. **Click Print Later if you want to print paper checks at a later time.**

   This field only applies when you plan to print checks from QuickBooks later on, so skip it if you use the QuickBooks Online Bill Pay service.

6. **Choose one or more bills to pay.**

   Click the checkbox in the first column of the bill list for any bills that you want to pay. The Filter button enables you to display open bills for a specific vendor or range of due dates or to display only overdue bills.

7. **Optional: Adjust the payment amounts.**

   Although QuickBooks assumes that you want to pay bills in full, you can override the payment amounts for any bills to reflect a partial payment.

8. **Choose Print Check, Schedule Payments Online, Save and Close, or Save and New.**

   Print Check appears in the bottom middle of the Pay Bills screen when you're making a payment from a bank account. Schedule Payments Online opens the QuickBooks Online Bill Pay service screen, which I discussed earlier in this chapter in the "Entering a bill" section. Choose Save and Close if you want to print later and have finished your work on this screen, or choose Save and New if you want to print later and enter another transaction.

   The only other option you have on this screen is Cancel, which causes QuickBooks to ask if you want to leave without saving.

REMEMBER

The Mark Paid command — which appears on the Bill screen and also in the Action drop-down menu of the Bills tab of the Expenses screen — opens the Pay Bills screen. In the past, this command displayed a Mark Paid task pane.

Recording Checks, Expenses, and Credit Card Charges

In the previous section you learned how to record bills in QuickBooks that you would then pay later. Conversely, this section covers the various payment method options you have for recording costs that you incur immediately. These options might not be readily apparent from the QuickBooks Online user interface, so understanding them will help ensure accurate and efficient expense tracking:

>> **Checks:** QuickBooks allows you to fill out a check form directly on the screen, providing a simple way to issue payments that need to be documented with a physical check. You can either print the check immediately or batch it for printing later, giving you flexibility depending on your workflow.

>> **Expenses:** This option covers direct debits from your bank account, including ACH transfers, wires, online bill payments, and transactions made with credit or debit cards. Choosing this method is ideal for payments that are made electronically or with cards, allowing for quick, efficient recording of everyday expenses without the need for checks.

>> **Credit card credit:** Although QuickBooks doesn't offer a specific transaction type for credit card expenses, it does allow you to record credits that post to your credit card account. This is useful when you receive refunds, rebates, or adjustments on your credit card, ensuring your credit card account balance reflects accurate transactions.

>> **Pay down card credit:** This transaction type is used when you need to pay down your credit card account balance, either in full or partially. Opting for this method is essential for managing your credit card debt, allowing you to track payments against your card balance and maintain a clear view of your financial obligations.

Tracking checks, expenses, and credit card charges

The process is practically identical for recording checks, expenses, and credit card charges, so I cover all three transaction types at once here:

1. **Choose + New ⇨ Check or Expense or choose Expenses ⇨ New Transaction ⇨ Check or Expense.**

Use the Check screen to record checks that you have handwritten or intend to print. Use the Expense screen to record electronic payments and credit card charges.

2. **Select a vendor or contractor from the Payee field or choose Add New from the drop-down list to add a new vendor.**

The vendor's or contractor's mailing address information appears if you choose an existing record; otherwise, a Vendor task pane opens. Fill in at least the Vendor Display Name and then click Save to create a new payee.

3. **Choose a Payment Account.**

This is always a bank account for Check transactions, but may be a bank or credit card account for expenses and credit card charges.

4. **Enter the Payment Date.**

   Use the date that the check was or is being written.

5. **Fill in the Check No. or Ref No. fields, respectively, for checks and expenses.**

   If you're recording a handwritten or printed check, make sure you use the actual check number printed on the check to make reconciling your bank account easier.

6. **If you're recording a check and want to defer check printing, turn the Print Later checkbox on.**

   Use this option when you want to enter one or more check transactions and then send the checks to the printer all at once, such as if you have a printer that uses MICR ink to generate checks on blank check stock. Print Later doesn't appear on the Expense screen because you're typically recording an electronic transaction.

7. **If you have enabled the Sales Tax feature, you can enter up to 20 characters in the Permit No. field.**

   The Permit No. field on the Check and Expense screens in QuickBooks Online is used to record a specific permit or reference number associated with a payment.

8. **To assign one or more custom labels to this transaction, fill in the Tags field and then choose Add, or select an existing tag.**

   Tags help categorize and track your transactions for more detailed reporting. I discuss the Tags feature in more detail in Chapter 6.

9. **If you are recording an expense, fill in at least one row of the Category Details section.**

   TIP

   If you need to receive inventory, refer to Chapter 10 for detailed instructions and guidance on the process.

   The Category Details section is comprised of the following columns:

   - **Category:** If you want to make a CPA's blood boil, label a column where one should choose an account from the chart of accounts as Category. Yes, I'm looking at you, Intuit. Okay, with that off my chest, let me elaborate and say that in Intuit's mind, you're choosing a tax category, or a line from your tax return where the expense will flow. No matter what, it's counterintuitive if you have any accounting experience at all, so just know that you'll pick an account from your chart of accounts in the Category column.

- **Description:** You can use up to 4,000 characters to describe what you exchanged for the money that you're about to send out the door.

- **Amount:** Enter the amount of money that will soon leave your hands.

Click Add Lines as needed to expand the Category Details section.

WARNING

Be cautious when clicking Clear All Lines because you won't receive a confirmation prompt, and the entire Category Details section will be erased immediately. This action is irreversible, so double-check before proceeding.

TIP

You can avoid frustration by clicking Save periodically at the bottom of the screen when entering complex transactions. If something goes wrong with a saved transaction, simply close it without saving, then reopen and edit the transaction to restore the most recent saved version. This practice helps safeguard your work and reduces the risk of losing important details.

REMEMBER

Plus and Advanced users may also see Customer and Class columns in the Category Details section. You can enter a customer's name if the charge being recorded is reimbursable, and you can use the Class field to associate the expense with a particular class, which I discuss in more detail in Chapter 11.

10. If you want to document this transaction further, enter up to 4,000 characters in the Memo field.

11. Use the Attachments field if you want to upload one or more supporting files.

I discuss the Attachments feature in detail in Chapter 1.

12. If you're entering a check that you want to print immediately, click Print Check. Otherwise, click Save and Close or Save and New.

The Print Check command saves the transaction and opens a print preview screen.

Unique commands that appear along the bottom of the Checks screen include:

- **Order Checks:** Opens a screen from which you can order QuickBooks-compatible checks from Intuit.

- **Make Recurring:** Sets up a recurring check, such as for a monthly rent check, on a schedule that you choose. See the section "Establishing Recurring Transactions" in Chapter 9 for more information.

- **More:** Initially this menu contains a single Void command, but additional commands appear after you save the check:

  - *Copy:* Creates a duplicate copy of the transaction that you then edit as needed.

- *Void:* Marks a check as voided but keeps it in your accounting records. Reasons for voiding checks are legion, but some examples include being jammed in the printer, lost in the mail, and eaten by a dog. The list goes on and on.

- *Delete:* Removes a check completely from your accounting records.

WARNING

While it's technically possible to delete checks from your accounting software, doing so is not recommended as it can create gaps in your financial records and make it difficult to track historical transactions. Instead, you should void the check to maintain a record of the transaction while indicating that it is no longer valid. This ensures the integrity of your accounting data and provides a clear audit trail.

- *Transaction Journal:* Opens a Transaction Drilldown Journal report that warms the cockles of any accountant's heart. The report breaks down the transaction into the nitty-gritty details of debits and credits.

- *Audit History:* Opens a Transaction History report that reflects when the transaction was first entered and any subsequent edits.

Conversely, Make Recurring is the only additional command that appears at the bottom of the Expense screen.

Posting credit card credits

This next transaction type is a borderline tongue twister, "Carol creates credit card credits on her computer." Think of credit card credits as a negative expense, with the twist that you enter them as positive amounts. Here's how to record credits that are posted to your credit card account:

1. **Choose + New ⇨ Credit Card Credit.**

2. **Select a vendor from the Payee field.**

   You can add a new vendor in the unlikely event that a credit appears from a vendor you haven't paid in the past.

3. **Choose a credit card from the Bank/Credit Account field.**

   Despite the name on the field, you'll only be able to choose a credit card account from this list.

4. **Record the date of the credit in the Payment Date field.**

   Use the date that the credit was posted to your account.

From here, the remaining steps are the same as you carry out for recording Check and Expense transactions, so refer to the previous section if you need further guidance.

Paying down credit cards

Although it's not strictly necessary, QuickBooks provides a screen from which you can ensure that you record your payment to your credit card company properly. Bear in mind that this screen assumes that you made your payment via bank transfer because you can't print a check from here. I give you the alternate steps to use if you want to print and mail a physical check to your credit card company instead of paying through the company's website.

Here's how to use the Pay Down Credit Card screen:

1. **Choose + New ⇨ Pay Down Credit Card or Expenses ⇨ Expenses ⇨ New Transaction ⇨ Pay Down Credit Card.**

   The Pay Down Credit Card screen opens, as shown in Figure 3-3.

2. **Choose a credit card from the Which Credit Card Did You Pay? drop-down menu.**

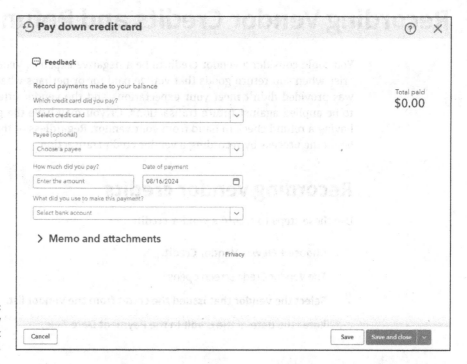

FIGURE 3-3: A blank Pay Down Credit Card screen.

3. **If you want to specify a payee, make a selection from the Payee (Optional) field.**

   You aren't required to establish your bank or credit card company as a vendor, but doing so can make certain reports easier to use.

4. **Enter an amount in the How Much Did You Pay? field.**

5. **Enter the payment date in the Date of Payment field.**

6. **Select a bank account from the What Did You Use to Make This Payment? field.**

7. **If you want to document the transaction further, expand the Memo and Attachments section and record up to 4,000 characters in the Memo field.**

   Perhaps write an affirmation here, something like, "Yes, I can pay this credit down; yes, I will pay this credit card down."

8. **Use the Attachments field to attach an unlimited number of supporting files related to this credit card payment.**

   I discuss the Attachments feature in detail in Chapter 1.

9. **Choose Save and Close or Save and New.**

Recording Vendor Credits and Refunds

You could consider a vendor credit to be a negative expense. Vendor credits may arise when you return goods that you've paid for or perhaps when a service that was provided didn't meet your expectations and the vendor offers you a credit to be applied against future transactions. Or you may have the good fortune of having a refund check in hand from your vendor. Regardless of the situation, you begin the process by recording a vendor credit transaction.

Recording vendor credits

Use these steps to record a vendor credit:

1. **Choose + New ⇨ Vendor Credit.**

   The Vendor Credit screen opens.

2. **Select the vendor that issued the credit from the Vendor list.**

3. **Enter the date of the credit in the Payment Date field.**

From here, the remaining steps are the same as you carry out for recording Check and Expense transactions (with one caveat that I discuss next), so refer to the previous section if you need further guidance.

REMEMBER

It's counterintuitive, but record vendor credits as *positive* amounts; otherwise, you'll record a negative credit, which in effect is like recording an expense instead of *offsetting* an expense.

TIP

Consider using the Attachments field to upload an electronic copy of any documentation you have for the credit. Your future self will likely be very appreciative.

Depending on how you choose to pay your bills, you might not even have to think about applying a credit against a future bill. The Pay Bills screen that I discuss earlier in this chapter automatically applies open credits against bills you want to pay. However, Pay Bills isn't the only way to pay a bill. In the "Paying one bill at a time" section, I explain that you can also use the Checks screen to pay bills. If you go that route, any open credits appear in the Add to Check task pane. Either way, it's a simple process to apply a credit memo against an unpaid bill.

Recording vendor refund checks

I cover two scenarios here. First, assume that you unexpectedly receive a check from your vendor, which means that you do not have an unapplied credit for this vendor. After that, I show you how to apply a refund check against an unapplied Vendor Credit transaction.

Posting refunds directly to your books

In this scenario, a vendor has sent you a check that you didn't anticipate, which means you don't have a vendor credit pending. You can record such payments in this fashion:

1. **Choose + New ⇨ Bank Deposit.**
   The Bank Deposit screen opens.

2. **Choose the bank account that you'll deposit the check into, or choose Payments to Deposit (Undeposited Funds) if you plan to take the check to the bank with one or more other checks.**

3. **Enter your vendor's name into the Received From column of the Add Funds to This Deposit section.**

4. **Choose an expense or cost of goods sold account from the Account column.**

WARNING

Do not choose Accounts Payable in this context because doing so will create an unapplied open credit.

5. **Use the Description field to document the transaction.**

6. **Make a selection from the Payment Method field or click Add New to create a new method.**

7. **Complete the Ref No. field if applicable.**

8. **Enter the refund check amount into the Amount field.**

9. **Choose Save and Close.**

Everything is now accounted for in this scenario where an unexpected refund check arrives. I cover Bank Deposit transactions in more detail in Chapter 5.

Offsetting vendor credits

The second scenario assumes that at some point in the past you entered a vendor credit because you anticipated applying the credit against a future bill. Perhaps your needs changed, or the vendor no longer provides the product or service you used in the past, so you requested a refund check. Here's how to apply the refund check in QuickBooks so that you can effectively zero out the open vendor credit:

1. **Choose + New ⇨ Bank Deposit.**

The Bank Deposit screen opens.

2. **Choose the bank account that you'll deposit the check into, or choose Payments to Deposit (Undeposited Funds) if you plan to take the check to the bank with one or more other checks.**

3. **Enter your vendor's name into the Received From column of the Add Funds to This Deposit section.**

4. **Choose Accounts Payable (A/P) from the Account column.**

REMEMBER

Make sure to choose Accounts Payable (A/P) from the list; otherwise, you may end up with some phantom amounts lingering on your Aged Accounts Payable report once you finish posting these transactions.

5. **Use the Description field to document the transaction.**

6. **Make a selection from the Payment Method field or click Add New to create a new method.**

7. **Complete the Ref No. field if applicable.**

8. **Enter the refund check amount into the Amount field.**

9. Choose Save and Close.

10. Choose + New ⇨ Pay Bills.

I know, I know. You're saying, "They just paid *me*, I don't need to pay *them*!" Hang with me here, as all will be revealed momentarily.

11. Select the bank deposit transaction that you saved in Step 9.

The vendor credit appears in the Credit Applied field, and the Total Payment becomes zero.

12. Choose Save and Close.

Whew! You made it! Your vendor refund check or payment is applied and properly accounted for.

Chapter **4**

Paying Employees and Contractors

As an employer, you have a responsibility to pay both your employees and any contractors who work for you. In this chapter, I explore both responsibilities. Running payroll is more than just issuing paychecks to your employees. After you've prepared paychecks, you need to remit amounts withheld for deductions and benefits to the appropriate parties. QuickBooks Payroll is a subscription service that offers automated payroll, tax deposits, and tax forms, but you can manually pay your employees, remit payroll taxes, and file your returns if you prefer. At the end of this chapter, I explore the ways that QuickBooks users typically pay — and report on paying — contractors who are vendors who perform work for a company but don't qualify as employees.

TIP

I discuss time tracking in Chapter 9. The QuickBooks Time service integrates seamlessly with QuickBooks Payroll if you have a QuickBooks Online Essentials, Plus, or Advanced subscription.

Getting Started with QuickBooks Payroll

When preparing payroll, the process starts with setting up the necessary details to ensure accurate payroll calculations. This includes accounting for payroll taxes that are withheld from each employee's paycheck. A payroll service may handle the remittance of federal, state, and sometimes local payroll taxes to the appropriate authorities. However, it is your responsibility to remit any required deductions and contributions that impact each employee's paycheck, such as 401(k) contributions, health insurance, and other similar deductions, to the appropriate institutions. Some of these can be automated by way of apps such as Guideline or Vestwell. I discuss apps for QuickBooks Online in Chapter 7.

You can add employees to QuickBooks without a payroll subscription if you plan to use a QuickBooks Time subscription for time tracking and process payroll manually or through another payroll service.

Subscribing to QuickBooks Payroll

Intuit tries hard to get you to subscribe to QuickBooks Payroll when you start your QuickBooks Online subscription, so you may already be signed up. Here's how to tell:

1. **Choose the Gear icon ⇨ Subscriptions and Billing.**

   If QuickBooks Payroll appears in the Billed to You or Billed to Accountant sections then you have an active payroll subscription. If not, scroll down to the Discover More section and click Find Out More in the QuickBooks Payroll section.

2. **Select one or more options within the Select What You Need and We'll Recommend a Plan section, or scroll down and compare the Core, Premium, and Elite plans.**

   Click the corresponding sign-up button, which often offers a 50 percent discount for three months.

   You may find yourself directed into the payroll subscription screen by clicking Get Started on any of the Payroll screens as well.

3. **Choose Payroll ⇨ Overview and then click Get Started to launch the payroll wizard.**

4. **Answer Yes or No when asked if you've incurred payroll expenses this year and then click Next.**

5. Specify the date for your next payday and then click Next.

6. Complete the company address field and then click Next.

The address you provided when you initially set up your company appears, which you can override if needed.

7. Fill in the payroll contact fields and then click Next.

8. Choose a method for adding your employees and then click Next.

The Add Your Team screen opens.

9. If you chose to manually set up your employees, click Add an Employee and fill in the contact fields and hire date.

Follow the onscreen prompts if you chose a different method for adding your employees.

10. If you have a payroll subscription, you can invite an employee to self-onboard in Workforce.

Please allow me to translate: *self-onboarding* means asking your employee to complete most elements of their personnel record online in the QuickBooks Workforce platform so that you don't have to fill in the blanks for them.

11. Click Add Employee.

12. Click Done if necessary to close the Add Your Team screen.

13. A Setup Tasks list appears on the Overview tab of the Payroll screen.

- **Setup Task 1: Get Ready to Pay Your Team**

  Here you confirm the date of your next payday, enter your business contact details, add employees, and connect your bank if you opt into using direct deposit.

- **Setup Task 2: Let's Handle Your Taxes**

  In this section, you enter your state and federal tax ID numbers, connect your bank so that you can remit payroll taxes, and set your tax preferences.

- **Setup Task 3: Take Care of Your Team**

  Here Intuit offers to help you secure workers' compensation insurance, a 401(k) plan, and health insurance.

  At a minimum, make sure that you complete Setup Tasks 1 and 2 of the checklist.

TIP

The date you start using QuickBooks Payroll determines the "as of" date of historical information you need to collect and determines that date to be the first day of the current quarter. Try to start using QuickBooks on January 1 of any year; that way, you don't need to enter historical information. If you can't start using QuickBooks on January 1, try to start using it on the first day of a quarter to make filing certain payroll tax returns easier. Historical payroll transactions can be summarized before that date but must be entered in detail after that date.

Configuring payroll preferences

In addition to adding employees, you should review payroll preferences and set up payroll taxes. You can't process your payroll and payroll tax returns fully until you complete all the setup fields.

To review payroll preferences, choose the Gear icon ⇨ Payroll Settings. The Payroll Settings screen includes a series of sections you can use to review or establish various settings related to payroll. Understanding this screen may make you feel less overwhelmed by what you see:

>> General Tax allows you to edit your company type, filing name, and filing address, as well as change your first payroll date if necessary.

>> Federal Tax allows you to indicate your employer identification number (EIN), opt out of workers' comp offers from Intuit partners, and specify a filing requirement and deposit schedule.

>> Special federal programs such as the CARES Act may appear here if payroll tax deferrals or other relief is available.

>> A State Tax section allows you to specify your state EIN, payroll tax deposit schedule, and state unemployment rates.

>> The Auto Payroll option indicates whether you have any employees set up on automatic payroll.

>> The Federal Forms Preference enables you to designate third parties and paid preparers authorized to represent you before the Internal Revenue Service.

>> Email notifications allow you to opt in or out of payroll-related email notifications.

>> Early Pay allows employees to access a payday lending program. While there's no cost to you, employees will incur fees for using the service.

>> Shared Data allows you to give your employees the option to import their W-2 data into TurboTax.

>> Bank Accounts requires you to connect your bank account to remit deductions, pay your employees via direct deposit, and e-file and e-pay your taxes.

>> Printing allows you to specify whether you want to print checks on plain paper (assuming that your printer allows you to use a MICR cartridge to generate the row of numbers at the bottom of a check) or on preprinted QuickBooks-compatible checks. This section also offers a link for ordering checks.

>> The Accounting preference enables you to map payroll tax payments, expenses, and liabilities to your chart of accounts.

TIP

Be sure to set aside a few minutes to review every section in Payroll Settings. This review helps you avoid surprises and frustration when you make a tax payment or attempt to e-file near a deadline.

QuickBooks also offers a Fill In Your Tax Info wizard that can walk you through some of these choices, although most sections in the Payroll Settings screen are limited to a few fields at a time.

Adding employees

You can't pay your employees through QuickBooks Payroll until you set them up in QuickBooks. Furthermore, you may need some paperwork from your employees, such as a Form W-4 form to document their withholding preferences. You may also need to get their approval to opt into any benefits that your company offers.

REMEMBER

Form W-4 is the Internal Revenue Service form that employees complete to specify their withholding allowance. If you need to complete Form W-4 for any employee, visit www.irs.gov and click the W-4 link in the Forms & Instructions section or use this link: www.irs.gov/pub/irs-pdf/fw4.pdf. You can confirm your state's payroll tax requirements by visiting your state's website and searching for **payroll taxes**. I live in Georgia, so I would search the Georgia Department of Revenue's site.

Setting up an employee can result in what feels like sorting through a blizzard of documentation, but you can minimize that by asking your employees to set themselves up in QuickBooks Workforce. Some of the information that either you or your employees need to enter includes the following:

>> Personal information, which includes the employee's address, Social Security number, birth date, gender, and phone number.

>> Tax withholding, which includes the employee's tax federal filing status (single, married, head of household, and so on) and withholding amount as well as

their state income tax, if applicable. QuickBooks prompts you to supply information for the state in which your business operates.

>> The method you want to use to pay the employee (such as paper check or direct deposit). If you choose direct deposit, specify the bank account information for the employee (account type, routing number, and account number).

TIP

For direct-deposit checks, you can choose to deposit the paycheck in its entirety in a single account, deposit the check into two accounts, or deposit a portion of the check directly and pay the balance as a paper check.

>> Employment details, which include employee status, hire date, pay schedule, work location, job title, employee ID, and workers' comp class.

>> Pay types, which include the amount you pay the employee (hourly, salaried, or commission only), along with time-off pay policies and additional pay types.

WARNING

Make sure to pay close attention when working in the How Much Do You Want to Pay section. For hourly employees, QuickBooks makes it easy and intuitive to enter regular time. Scroll down on this screen and enable any other types of pay that the employee might accrue, such as overtime, holiday pay, bonuses, and so on. If you don't enable the fields here, you can't enter the amounts when you process payroll.

>> Deductions or contributions. (Add in whether the employee has any.)

Here's how to add employees to QuickBooks:

1. **Choose Payroll ⇨ Employees.**

2. **Click Add an Employee.**

   The Who's Your New Team Member? dialog appears. If you haven't yet opted in to a QuickBooks Payroll subscription, click the Add Employee link at the top of the screen.

3. **Provide the employee's name, email address, and hire date.**

4. **The next steps depend upon whether you have an active QuickBooks Payroll subscription.**

   If you *do* have an active payroll subscription, follow these steps:

   a. *If you want the employee to enter their own personal information, click Yes, Allow Employee to Enter Their Tax and Banking into Workforce.*

   Enabling this option will generate an email to your employee with further instructions.

   b. *Click Add Employee.*

   The employee record appears.

c. *Click Edit in the Personal Info section.*

The Edit Personal Info screen appears.

d. *Complete as many fields as you want and then click Save.*

If you do *not* have an active payroll subscription, follow these steps:

a. *Click Add Employee.*

The Employees screen opens.

b. *Click Edit in the Personal Info section.*

The Edit Personal Info screen appears.

c. *Complete as many fields as you want and then click Save.*

d. *Click Edit in the Employment Details section.*

The Edit Employee Details screen opens.

e. *Complete as many fields as you want and then click Save.*

Notice that no employee compensation fields appear here, although you can establish a billable rate for the employee.

f. *Click Start in the Emergency Contact section.*

The Edit Emergency Contact screen opens.

g. *Complete as many fields as you want and then click Save.*

5. **Click Employee List at the top of the screen to return to the Employees screen or select from the sidebar menu to move on to another task.**

Removing employees

All good things eventually come to an end and the day will arise where either you or an employee decides that it is time to part ways. As is the case across QuickBooks, you generally must mark an employee as inactive, particularly if you have paid them at least once.

To change an employee's status from Active to Inactive, click Actions ⇨ Delete Employee if an employee ghosts you, as unlikely as that may seem these days, or if you have other reasons for removing an employee from the list. This is a true deletion, as opposed to making an employee inactive, which is generally the case for list items in QuickBooks.

Preparing Payroll

Processing payroll in QuickBooks Online involves a three-step process:

1. Record paycheck information.

2. Review paycheck information.

3. Generate paychecks.

TIP

Mobile users should consider trying the QuickBooks Payroll mobile app to pay employees. You can optionally pay payroll taxes and file payroll tax forms electronically if you opt out of letting Intuit do this for you, and review employee information and paycheck history. Data syncs automatically between the mobile app and your Intuit payroll account. I discuss the mobile app in more detail in Chapter 7.

Recording payroll information

Choose Payroll ➪ Employees ➪ Run Payroll to start processing payroll. The Run Payroll wizard appears and lists all your employees.

WARNING

Run Payroll isn't displayed until you've completed the tax setup step, entered your payroll history, and, depending on your automation choices, connected your bank account. Check the bottom of the setup list for any required tasks you haven't completed. If you try to do an end-run by choosing + New ➪ Payroll, you're simply returned unceremoniously to the payroll setup list.

TIP

Click the arrow next to Run Payroll to review a Bonus Only option for generating bonus checks. You can enter bonus amounts as net pay, meaning that you specify how much you want the employee to receive, and QuickBooks works backward to figure out the gross pay, or you can choose the As Gross Pay option and have QuickBooks calculate the net pay.

Verify the bank account from which to pay employees and double-check the pay period and pay date. By default, a checkmark appears to the left of each employee scheduled to be paid, but you can remove the check if appropriate. Enter the hours that any hourly employees worked during the pay period.

TIP

You can squeeze more employees onscreen by choosing the Gear icon ➪ Compact just above the top-right corner of the employee list.

Reviewing and generating payroll checks

When everyone's favorite days of the month, known as paydays, come around on the calendar, it's time to process payroll:

1. **Choose Payroll ⇨ Overview from the sidebar.**

   The Payroll Overview screen opens.

2. **Click Let's Go beneath the large It's Time to Run Payroll banner.**

   QuickBooks really doesn't want you to miss payday. Your employees don't either. The Run Payroll screen opens to help you with this process.

3. **Enter regular pay hours and an optional memo.**

   Your active employees appear in individual rows. If you need to override federal or state withholdings for a single paycheck, click Edit at the right side of an employee's row.

   REMEMBER

   QuickBooks only shows you fields for pay types that you've enabled within each employee's record. Infrequent pay types, such as holiday pay or bonuses, can suddenly feel like a pop quiz when there's no place to enter the information. To enable additional pay types on the fly, click the employee's name on the Run Payroll screen, and then scroll down to the How Much Do You Pay section. Within this screen, you see checkboxes for enabling additional pay types.

4. **Click Preview Payroll.**

   If you need more time, click the arrow on the Preview Payroll button and choose Save for Later to save your work in progress rather than abandoning a payroll run completely.

5. **Use the Review and Submit screen to make sure everything looks in order.**

   Click Edit next to each employee's Net Pay amount if you need to edit their check, or click the Compare to Last icon to display a chart that compares this paycheck to the employee's previous check.

   WARNING

   If you use the Compare to Last Payroll screen, make sure you click the Close (X) button in the upper-right corner. If you're like me and press the Escape key to close windows on your computer, you not only close the Compare to Last Payroll screen, but cancel your payroll run as well.

6. **Click Preview Payroll Details if you want to review the employee's compensation details.**

   This command is a little tricky because it doesn't look clickable but is. A detailed report shows every aspect of your employee's compensation, withholdings and deductions, and any employer costs such as the employer portion of payroll taxes.

7. **Click Submit Payroll to finalize your payroll.**

If you have any issues that you need to resolve before submitting your payroll, you can click the arrow beside Submit Payroll and choose Save for Later.

The Payroll Is Done screen opens.

Hold your horses, though; you might not be completely done yet. If you use direct deposit and don't need to print pay stubs, you can skip the next two steps. Otherwise, you still have some unfinished business to attend to.

8. **Optional: Click Auto-Fill to assign check numbers, or manually enter check numbers if you use handwritten checks.**

If you happen to catch a last-minute issue, you can click an employee's pay amount to display a screen from which you can edit their check. Payroll isn't over until it's over.

9. **Optional: Click Print Pay Stubs to preview paychecks and stubs and print them.**

This report opens in an additional browser tab.

10. **Optional: Click View Payroll Reports.**

The Your Payroll Reports Are Ready screen allows you to pick the reports that you want to export to Excel. Each report is placed on a separate worksheet that you can open in Microsoft Excel or Google Sheets. Click OK to close this screen.

WARNING

When you open your payroll report workbook, you might encounter a warning prompt in Excel that informs you that the file format and extension don't match and that the file could be corrupted or damaged. You can safely click Yes to open the report. The geeky details are that the programmers at Intuit are generating a workbook that has an XLS file, but the workbook itself is in the modern XLSX format. In short, you have nothing to worry about here. Click Yes and move along.

11. **Click Finish Payroll.**

Take a deep breath. Now, my friend, you're truly done with payroll.

TIP

You can click Edit at the right edge of the line for any employee to see the details associated with the employee's paycheck. If necessary, you can change certain paycheck details, such as hours worked and federal/state tax amounts.

TIP

If you pay your employees by direct deposit, expect next-day deposits for Payroll Core, or same-day deposits for Premium or Elite for transactions initiated by 7 a.m. Pacific time.

Adjusting payroll exemptions

Although it's most likely unnecessary, you can establish payroll tax exemptions when necessary by following these steps:

1. Choose Payroll ➪ Employees and select the name of the employee whose status you need to change.

2. Click the Edit link in the Tax Withholding section of the Employee Details screen that opens.

3. On the What Are [Employee's] Withholding screen, scroll down and expand Tax Exemptions.

4. Click Done when you finish editing.

TIP To void or delete a paycheck, click Paycheck List in the top-right corner of the Employee screen, select a paycheck, and then click Void or Delete above the list. A series of questions helps you get the job done.

Printing payroll reports

When you complete payroll, you may want to print payroll-related reports. Choose Reports ➪ Reports (Business Overview ➪ Reports) on the left menu bar to display the Reports screen. Scroll down to the payroll reports. Along the way, you may see an Employees section that has reports related to time tracking. You can click any payroll report to print it to the screen and, subsequently, to your printer. See Chapter 6 for more details.

Administering Payroll Taxes

As I mention at the beginning of this chapter, the payroll process doesn't end with preparing and producing paychecks. You need to remit payroll taxes and file payroll tax returns on schedules mandated by the Internal Revenue Service, your state, and possibly your locality.

Paying payroll taxes

Using rules established by the IRS, most employers pay payroll taxes semiweekly, monthly, or quarterly, depending on the amount owed (called your *payroll tax liability*). All versions of QuickBooks Payroll now include the option of automated tax deposits and forms, so your payroll tax compliance can be automated, or you can file your returns on your own. Payroll Premium and Elite handle local taxes where applicable.

To manage how payroll taxes are paid:

1. **Choose the Gear icon ➪ Payroll Settings ➪ Taxes and Forms, and then click Edit.**

2. **Clear the Automate Taxes and Forms option if you *don't* want QuickBooks to handle your taxes and forms for you.**

3. **Optional: If you're handling taxes on your own, choose between I'll Initiate Payments and Filings Using QuickBooks and I'll Pay and File the Right Agencies through Their Website or by Mail.**

WARNING

Don't wait until the 11th hour to file payroll tax returns because you may end up with late filings due to buffers needed for both electronic filing and electronic payments.

You must make federal tax deposits by electronic funds transfer by connecting your bank account to QuickBooks Online. If you opt out of this service, you need to make federal tax deposits using the Electronic Federal Tax Payment System (EFTPS; www.eftps.gov), a free service provided by the U.S. Department of the Treasury. QuickBooks Payroll doesn't use EFTPS but pays directly on your behalf. For this reason, you need to complete and sign IRS Form 8655 (Reporting Agent Authorization) before your tax deposits and form can be filed on your behalf.

Choose Taxes ➪ Payroll Tax to display the Payroll Tax Center, which keeps you in the loop on the amount of taxes slated to go out the door. Once you've paid employees, the Payroll Tax Center displays taxes that are due, along with their due dates and e-payment cutoff dates. You can preview how much you owe by printing the Payroll Tax Liability report; click the View Your Tax Liability Report link on the Payroll Tax Center screen.

Accessing payroll tax forms

Quarterly, you must complete and submit a federal payroll tax return by using Form 941, which identifies the total wages you paid, when you paid them, and the total taxes you withheld and deposited with appropriate taxing authorities throughout the quarter. The IRS permits you to file the form electronically or to mail it. If you connect your bank account, QuickBooks Payroll automatically files these returns for you. When you click Filings on the Payroll Tax Center screen, the reports you need to prepare and submit appear.

TIP

If you live in a state that imposes a personal income tax, you typically also must file a similar form for your state; check your state's website for the rules you need to follow for payroll tax reporting. Your state probably has a state unemployment form that you need to prepare and submit as well.

Facilitating Contractor Compensation

In this section, I focus on setting up 1099-eligible contractors, paying them (without using direct deposit), reporting on 1099 payments you've made, and preparing 1099s for your contractors who need them. You don't need to change anything if you've already set up a contractor as a vendor. The contractor list just makes it easier to identify the contractors you work with and pay them if you opt for an Intuit service that I mention later in this chapter.

Paying contractors is generally a straightforward experience. You can wait until you receive a bill from a contractor, enter it, and then pay it, as described in Chapter 8 if you have an Essentials, Plus, or Advanced subscription. QuickBooks Simple Start users can't enter bills, but they can write checks to pay contractors. Either way, you need to ensure that contractors are set up as vendors who will receive Form 1099-NEC. I call these folks *1099-eligible contractors* going forward. Previously, nonemployee compensation was reported in Box 7 of Form 1099-MISC.

REMEMBER

I use the term *1099-eligible* because if you hire someone as a contractor but don't pay that person at least $600 — the threshold established by the IRS — technically, you don't have to produce a 1099 for that contractor. Further, if you don't pay a contractor more than $600, QuickBooks doesn't show payments to that contractor on certain reports.

1099-eligible contractors are people who work for you but who aren't your employees. Specifically, the IRS distinguishes between 1099-eligible contractors and employees based on whether you, the employer, have the means and methods of accomplishing the work or simply have the right to control and direct the result of the work. If you have the means and methods to accomplish the work, the person who works for you is an employee, not an independent 1099-eligible contractor. If you're at all uncertain, ask your accountant, or visit https://quickbooks.intuit.com/find-an-accountant/ to engage an expert.

TIP

If you use QuickBooks Payroll, you can pay contractors (as well as employees) via direct deposit for a fee of $5 per contractor per month after you complete the direct-deposit setup for your company's payroll subscription. To set up a contractor as a direct-deposit recipient, choose Workers ⇨ Contractors. Click Check It Out, and follow the onscreen directions to add a contractor's banking information.

Keep in mind that it may be far less expensive to add ACH capabilities to your bank account and pay contractors directly unless you have only one or two contractors you want to pay this way. Or you can subscribe to Contractor Payments for $15/month to pay up to 20 contractors, plus another $2/month for each additional contractor you add. All plans include 1099 e-filing.

Establishing contractor records

You can set up 1099-eligible contractors in two ways, with the same result:

» You can use the information in Chapter 3 to set up a new vendor. Make sure that you select the Track Payments for 1099 checkbox.

» You can use the Contractors screen to set up a contractor. Any contractor you add from this screen becomes a 1099-eligible contractor.

Follow these steps to create a contractor (as opposed to a vendor):

1. **Choose Payroll ⇨ Contractors.**

    The Contractors screen opens.

2. **Click Add Your First Contractor.**

3. **Provide the contractor's name, and if you want the contractor to complete their profile, enter their email address.**

TIP

    If you provide the contractor's email address, Intuit contacts the contractor and gets their 1099 information for you, including the contractor's signature on the W-9 form that the IRS requires you to keep on file. Intuit uses the form information to populate the contractor's record and leaves a PDF of the W-9 form for you on the Contractors screen in the Documents section.

4. **Click Add Contractor.**

    The contractor's details screen opens.

5. **Click Add (or Waiting for Info if you opted to send the contractor an email) to provide details about the contractor type.**

    This information is used when you prepare 1099s for the year.

6. **Click Save.**

    The contractor's details screen opens again, showing the details you just provided.

Paying contractors

You can pay contractors the same way you pay any other vendors; see Chapter 3 for details on expense transactions and checks, or Chapter 8 for entering and paying bills. As noted elsewhere in this chapter, you must have a QuickBooks Online Essentials, Plus, or Advanced subscription if you want to enter contractor bills to pay later. You can use check or expense transactions in any version of QuickBooks to make an immediate payment.

Alternatively, if you opt into one of QuickBooks Payroll or Contractor subscriptions that offers direct deposit, you can choose Payroll ➪ Contractors ➪ Pay Contractor to display a screen that enables you to pay all contractors from a single screen.

Submitting 1099 Forms for Contractors

At the end of each calendar year, the Internal Revenue Service expects you to provide an accounting of every person you've paid $600 or more to during that period. QuickBooks makes the process relatively painless, albeit for a $15/month fee for the Contractor Payments subscription, which enables you to pay up to 20 contractors by direct deposit, plus $2 for each additional contractor, and includes e-filing of 1099 forms.

Reviewing your vendor list

As the end of each year approaches, review your vendor list and make sure you've tagged all the vendors who should receive a 1099 form. The IRS takes these information returns seriously, and in 2024 can charge the following penalties for each 1099 that's filed late or not at all:

>> **Up to 30 days late:** $60

>> **31 days late through August 1:** $120

>> **After August 1 or not filed:** $310

>> **Intentional disregard:** $630

As the saying goes, the best defense is a strong offense, so here's how to review your vendor list to determine which should receive 1099s. This is going to be a bit of a ride because the New Enhanced Experience version of the report is far from enhanced, and in fact you have to return to Classic View to get to the information you need.

REMEMBER

QuickBooks reclassifies vendors whom you click the Track 1099 checkbox for within their vendor record as contractors. Such vendors still appear on your vendor list, as do contractors you set up through the Contractors command.

Here's how to audit your vendor list to identify contractors who have missing information and to identify vendors you should classify as contractors:

1. **Choose Reports on the sidebar menu.**

   The Reports screen opens.

2. **Use the Search box to find the Vendor Contact List report.**

   You can also find this report in the Expenses and Vendors section. You need to add two columns to this report: Track 1099 and Tax ID. In a perfect world, you would click Customize, scroll down the list, and click the icons for Track 1099 and Tax ID. Unfortunately, only the Track 1099 field is available on the Modern View version of the report. A crucial aspect of a 1099 audit is to ensure that the Tax ID, meaning Federal ID or Social Security Number, has been entered for every vendor who should receive a 1099.

   A secondary part of a 1099 audit is to look at every vendor and determine if the Track 1099 checkbox should be turned on if it currently isn't.

REMEMBER

3. **Choose Columns.**

   The Columns task pane opens.

4. **Locate and turn on click the checkboxes for Track 1099 and Tax ID.**

   Track 1099 and Tax ID columns should now appear.

TIP

In Chapter 20, I discuss how you can export reports like this to Excel and then use Filter to display only records where Track 1099 is set to Yes. This makes for an easy way to identify any missing Tax IDs. However, you still need to do a line-by-line review of your vendors to identify any that should have the Track 1099 checkbox turned on within their vendor record.

REMEMBER

The Track 1099 field is automatically selected for all contractors who also appear on the Vendor Contact List, so you at least get a two-for-one with regard to reviewing contractors and vendors in one fell swoop.

Initiating 1099 forms

Typically, you prepare 1099s each January. Here's how to start the process:

1. **Choose Taxes ⇨ 1099 Filings.**

The Get Ready to File Your 1099 Forms screen opens. It's not quite as fun as hearing "The ice cream truck is coming!" but hey, we're talking about filing a tax form.

2. **Click the button to start or continue your 1099s.**

Confirm that all information is correct on the Review Your Company Info, and then click Next.

3. **Click Edit for any section where you need to add or edit information.**

4. **Map your accounts (notice how suddenly QuickBooks refers to them as accounts instead of categories) to the 1099 form.**

Typically, you click the Non-Employee Compensation checkbox and then choose the accounts(s) where you've posted expenses that should be reported on Form 1099. You may need to click the checkbox for Rents and do the same, as well as for any of the items in the Other Payments or Federal Tax Withheld sections, and then click Next.

TIP

If you suddenly feel an overwhelming sense of dread, click Save and Finish Later. This may be an indication that you're best served by outsourcing this task, and perhaps other bookkeeping tasks, to an accountant. This page is a great place to start: https://quickbooks.intuit.com/find-an-accountant/.

5. **The next screen displays all contractors. It includes vendors you've clicked the Track 1099 checkbox for within their Vendor profile. Click Next once you've completed your review.**

Such vendors are automatically reclassified as contractors by QuickBooks. Don't worry; any such vendors still appear on the Vendor list, as do any contractors you add to QuickBooks by way of the Contractors menu.

6. **Check that the Payments Add Up screen opens and enables you to review the contractors who were paid $600 or more.**

The list shows you contractors who met the criteria for needing a 1099, but you can filter the list two other ways:

- Show 1099 Contractors Below Threshold

- Show Contractors Not Marked for 1099

The second choice presents all vendors on your vendor list who aren't currently flagged as 1099 vendors. You can click the vendor name to display their record and change their 1099 status, if needed.

7. **Once you've completed your review, click Finish Preparing 1099s to get to the screen where you're walked through the filing or printing process.**

    If you've missed the e-filing window for a given year, QuickBooks enables you to print your 1099s on preprinted forms that you can purchase online or find at most office supply stores. You may also order up to a hundred 1099 forms from the IRS at: www.irs.gov/businesses/online-ordering-for-information-returns-and-employer-returns. Then you need to submit the paper copies through the U.S. Postal Service.

Chapter **5**

Mastering Banking Tasks and Account Reconciliations

I n this chapter, I guide you through setting up bank and credit card accounts in QuickBooks, as well as reconciling those accounts. If you're curious about recording credit card transactions, refer to Chapter 3, where you learn that credit card transactions are recorded in the same fashion as expense transactions that post to your bank account.

Establishing Bank and Credit Card Accounts

In Chapter 1, I cover how to add new accounts to your chart of accounts. QuickBooks uses the term *account* on setup or list screens, while the word *category* appears on transaction screens. This distinction can sometimes be confusing, but it's important to understand that they refer to the same thing. Adding a bank or credit card account is similar to creating a revenue or expense account, but with an extra step: entering an opening balance.

Adding bank and credit card accounts

Here's how to add a bank or credit card account to your chart of accounts:

1. **Choose Settings ⇨ Chart of Accounts from the Your Company column.**

2. **Click New to open the New Account task pane.**

3. **Enter a label, such as Treasure Chest Checking or Debt Defying Credit Card, in the Account Name field.**

   You can use up to 100 characters to describe your bank account. If you have multiple accounts at the same bank, it can be helpful to include the last four digits of the bank account to distinguish one from the other.

4. **If the Account Number field is displayed, assign an account number.**

   Account numbers are optional unique identifiers that help you organize and locate accounts quickly while streamlining data entry if you find it easier to type account numbers versus names.

5. **Select Bank or Credit Card from the Account Type list.**

6. **Make a selection from the Detail Type drop-down list to further describe the account.**

   Choose one of these detail types for bank accounts: Cash on Hand, Checking, Money Market, Rents Held in Trust, Savings, or Trust Account. If the Account Type is Credit Card, then your only available Detail Type is Credit Card.

7. **If you want to combine two or more bank or credit card accounts into a single line item on your balance sheet, turn the Make This a Subaccount checkbox on. Then specify a parent account.**

8. **Input the account balance in the Opening Balance field.**

   Typically you'll use the ending balance from your most recent bank or credit card statement.

9. **Enter the date of the statement that you derived the opening balance from in the As Of field.**

   Always defer to your accountant or bookkeeper if you're unclear how to answer a question like this.

10. If you're feeling detailed, use up to 100 characters in the Description field to explain the account's purpose in life.

11. Click Save to close the New Account task pane, or choose Save and New from the drop-down menu if you have multiple accounts to add.

Recording bank deposits

It's crucial to remember to record bank deposits transactions to prevent customer payments from getting stuck in your Payments to Deposit or Undeposited Funds account. Your holding account should always have a zero balance after you've recorded any current bank deposits. Here's how to post a bank deposit:

1. Choose + New ▷ Bank Deposit or select Home ▷ Dashboard ▷ Add Bank Deposit.

The Bank Deposit screen opens, as shown in Figure 5-1. Undeposited customer payments appear in the Select the Payments Included in This Deposit section. You can use the lines in the Add Funds to This Deposit to add new payment transactions that aren't associated with an outstanding invoice, such as refund checks, reimbursement payments, the check for $1.63 that you received from a class-action lawsuit settlement, and so on.

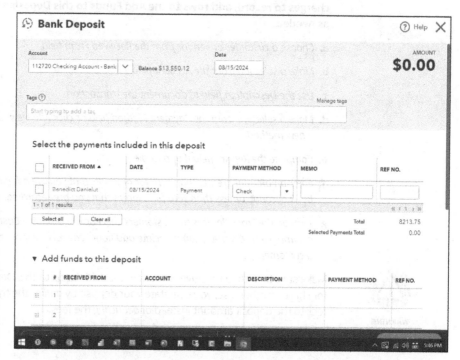

FIGURE 5-1:
The Select the Payments Included in This Deposit section appears when you have one or more undeposited Receive Payment or Sales Receipt transactions.

While it might be tempting, do not record customer invoice payments in the Add Funds to This Deposit section. Instead, create a Receive Payment transaction, as discussed in Chapter 2. Recording a customer payment in the Add Funds to This Deposit section doesn't mark the invoice as paid, which can inflate your accounts receivable balance and risk annoying your customer by mistakenly attempting to collect payment again.

2. **Select a bank account from the Account field if needed.**

3. **Override the Date field if applicable.**

4. **To assign one or more custom labels to this transaction, fill in the Tags field and then choose Add, or select an existing tag.**

   Tags help categorize and track your transactions for more detailed reporting. I discuss the Tags feature in more detail in Chapter 6.

5. **The Select the Payments Included in This Deposit section will appear when you have one or more customer payments being held in the Payments to Deposit Account, from which you can choose what you want to include in the deposit.**

   Turn on the checkbox next to each payment that you're including in this deposit, or click Select All.

6. **If you have additional checks or deposits to record, or bank or processing charges to record, add rows to the Add Funds to this Deposit section as needed.**

   a. *Choose a customer or vendor from the Received From field.*

   b. *Make a selection from the Account field.*

   c. *Use the Description field to document the transaction.*

   d. *Make a selection from the Payment Method field or click Add New to create a new method.*

   e. *Complete the Ref No. field if applicable.*

   f. *Enter an amount greater than zero for amounts that you are adding to your bank account, or less than zero for charges that you are recording.*

   g. *Turn on the Track Returns for Customers checkbox to display a Customer column from which you can associate additional checks or deposits with a customer.*

Make sure to enter a negative amount in the Add Funds to This Deposit section for charges; otherwise, you overstate your deposit by *adding* the transaction fees to the deposit amount instead of *deducting* the fees.

TIP

Intuit Payments automatically posts deposits in a QuickBooks Payments section, which is collapsed by default for users who don't rely on that service. If you use your own merchant account, credit card transaction receipts may be deposited into your bank account daily. Ensure you record a separate deposit for each day so the amounts match what's hitting your physical bank account. Additionally, create a separate deposit to group any checks and cash payments together.

7. **Enter up to 4,000 characters in the memo field if applicable.**

8. **If you are taking cash back from the bank deposit, fill in three additional fields:**

   a. *Select an account from the Cash Back Goes To field if you are taking cash from the bank deposit.*

   b. *Document the withdrawal in the Cash Back Memo field.*

   c. *Record the cash withdrawal in the Cash Back Amount field.*

9. **Use the Attachments field to attach an unlimited number of supporting files related to this deposit.**

   I discuss the Attachments feature in detail in Chapter 1.

10. **Confirm that the deposit total matches the net amount that posts to your bank account.**

    If you deposit $12,075.00 and post –$350.18 in the Add Funds to this Account section, the net deposit is $11,724.82. Conversely, if you're simply depositing paper checks that you take to your bank, you likely don't need to enter anything in the Add Funds to This Deposit section, so the Total should match the sum of the checks that you're about to deposit.

11. **Click Save and Close or click Save and New.**

    Click the arrow on the Save button to toggle between those two settings. Your choice then becomes the default for future transactions.

All that's left to do is to take a trip to the bank. Or, if you're tech-savvy, ask your banker about depositing checks remotely through your mobile device or a check scanner.

Synchronizing with Financial Institutions

Synchronizing your QuickBooks accounts with a financial institution means that transactions posted to your bank or credit card are automatically entered into your books, greatly simplifying the reconciliation process. Ideally, you can connect directly to your bank, but if your bank doesn't offer direct integration with QuickBooks, you can manually import transactions by using QuickBooks Web Connect or by importing files from Microsoft Excel or Google Sheets.

REMEMBER

You must set up your bank and credit card accounts in QuickBooks *before* you can connect to your financial institution.

TIP

For details on entering transactions that affect a bank or credit card account, see Chapter 2 for sales transactions like customer payments and sales receipts, and Chapter 3 for expense transactions, checks, and credit card transactions. Chapter 4 covers payroll.

AVOID STEPHANIE'S COSTLY MISTAKE

My friend Stephanie Miller learned a tough lesson about connecting bank accounts to QuickBooks. A couple of years ago, she connected her bank account to QuickBooks and downloaded a significant number of transactions. Life got in the way, and she didn't review them. These unreviewed transactions lingered in the For Review list, which I discuss in the section "Reviewing Your Bank and Credit Card Transactions" later in this chapter.

Stephanie later disconnected her bank account, thinking all was well. However, a well-meaning temporary bookkeeper reconnected the account and downloaded the original transactions again, along with all subsequent transactions. The real trouble began when the bookkeeper selected all the transactions and clicked Accept, leading to hundreds of duplicate entries. Stephanie was then faced with the daunting task of either manually deleting each duplicate transaction or starting a new set of books.

Connecting your QuickBooks accounts to your financial institution isn't something you can approach halfway. It's essential to fully commit by reviewing and accepting the transactions each time you connect or import, or you risk compromising your accounting records. The download and import processes I'm about to share bring in new transactions each time; they don't overwrite existing ones in the For Review list. If you can't address downloaded transactions immediately, it's best to select all and choose Exclude. This way, you can undo the exclusion later without creating a potential accounting nightmare.

Connecting directly with your bank

Before proceeding, make sure that you have online banking credentials handy. You'll also want to set aside a few minutes to allow the transactions time to download. Unfortunately, there's no meaningful progress indicator, so it's hard to forecast exactly how long the initial download will take.

GET THEE A PASSWORD MANAGER

If you don't currently have a password manager, I strongly encourage you to install one today. Personally, I am a fan of 1Password (https://1password.com/), and millions of other users rely on Dashlane (www.dashlane.com). I no longer recommend LastPass (www.lastpass.com) due to repeated hacking incidents. There are no perfect solutions when it comes to Internet security, so there is always risk involved in storing all your passwords in one place. However, I contend that there is *much greater risk* in not using a password manager at all. Identity thieves make hay from users who reuse the same password across multiple platforms. Unlike the other two platforms that I recommend, LastPass was guilty of storing certain user information, including passwords, in an unencrypted form. 1Password has integrated two-factor authentication into their product, which means logging into sensitive platforms is much more secure and easier than having a verification code emailed or texted to you.

I resisted using password management software for far too long. One day, I was struggling to remember a password when the person I was meeting with said, "My password manager software saves me so much time." I heard that advice at the right moment and writing this reminds me that I need to finish getting my two teenagers set up on a password manager as well.

You have a choice: reuse passwords on more than one site — an enormous identity-theft risk — or use a password manager to have unique and complex passwords for each site, including QuickBooks. Once installed on all of your devices, the password manager allows you to create a passphrase that serves as a master key. You'll be surprised at the number of sites you're logging into once they're all in one place.

Use the following steps to synchronize your bank or credit card account transactions directly with QuickBooks.

1. **Choose Transactions ⇨ Bank Transactions ⇨ Link Account.**

TIP

You create faster access to this screen by clicking Edit next to the Menu or Bookmarks headings in the sidebar. Choose Bank Transactions on the Bookmarks tab, and then click Save to create one-click access to your Bank Transactions screen. If you change your mind later, return to the Bookmarks tab, clear the Bank Transactions checkbox, and then click Save.

2. **Choose a logo from the list if your financial institution is one of the eight choices; otherwise, type a name in the Search box and then select a match from the list.**

TIP

When I searched on one of my banks, QuickBooks returned 9,869 choices until I removed the word *Bank* from my search. That narrowed the list to 141 choices. The list shows the website address for each bank to ensure that you're making the correct choice.

REMEMBER

If your bank isn't on the list or if you're hesitant about connecting QuickBooks to your financial institution, remember that it's a one-way feed, meaning *their* transactions come into *your* books, not the other way around. For an alternative to a direct connection, see the section "Handling indirect banking connections" later in this chapter.

3. **Follow the onscreen instructions, which vary.**

You may be directed to go to your bank's website and sign in, after which you're returned to the connection process. Or if you're connecting to PayPal, you're walked through a three-step process.

TIP

You may have to prove you're not a robot by way of a reCAPTCHA — because who doesn't like looking for stoplights in grainy photos? Fortunately, this method is falling out of favor. Instead you may be prompted to authorize an OAuth connection, such as through a service like Plaid, to connect to your bank or credit card account. Simply follow the onscreen prompts.

If all goes as expected, a new screen displays the accounts you have at the financial institution and lets you choose which ones you want to connect to QuickBooks.

4. **Choose the accounts you want to connect.**

For each account you choose, QuickBooks asks you to select an existing Bank or Credit Card account or create a new account. QuickBooks also asks you how far in the past you want to pull transactions for the account. Depending on your bank, options may include Today, This Month, This Year, or Last Year, or you may be able to specify a custom range.

5. Click Connect, and then wait while your accounts download.

The Connect button is disabled until you select an account, specify a type, and choose a date range for downloading transactions.

6. Follow any additional onscreen prompts you see to finish setting up the account.

The automatic download of transactions is only the first phase of the process; you must still review and accept the transactions, which I discuss in the "Reviewing Your Bank and Credit Card Transactions" section later in this chapter.

TIP

You can use the Rules feature to automatically process synchronized transactions, as discussed in Chapter 7.

Handling indirect banking connections

You can manually import your banking and credit card transactions if your bank doesn't support direct connections or if you're uncomfortable setting up such a connection. Ideally, you'll download a QuickBooks Web Connect file, but even if you can only download the transactions to an Excel spreadsheet or text file, you can transform the data into a format that QuickBooks can import. The end result is the same as an automatic synchronization, as long you're willing to carry out the necessary repetitive actions.

WARNING

Do not use a public computer to download Web Connect or transaction files from your bank. The files are not encrypted and contain sensitive information about your bank or credit card account. Deleted files are not ever truly deleted on your computer until other data has been saved over that location.

Follow these steps to download transactions from your financial institution:

1. Log in to your financial institution's website and look for a link that enables you to download to QuickBooks or to a text file.

Some websites have a Download button associated with each account, whereas others offer a Download to QuickBooks or CSV/TXT link. Others may offer a QuickBooks Web Connect link. If you can't find a link, odds are that your financial institution doesn't offer this functionality, but check with the customer service department to make sure.

TIP

If you can't download the transactions, try copying and pasting your banking activity into a Microsoft Excel workbook or Google Sheets spreadsheet and then carry out the instructions in the "Opening unsupported download files" section. You truly can get there from here.

2. **Select any of the following file formats that your financial institution offers:**

- QBO (QuickBooks)
- QFX (Quicken)
- OFX (Microsoft Money)
- Any file format that references QuickBooks or QuickBooks Online
- CSV (comma-separated value file)
- TXT (tab-delimited text file)

TIP

I've listed these files in priority order, meaning you should always choose one of the first four types if available so you don't have to edit the file. The last two types are last-resort options that may require some editing before you can import them into QuickBooks.

3. **Specify a date range for the transactions you want to download.**

WARNING

The account's opening balance changes if you download transactions with dates that precede the opening balance, so double-check the dates you choose here, and don't go too far back in time.

4. **If prompted, save the file to a location on your computer where you can find it later.**

The file will appear in your Downloads folder if you're not given a choice to save the file in a specific location.

If you downloaded a Web Connect file, which includes QuickBooks (QBO), Quicken (QFX), or Microsoft Money (OFX) files, skip ahead to the "Uploading your transactions into QuickBooks" section. Otherwise, read on to see the hopefully minor changes you may have to make to the text file that you download.

Opening unsupported download files

If your transactions are in a text-based file format, such as a CSV or TXT file, you need to transform the data into a three- or four-column CSV format that QuickBooks can upload. You can skip the next part if your data is already in an Excel workbook — whether you downloaded it in that format or copied and pasted it into a workbook. To get the data into Microsoft Excel, follow these steps:

1. **In Microsoft Excel, choose File ⇨ Open.**
2. **Change the File Type field to Text Files.**
3. **Browse to the folder where your CSV or TXT file resides, select the file, and then click Open.**

Then, in Google Sheets, follow these steps:

1. **Create a blank spreadsheet.**
2. **Choose File ⇨ Import ⇨ Upload.**
3. **Click Select a File from Your Device, browse for the file, and then click Open.**
4. **Make a choice from the Import Location list, and then click Import Data.**
5. **Change the File Type field to Text Files.**
6. **Browse to the folder where your CSV or TXT file resides, select the file, and then click Open.**

Read on to see how to edit your text file to conform to what QuickBooks expects.

Transforming the transaction files

QuickBooks can upload your transactions if you rearrange the data into one of the formats shown in Tables 5-1 and 5-2. What's key is to create a single row of titles and specify the column headings shown. The order of the columns does not matter.

TABLE 5-1   **An Acceptable Three-Column Format**

Date	Description	Amount
1/1/2025	Example check, fee, or credit card charge	–100.00
1/1/2025	Example deposit or credit card payment	200.00

TABLE 5-2   **An Acceptable Four-Column Format**

Date	Description	Debit	Credit
1/1/2025	Example check, fee, or credit card charge	200.00	
1/1/2025	Example deposit or credit card payment		100.00

REMEMBER

Keep in mind that these columns are the minimum required. QuickBooks ignores any extraneous columns, so don't obsess about making the file just so.

REMEMBER

Deductions from your bank account need to be listed as negative amounts in the three-column format and as positive amounts in the Debit column of the four-column format. Credit card charges need to be formatted in this same fashion. Conversely, bank deposits and refunds posted to your credit card account need to be entered as positive amounts in the three-column format and credits in the four-column format.

WHY BANK STATEMENTS SEEM BACKWARDS

Remember, banks counterintuitively report transactions from their perspective rather than yours. Your money is a liability on the bank's books, because they have to give your money back to you upon request. As a result, when you record an increase to your bank account on your books, you debit the account, but your bank statement reflects this increases as a credit. Similarly, a credit to your bank account on your book reduces your account balance, while a debit on the bank's side does the same thing.

In either case, edit the spreadsheet to conform with the format in Tables 5-1 or 5-2 by adding or removing columns. Remember, QuickBooks ignores any additional columns beyond the minimum requirements.

You must resolve three special situations before saving a CSV file that QuickBooks can upload:

>> **Amounts:** Ensure your transaction amounts are correctly entered as positive or negative values, or appear in the proper columns (Debit or Credit), as shown in the tables.

>> **Date formats:** Ensure the date column contains only dates, without times. For example, if cell A2 contains 01/01/2026 08:00 AM, you can enter =ROUND(A2,0) in a blank cell, such as E2, and then copy the formula down the column. Once done, copy the formulas in Column E, choose Home ⇨ Paste ⇨ Paste Special ⇨ Values, and then click OK.

WARNING

Dates within spreadsheets are serial numbers that represent the number of days that have elapsed since December 31, 1899. That means that 1/1/2026 may appear as 46,023 instead. In Excel, select dates formatted as serial numbers and then choose Home ⇨ Format ⇨ Format Cells, select a date format from the Date section of the Number tab, and then click OK. In Google Sheets, choose Format ⇨ Number ⇨ Date. QuickBooks rejects serial number-based dates.

>> **Splitting columns:** You can remove extraneous text by splitting description or memo columns and then discarding the extraneous text. Copy the data in question to an unused area of your spreadsheet and then select the cells. Choose Data ⇨ Text to Columns in Microsoft Excel, and then work through the wizard, or choose Data ⇨ Split Text into Columns in Google Sheets, and then select or enter a separator from the list that appears.

FLIPPING THE SIGN ON NUMBERS

You can use spreadsheet formulas to flip positive numbers to negative or vice versa. Here are two approaches:

Microsoft Excel: Enter **–1** in a blank worksheet cell, such as cell E1. Select cell E1 and then choose Home ⇨ Copy. Next, select the numbers that you want to flip the sign on and then choose Home ⇨ Paste ⇨ Paste Special ⇨ Multiply ⇨ OK.

Google Sheets: If column C contains positive amounts that you want to make negative and the first amount appears in cell C2, type **–C2** into any blank cell, such as D2, and then copy the formula down as many rows as needed. Select and then copy the formulas from Column D and choose Edit ⇨ Paste Special ⇨ Values Only. At this point, you can delete column D or erase the worksheet cells to avoid confusion.

The next step is to save your transactions as a comma-separated value (CSV) file.

Saving comma-separated value (CSV) files

A comma-separated value (CSV) file is simply a text file that has a comma between each field. This format is an alternative to the Web Connect formats that do not require any transformation.

Here's how to save your three- or four-column format as a CSV file in Microsoft Excel:

1. **Choose File ⇨ Save As.**

2. **Change the File Type field to CSV (Comma Delimited).**

3. **Browse to the location where you want to save the file, and then click Save.**

   Make sure you choose a location you can remember because you'll be choosing this file in QuickBooks.

4. **Choose File ⇨ Close.**

   This step is crucial to a successful upload. First, it ensures that your changes are saved. Second, it prevents your operating system from locking open files, which could prevent the upload.

To save a CSV file in Google Sheets, use these steps:

1. **Choose File ⇨ Download ⇨ Comma Separated Values (.csv).**

2. **Browse to the location where you want to save the file and then click Save.**

   Make sure you choose a location you can remember because you'll be choosing this file in QuickBooks.

3. **Choose File ⇨ Close.**

   It's not as crucial to close a Google Sheets spreadsheet as it is in Excel but doing so ensures that you don't make any changes onscreen that aren't in the copy you downloaded.

WARNING

Don't be fooled by QuickBooks' assertion that you can upload TXT files. Most TXT files use tab-delimited or fixed-width formats, although you can certainly save a comma-separated value file with a .TXT file extension.

You're now ready to upload your transactions to QuickBooks.

Uploading your transactions into QuickBooks

At this point you should either have a Web Connect file — meaning a .QBO, .QFX, or .OFX file — in hand or a .CSV file that you have formatted in either the three- or four-column formats described earlier in this section. Here's how to upload:

1. **In QuickBooks choose Transactions ⇨ Bank Transactions.**

   The Bank Transactions screen opens.

2. **Click the Link Account drop-down menu and choose Upload from File or choose Settings ⇨ Import Data ⇨ Bank Data.**

   The Import Bank Transactions screen opens.

3. **Click the Select Files link, and then browse and select your transaction file. Click Open.**

4. **Click Continue.**

   Depending upon your screen resolution you may need to scroll the Import Bank Transactions screen down to locate the Continue button.

5. **On the next screen, select the bank or credit card account where the transactions should appear, and then click Continue.**

Your transactions are imported, which may take seconds or minutes, depending on the speed of your Internet connection and the number of transactions you're importing.

6. **At this point, the steps differ between Web Connect and CSV files.**

   - **Web Connect:** Click Done and move on to Step 7.

   - **CSV file:** The Let's Set Up Your File in QuickBooks screen opens. From here, you do the following:

   a. *Confirm if the first row of your file is a header.*

   b. *Indicate whether your file has one amount column or two.*

   c. *Select a date format.*

   d. *If needed, map the columns in your CSV file to the corresponding QuickBooks fields.*

   e. *Click Continue.*

   f. *Click Yes to confirm that you want to import the transactions.*

      In some cases, QuickBooks shows you the list of transactions and allows you to pick which ones you want to import. In other cases, a simple confirmation prompt appears.

   g. *Click Done.*

7. **You're now ready to review and accept the transactions by following the instructions in the "Reviewing Your Bank and Credit Card Transactions" section.**

WARNING

Always delete Web Connect files after importing them because they contain sensitive information about your financial accounts that anyone who gains access to the file can view.

REMEMBER

When you import transactions from a CSV file, the bank balance in QuickBooks may be reported as zero. No need to worry — this simply means that the balance amount isn't available in the CSV file.

Customizing your Bank Transactions screen

When you upload files manually, you control the schedule for when they're added. In contrast, QuickBooks typically downloads activity from your financial institution nightly, but the timing of updates depends on your financial institution.

You can control the following aspects of the transaction listing on the Banking screen by clicking the Gear icon above the Action column. Available customizations include:

>> Displaying or hiding the following fields:

- Check numbers

- Payee names

- Tags

- Bank details

- Class names (Plus or Advanced companies only)

- Location names (Plus or Advanced companies only)

>> Grouping transactions by month

>> Viewing 50, 75, 100, or 300 transactions per screen

>> Displaying a single Amounts column or separate Spent and Received columns

>> Making the Date field editable

>> Copying bank detail information into the Memo field

>> Suggesting categories (meaning accounts from your chart of accounts) based upon your past transaction history

REMEMBER

You can also adjust the column widths with the transaction list by hovering your mouse between column headings to display a double-headed arrow that you then drag. Any adjustments you make are a sticky preference that will be remembered going forward.

Reviewing Your Bank and Credit Card Transactions

Your bank and credit card transactions don't post directly to your books; instead, they land in a holding area where you must explicitly accept them. This applies to both direct feeds, where synchronization is automated, and indirect feeds, where you manually upload the transactions into QuickBooks. Accordingly, here are the steps you need to carry out on an ongoing basis to match, exclude, or add bank and credit card transactions:

1. **Choose Transactions ⇨ Banking Transactions.**

   The Banking Transactions screen opens.

2. **Choose a bank or credit card account to display any related transactions you need to review.**

   Three tabs appear just below your account(s).

   - **For Review:** Unreviewed transactions that await your attention.

   - **Categorized:** Transactions that you've reviewed and accepted or confirmed, either manually or by way of a rule. I discuss rules in Chapter 7.

   - **Excluded:** Transactions that you've opted not to post to your books at the present time. You can select one or more transactions and choose Undo to return the transactions to the For Review list, or you can choose Delete to remove the transactions from QuickBooks.

TIP

Note that the Delete command doesn't ask you if you're sure, so think twice before clicking Delete. See the "Handling indirect banking connections" section earlier in this chapter if you inadvertently delete transactions directly downloaded into QuickBooks. You may be able to recover what you deleted by manually downloading the transactions from your financial institution to an Excel spreadsheet or text file and then uploading them into QuickBooks.

3. **QuickBooks automatically classifies as many transactions as it can, based on built-in rules that you can override with your own specifications.**

   a. *When you select one transaction at a time, you can use the following commands:*

   - *Accept (or Confirm):* Accepts the category/account that QuickBooks assigned the transaction to and posts the transaction to your books.

   - *View (Review, or click on the transaction):* Displays a screen from which you can do the following:

   - Choose the Categorize radio button to change the vendor/customer, category, location, class, tags, or memo.

   - Choose the Find Match radio button to view potential matches or search for other matches.

   - Choose the Record As Transfer radio button to select an offsetting account for the transfer.

   - Add an attachment, such as a PDF copy of a receipt.

   - Create a rule, which I discuss in Chapter 7.

QuickBooks may ask if you want to create a rule to automatically apply the transactions in the future. Click Don't Show Me This Again if you don't want QuickBooks to suggest creating rules.

- Exclude a transaction so that it doesn't post to your books.
- View the categorization history for similar transactions when you choose the Categorize option.
- Split a transaction that you're categorizing among two or more categories.

b. *When you select two or more transactions on the list (using the checkboxes along the left), you can then confirm, update, or exclude them.*

- *Confirm:* Accepts the transactions, which means that they post to your books and appear on the Categorized tab.
- *Update:* Displays the Update Selected dialog box.
- *Exclude:* Moves the transactions to the Excluded tab. As noted previously, you can later select one or more transactions and choose Undo to move transactions back to the For Review tab, or you can delete the transactions.

4. **Keep working the list until you've reviewed all transactions.**

You may be able to speed up the process by making one of the following choices from the All Transactions filter:

- **Recognized:** View transactions that have been recognized. (You updated the category manually.)
- **Matched:** See transactions in which a match was made between the transaction downloaded from your financial institution and your accounting records.
- **Transferred:** See transactions that are deemed to be a transfer between accounts, such as a credit card payment, or a transfer of funds between two bank accounts.
- **Rule Applied:** View transactions that are automatically updated by a rule, which I discuss in Chapter 7.
- **Missing Payee/Customer:** See a list of transactions for which the payee or customer can't be identified.
- **Unassigned:** View a list of transactions that have a status other than Add and haven't been processed yet.

Reconciling Bank or Credit Card Accounts

For many, reconciling a bank statement is a dreaded task, but I appreciate the peace of mind that comes from knowing my books are aligned with my bank — it's a great way to avoid surprises. On the other hand, reconciling credit card statements isn't my favorite chore, but it's necessary to face the music. Fortunately, if you've been diligent about entering transactions in QuickBooks and recording bank deposits and credit card payments as outlined in the previous section, reconciling your bank or credit card statement should be straightforward. Grab your most recent statement and follow these steps:

1. **Choose Settings ⇨ Reconcile from the Tools section.**

   Make sure you click the Gear icon and not + New.

2. **Select the account you want to reconcile from the Account field drop-down menu.**

REMEMBER

   The fields related to recording service charges and interest don't appear for accounts you've connected to your bank because this information downloads automatically.

TIP

   You may see a Get Started button that you can click to view a summary, road map-style, of the reconciliation process. At the end of the wizard, click Let's Get Reconciled to continue.

3. **Enter the ending date and balance from your statement and click Start Reconciling.**

   The Reconcile screen opens.

REMEMBER

   Enter bank and credit card balances so they're the same as the balance on your bank and credit card statements. For example, if the bank says you owe $750 on your credit card, enter **$750** in the Ending Balance field. However, if you overpaid and your credit card statement reports a balance of –$125, enter **–125** as the ending balance. Typically, you always enter a positive number for your bank account balance — that is, unless you're reconciling an overdrawn or overpaid account.

TIP

   Click Edit Info if you need to return to the initial screen to correct your ending bank balance or to record a service charge or interest. Click Save to return to the reconciliation screen.

4. **Select each transaction that appears in your statement and on the Reconcile screen by clicking the rightmost column.**

TIP

   Paychecks divided between two bank accounts show up as two distinct transactions in QuickBooks, so they should be easy to match up during reconciliation.

By selecting a transaction, you're marking it as having cleared the bank. Your goal is to have the Difference amount at the top-right corner of the Reconcile screen equal $0. If your account is connected to your bank, many transactions might already display a checkmark in the rightmost column because the transactions have been downloaded from the bank and matched with your accounting records, as I discussed in the "Synchronizing with Financial Institutions" section earlier in this chapter.

By default, the Reconciliation screen displays all uncleared transactions dated before the statement ending date, but you can click Payments or Deposits to filter by either of those options, like the way most bank statements are organized. Any transactions with dates later than the statement ending date are hidden by default. If, after you select all the transactions you see, the Difference amount isn't $0, click the X next to Statement Ending Date to look for additional transactions to mark as cleared. You can also take advantage of the Filter icon (which looks like a funnel) to limit the transactions in a way that works best for you. Be sure to compare the total payments and deposits with the corresponding numbers on the bank statement. This comparison can help you determine whether deposits or payments are missing.

TIP

You can click the Bank Register or Credit Card Register link in the top-left corner of the screen to view the register for the account you're reconciling. When you finish viewing the register, click Reconcile in the top-right corner of the register screen. If you want to see more transactions on the reconciliation screen, click the upward-pointing arrow to collapse the header.

5. **Click Finish Now when the Difference equals $0, as shown in Figure 5-2.**

A Success message gives you the opportunity to view the Reconciliation report by clicking the View Reconciliation Report link. The Reconciliation report is broken into a summary section and a detail section that lists all transactions you cleared.

REMEMBER

You don't have to finish your reconciliation in a single sitting. Click the drop-down arrow on the Finish Now button and then choose Save for Later if you get interrupted or you simply can't get the reconciliation to zero out. Returning with a fresh eye can often make discrepancies jump off the screen. You can also choose Close Without Saving if you want to abandon the entire process.

TIP

There's an age-old bookkeeping trick that calls for dividing the unreconciled difference by 9. If it divides cleanly, the chances are exceedingly high that your difference is caused by a transposition. For instance, if your unreconciled difference is $90, you may have entered $450 when you should have entered $540 for a transaction.

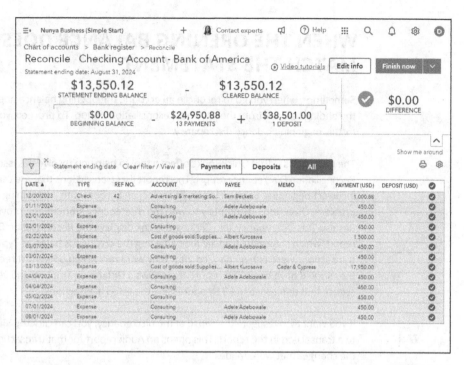

FIGURE 5-2:
The Bank
Reconciliation
screen.

You can click any transaction in the report to view it in the window where you created it. To produce a paper copy of the report, click Print in the top-right corner of the report window.

You can view the Reconciliation report at any time. Just redisplay the Reconcile screen by choosing Settings ⇨ Reconcile. After you reconcile an account, a History by Account link appears in the top-right corner of the screen. When you click the link, the History by Account screen opens, listing earlier reconciliations for an individual account. Click the View Report link beside any reconciliation on this screen to see its Reconciliation report.

To view reconciliations for other accounts, choose a different account from the Account drop-down list.

REMEMBER

QuickBooks does not allow Simple Start, Essentials, Plus, or Advanced users to undo a bank reconciliation. However, as I discuss in Chapter 19, the Accountant version of QuickBooks Online does offer the ability to undo bank reconciliations.

WHEN THE OPENING BALANCE DOESN'T MATCH THE STATEMENT

Sometimes, when you go to reconcile an account, the opening balance doesn't match the ending balance from the previous reconciliation period. To proceed, you need to fix this beginning balance discrepancy.

The good news is that QuickBooks offers a tool to help you resolve this issue: the Reconciliation Discrepancy report. This report lists transactions that are causing the incorrect beginning balance. When you select an account with a beginning balance problem, QuickBooks prompts you with the discrepancy amount and provides a Let's Resolve This Discrepancy link. Clicking this link displays the Reconciliation Discrepancy report, which shows the transactions affecting the erroneous balance. Typically, these transactions were either changed after they were reconciled or weren't reconciled when they should have been. The report also shows a Difference amount, and your goal is to reduce that difference to $0 by addressing the listed transactions.

If you want to investigate the cause of the discrepancy, you can click the View link next to a transaction in the report. This opens an Audit report for that transaction, detailing the changes that were made.

Chapter **6**

Leveraging QuickBooks Reports

A ccounting reports help you monitor the financial health of your business by enabling you to dive into detailed data when needed. In this chapter, I guide you through the accounting reports that are available to all subscription levels and show how you can export reports to Microsoft Excel, comma-separated value (CSV) files, and PDFs. If you have an Advanced subscription, be sure to out the custom report writer and chart capabilities that I discuss in Chapter 14.

TIP

A detailed listing of the reports available to each subscription level is available at https://quickbooks.intuit.com/learn-support/en-us/help-article/purchase-orders/reports-included-quickbooks-online-subscription/L0s4KrGgr_US_en_US.

I used the QuickBooks Online sample company at https://qbo.intuit.com/redir/testdrive to provide you with an easy way to generate reports that containing actual data, especially if you haven't entered a significant number of transactions into your accounting records. This sample company lets you test-drive the Plus subscription level, so you may see more reports than are available if you have a Simple Start or Essentials subscription.

Reviewing the Reports Screen

Choose Reports on the sidebar to open the Reports screen, which has three tabs: Standard, Custom Reports, and Management Reports. The following sections dive into the various features of the Reports screen.

Exploring standard reporting

Basic/standard reporting is organized into the following categories:

>> Favorites

>> Business Overview

>> Who Owes You

>> Sales and Customers

>> What You Owe

>> Expenses and Vendors

>> Sales Tax (if the Sales Tax option is enabled)

>> Employees

>> For My Accountant

>> Payroll (if you have a payroll subscription)

 I find it easiest to locate reports by typing a portion of the report name in the Find a Report field. You can also toggle the star next to any report name on or off to determine if a report appears in the Favorites section.

 You also can use the Search tool, in the top-right corner of the screen, to search for a report from anywhere in QuickBooks.

Exploring Modern View reports

Modern View reports have been creeping into QuickBooks over the past two years, replacing what has been known as Classic reports. Intuit has set a goal to apply Modern View to all reports by December 2024, so I'm going to take it on faith that they follow through on this endeavor and assume that by the time you're reading this that Classic reports are no longer available.

Modern View reports enable you to group data based on a single criterion and allow you to apply more levels of filtering. You can export reports to Excel, CSV (comma-separated value) files, or PDF files. You can also create report groups comprised of two or more reports. The following steps walk you through customizing the Transaction List by Date report:

1. **Choose Transaction List by Date from the For My Accountant section.**

   Alternatively, you can type **by date** in the Find Report by Name field and then press Enter.

2. **To set a date range for the report, select from the This Month to Date field.**

   Scroll to the top of the time period list and choose Custom if you don't see the time period you want on the list.

TIP

3. **To group the report by one or more criteria, select from the Group By field.**

   The Group By feature allows you to organize and categorize data by specific criteria, such as customer, vendor, or account.

TECHNICAL
STUFF

   The +Add Subgroup button is available exclusively to Advanced users, so if you have a different subscription level it may appear as a tease. Advanced subscribers can specify a group and add up to two subgroups for more detailed reporting.

4. **To narrow down the report, click Filter and specify criteria that you want to apply.**

   You must specify an operation and value for each filter that you apply. All subscription levels can add multiple filters to a report.

5. **To add or remove fields from the report, click Columns.**

   As shown in Figure 6-1, you can hide or display columns by toggling the checkbox to the left of each column name. You can reorganize the report by dragging the six dot button to the right of each column name into a new position on the list.

6. **To change the name of a report, click Edit and update the report title.**

7. **To email a report, choose More Actions ⇨ Email Report.**

   This command opens a Send dialog box, where you can compose an email by filling in the To, CC, Subject, Message, and File Name fields, as well as choose from Excel, CSV, and PDF formats.

8. **To add the report to the Custom Reports list, click Save As.**

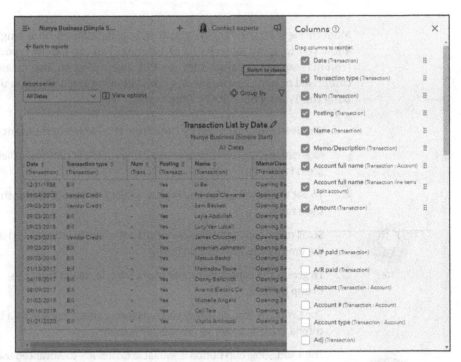

FIGURE 6-1:
The Columns
task pane.

TIP
Once you save a report, Save As changes to a Save button, which enables you to save a report with another name or add the report to a report group.

Creating custom reports

You can share customized classic reports with other users in your QuickBooks Online company. This means your Custom Reports tab may display custom reports that other users have elected to share. You can do the following from the Custom Reports tab shown in Figure 6-2:

>> Click the report name to display the report onscreen. You can modify the report and then click Save. Keep the report name intact if you want to overwrite the previously saved custom report.

>> Click Delete to remove the report from your Custom Reports list.

>> Choose Add to Management Reports from the Actions column to add the report to a new or existing management report.

>> Select Add to Group or Change Group from the Actions column to add or adjust the group that a report is assigned to.

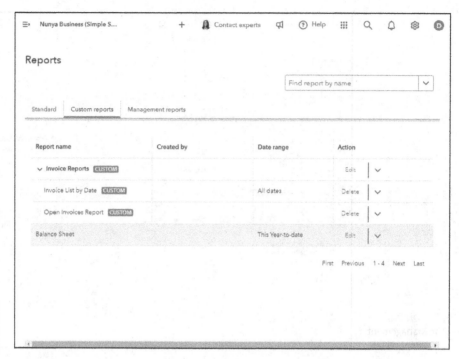

Report name	Created by	Date range	Action	
⌄ Invoice Reports CUSTOM			Edit	⌄
Invoice List by Date CUSTOM		All dates	Delete	⌄
Open Invoices Report CUSTOM			Delete	⌄
Balance Sheet		This Year-to-date	Edit	⌄

First Previous 1 - 4 Next Last

FIGURE 6-2:
The Custom
Reports tab of the
Reports screen.

TIP

Report groups can be used to organize related reports, but you can only view one report onscreen at a time unless you first save the report group to a PDF. To do so, Choose Export as PDF from the Action column for a report group title. You can also choose Delete Group to unbundle the reports.

Analyzing management reports

The Management Reports tab of the Reports screen, shown in Figure 6-3, lists three predefined management report packages that you can prepare and print by selecting the Preview link in the Action column.

These report packages are quite elegant. Each package contains a professional-looking cover page, a table of contents, and several reports that correspond to the report package's name:

>> The Company Overview management report contains the Profit and Loss report and the Balance Sheet report.

>> The Sales Performance management report contains the Profit and Loss report, the A/R Aging Detail report, and the Sales by Customer Summary report.

>> The Expenses Performance management report contains the Profit and Loss report, the A/P Aging Detail report, and the Expenses by Vendor Summary report.

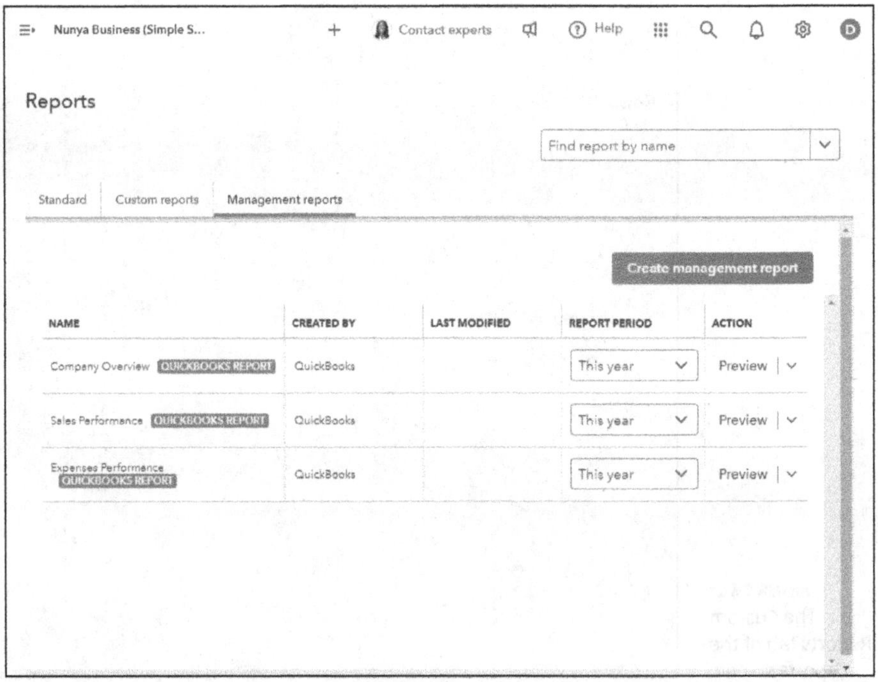

FIGURE 6-3:
The Management
Reports tab.

Click Preview in the Action column to display the Print or Save as PDF dialog box shown in Figure 6-4 to generate an electronic or hard copy. The Action column also contains the following commands:

>> **Edit:** Allows you to customize titles, add your logo to the cover page, add more reports or charts to the package, include text on one or more preliminary pages, and add endnotes to the package. Click any page along the left side of the screen to modify each section of the report.

Toggle the eye icon at the center of a page to exclude or include the page in the final report package.

>> **Send:** Opens a Send dialog box, where you can compose an email by filling in the To, CC, Subject, Message, and File Name fields, as well as choose from PDF and Microsoft Word formats.

>> **Export as PDF:** Downloads a copy of the report package to your computer as a PDF file.

>> **Export as DOCX:** Downloads a copy of the report package to your computer in a format compatible with Microsoft Word, Google Docs, and other word processing platforms.

>> **Duplicate:** Replicates a report package while keeping the original intact.

>> **Delete:** Available for management reports that you've copied or created. You can't delete the three default report packages.

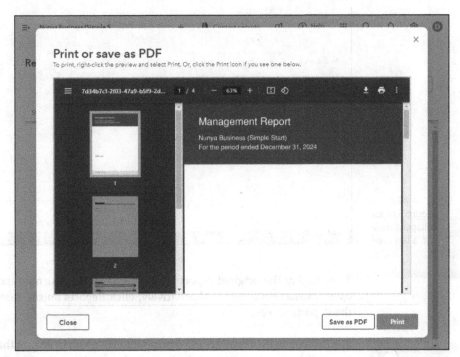

FIGURE 6-4:
Print Preview
screen of a
management
report.

Interacting with Reports

Some reports enable you to manage information overload by collapsing sections of the report, and most every report allows you to drill down into the underlying details. Let's look at a report that offers both of these features:

1. **Choose Journal from the For My Accountant section of the Standard tab on the Reports screen.**

2. **Click collapse/expand arrow shown in Figure 6-5 to collapse that level of the report or click the arrow a second time to expand the level.**

3. **Click any text or numeric amount for a line item on the Journal report to display the underlying transaction.**

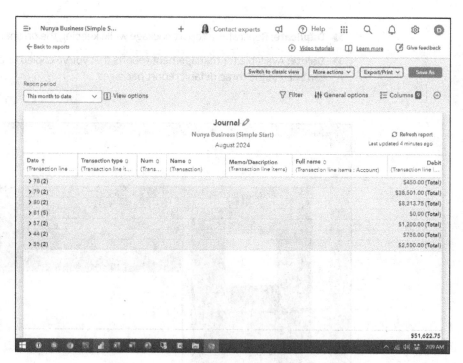

FIGURE 6-5:
A Journal report
collapsed down
to a few rows.

To redisplay the original report — in this case, the Journal report — close any open transaction screens. Alternatively, click Reports on the sidebar to return to the Reports screen.

TIP

You can duplicate a browser tab before you drill down to ensure that you're always just a click away from the original report that you're reviewing. To duplicate a tab in Google Chrome, right-click a tab and choose Duplicate from the shortcut menu. For all other browsers, consult the browser's Help menu for instructions on duplicating a tab.

Charting Your Business

For most QuickBooks users, charts present a good news/bad news scenario. Let's get the bad news out of the way first. Unless you have an Advanced subscription, your ability to create charts is limited to a handful of widgets on the Home screen. The good news is that your accountant can create up to 25 charts based upon your accounting records and share these charts with you in PDF form. With that said, here's how to access the limited charts that are directly available:

1. **Choose Dashboards ⇨ Home.**

   The Home screen appears. Widgets also appear that show the following information:

   - Tasks that need to be completed within your accounting records.
   - Shortcuts to frequently used features, such as creating checks, recording expenses, and so on.
   - Expenses for the past 30 days or for selected time periods.
   - The number of apps connected to your QuickBooks company.
   - Bank balances.
   - Unpaid invoices for the past year, and paid invoices for the past 30 days.
   - Profit and Loss for the past 30 days or selected time periods.
   - Accounts receivable as of today.
   - Mileage for the past 30 days or selected time periods.
   - Sales for the past 30 days or selected time periods.

2. **Optional: Click the Customize button and then hover your mouse over any widget to reposition or delete the object.**

   The Add or Remove Widgets button enables you to turn widgets on or off but not move them.

TIP

The Recommended Charts feature on the Insert tab of Microsoft Excel's ribbon suggests charts suitable for presenting data that you've exported from QuickBooks. The Analyze Data command appears on the Home tab of the Microsoft 365 version of Excel and enables you to create charts by asking plain-English questions.

The Cash Flow tab of the Dashboard screen enables you to view an automated cash flow forecast once you link one or more bank accounts. The Planner tab of the Dashboard screen enables you to add or remove items from the cash flow forecast without affecting your accounting records.

Tagging Transactions

Tags offer an additional dimension for categorizing and reporting on related transactions. They're similar to the project tracking feature that's available to Plus and Advanced subscribers. You can tag just about every type of transaction except for transfers and journal entries. Tag groups are collections of one or more tags, for which you can run a Profit and Loss by Tag report or a Transaction List by Tag Group report. You can also view lists of transactions by individual tags, sometimes referred to as *flat tags*.

I recommend that you keep the Profit and Loss by Tag report in mind when planning your tags. For example, let's say that you're completing a project for a customer named Sure Lock Homes. You can create a tag group called Sure Lock Homes, which you can apply to any invoices that you send to that customer, as well as to any expenses that you incur related to that customer. You don't need to create a Revenue tag or Expense tag for two reasons:

>> The Profit and Loss by Tag report automatically groups revenue and expenses and gives you a net income figure by tag.

>> You can assign the Revenue and Expense tags I'm discussing only to a single tag group. You can create Sure Lock Homes Revenue and Sure Lock Homes Expense tags, but doing so makes your tracking harder because the Profit and Loss by Tag report contains two columns: one for Sure Lock Homes Revenue and one for Sure Lock Homes Expenses — each with separate net income amounts.

However, maybe you're building a fence for Sure Lock Homes, and you're separately installing a gravel sidewalk. This is the level where tags (subtags) makes sense, because then on the Profit and Loss by Tag report you see one column for the fence and a second column for the sidewalk.

In short, tags are beneficial when you want to group related accounting transactions in a manner that isn't already available. For instance, you likely don't need an Insurance tag because you're probably already grouping insurance expenses into one or more accounts and perhaps sub-accounts. On the other hand, if you're sponsoring a booth at an industry conference, you likely have an array of expenses that you want to group into something like a 2025 Conference Sponsorship tag group. If you gain new business from the conference, you can tag invoices for those customers with that tag group as well. You can then use tags (subtags) to group related expenses, such as Booth Materials, Customer Swag, and so on.

REMEMBER

Tags can only be assigned at the transaction level, which means you cannot assign a tag to individual rows within the transaction itself.

Creating tag groups and tags

You can quickly add tags on the fly when creating new transactions by typing a tag name in the Tags field of a transaction screen and clicking Add. However, you need to create any tags in advance that you want to assign to existing transactions:

1. **Choose the Gear icon ⇨ Tags to display the Tag list.**

2. **Click New, and then choose Tag Group or Tag.**

   In QuickBooks vernacular, tag groups are parent tags, whereas tags are treated as children tags, or subtags. Each tag group can optionally have one or more subtags associated with it.

3. **Create a tag group or tag.**

   You can choose one of the following:

   - **Tag Groups:** As shown in Figure 6-6, you assign a tag group name, optionally assign one of 16 colors to the tag group, and then click Save. You can then fill in the Tag Name field and click Add as needed to add subtags to the group. Click Done to close the Tag Group task pane.

TIP

   Simple Start, Essentials, and Plus users can create 40 tag groups while Advanced users can create unlimited tag groups.

   - **Tags (subtags):** The Create New Tag task pane has only two fields: Tag Name and Group. You're returned to the Tag list when you click Save. Accordingly, it's more efficient to use the Tag Groups command when you need to create multiple tags. All versions of QuickBooks, including Advanced subscriptions, are limited to assigning 300 tags across all tag groups.

TIP

   Plus and Advanced users can use the project tracking capability that I discuss in Chapter 11 instead of tags to track projects that are completed on behalf of customers.

REMEMBER

   You can associate each tag with only a single group. For instance, if you sell fruit baskets internationally and domestically, you might create tag groups for Domestic Sales and International Sales. In this case, a Fruit Basket tag (subtag) can be associated only with Domestic Sales or International Sales, but not both. One solution might be to have Fruit Baskets be the tag group and to set up Domestic Sales and International Sales as tags (subtags). Fortunately, you can delete tags and tag groups (as opposed to marking them inactive, which is what QuickBooks requires for most list items).

   - **Tags (flat tags):** Flat tags are tags that aren't associated with a tag group. To create a flat tag, simply leave the Group field blank in the Create New Tag task pane, and then Click Save.

REMEMBER

   You can't choose flat tags in your reports, but you can use the various transaction filter options in QuickBooks to unearth transactions that have flat tags assigned.

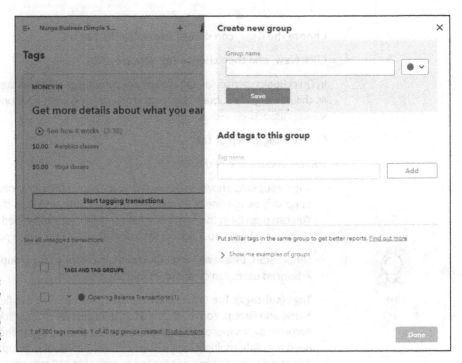

FIGURE 6-6:
The Create New
Group task pane
enables you to
establish new tag
groups and tags.

Tagging existing transactions

After you have at least one tag or group created, you can start tagging existing transactions:

1. **Choose Settings ⇨ Tags, if necessary.**

2. **Click Start Tagging Transactions in the Money In or Money Out sections or choose See All Untagged Transactions above the list of Tags and Tag Groups.**

   A list of your transactions appears.

3. **Use the checkboxes to the left of the transactions to select one or more transactions that you want to tag, which causes an Update Tags button to appear at the top of the list.**

   You can use the Filters button to the left to select groups of transactions if you like.

4. **Choose Update Tags ⇨ Add Tags.**

   You can also choose Remove Tags from the Update Tags drop-down menu if you want to untag one or more transactions.

5. **Choose or type the name of the tag and click Apply.**

Tags appear in the new Tags column.

You can assign as many tags as you want to a transaction, but you can choose only one tag (subtag) per tag group (parent tag). The nuance goes further: You can't assign a tag group (parent tag) to a transaction. You must choose a tag (subtag) that's associated with a tag group (parent tag).

Tagging new transactions

The Tag field appears on just about every transaction screen except for transfers and journal entries. When creating a new transaction, simply choose one or more tags from the Tags field or start typing the name of a new tag, and then choose Add Tag from the drop-down menu.

You can assign only tags, versus tag groups, to transactions.

Running tag reports

You can choose between two tag-related reports:

>> **Profit and Loss by Tag Group:** The report generates a Profit and Loss report for the time period of your choice.

>> **Transaction List by Tag Group:** This report lists all transactions within a tag group of your choice.

Throughout the following steps, I draw your attention to a couple of nuances related to these reports:

1. **Choose Reports from the sidebar menu.**

Normally I suggest that you click the Search button at the top of the screen and then enter the word **Tags**. Although you can search for most reports in this fashion, inexplicably tag-related reports don't appear here.

2. **Type the word** Tag **in the Find Report by Name field and then choose a report name.**

The report names vanish if you type *Tags* instead of *Tag*.

3. **Select a tag group from the Display Columns By field, change the report period if needed, and then click Run Report.**

Removing the Tags field from transaction screens

You can't disable the Tags feature, but you can remove the Tags field from your transaction screens:

1. **Choose the Gear icon ⇨ Account and Settings ⇨ Sales ⇨ Sales Form Content.**

2. **Toggle off the Tags feature and then click Save.**

3. **Choose Expenses ⇨ Bills and Expenses in the Accounts and Settings screen.**

4. **Toggle off the Show Tags feature and then click Save.**

5. **Click Done to close the Account and Settings screen.**

REMEMBER

The Tags command still appears in the Settings menu and cannot be removed, even if you're not using the Tags feature.

IN THIS CHAPTER

» **Discovering mobile and online apps**

» **Establishing automated rules**

» **Converting paper receipts to electronic transactions**

» **Importing data into QuickBooks**

Chapter **7**

Implementing Apps and Automation

S ometimes it seems that our society has gone app-crazy, and QuickBooks Online is a willing participant in the frenzy. In this chapter, I talk about apps that enable you to access your books from your mobile device, as well as apps that add new functionality. I also cover some automation aspects for QuickBooks, including importing certain lists and transactions, adding automatic subtotals to sales forms, and transforming paper or electronic bills and receipts into transactions.

The automation techniques that I discuss in this chapter are available to all QuickBooks Online subscription levels. In Chapter 9, I explore how Essentials, Plus, and Advanced users can utilize the Recurring Transactions feature to eliminate repetitive data entry. Chapter 10 focuses on how Plus and Advanced users can streamline invoicing tasks with pricing rules, while Chapter 15 covers the automation features that are exclusive to companies with an Advanced subscription.

Investigating QuickBooks Online Apps

QuickBooks Online Apps come in three different varieties. I discuss the first two in this chapter and the third in Chapter 13:

» **Mobile app:** You can log into QuickBooks Online through the web browser on your mobile device, but you're likely to have a much better experience if you download and install the mobile app.

» **Online apps:** Think of these as plug-ins that fill functionality gaps in QuickBooks. Some are free, but you pay for most of them on a subscription basis.

» **Desktop app:** In Chapter 13, I discuss how QuickBooks Online Advanced users can download and install a desktop app for Windows that enables users to access multiple companies at once and avoid the infuriating situation that arises when you close the wrong browser tab in QuickBooks and have to log in again.

TIP

If you close the wrong browser tab, press Ctrl+H (Cmd+H in macOS) in many browsers to display the History screen, from which you can reopen the errant tab that you closed by mistake.

Engaging with mobile apps

Your QuickBooks subscription includes mobile apps for iOS/iPadOS and Android devices. These apps are optimized for touch interaction and on-the-go workflows such as customer management, invoicing, estimates, and signatures. You can also use the mobile apps to track the status of invoices, take payments, reconcile bank accounts, capture expenses, record mileage, and check reports. Pinch-and-zoom functionality works in both the apps and browsers on mobile devices.

WARNING

Mileage tracking in QuickBooks Online Mobile is available only to administrative users. This is a whack-a-mole situation where you solve one problem — making it easy for employees to track mileage — and replace it with another: granting employees administrative access to your books.

You can get the mobile apps from the app store for your device or request a link at `https://quickbooks.intuit.com/accounting/mobile`. Alternatively, you can use your browser to log into your books at `https://qbo.intuit.com` without installing anything. Keep in mind that the mobile apps offer a subset of Quick-Books functionality, so you still need to use a web browser to carry out certain tasks, such as customizing templates.

Browsing the QuickBooks App Store

As I discuss in Chapter 1, QuickBooks is all about the add-ons, such as QuickBooks offerings, including Payroll, Time, Payments, and Commerce, along with countless third-party apps. Choose Apps in the sidebar menu to explore the free and paid options that can enable new functionality.

Capitalizing on Commerce

QuickBooks Commerce started out as an app that could be added to QuickBooks Online, but now it's a feature of the software platform. Presently you can connect the following platforms to your books:

>> Amazon

>> eBay

>> Shopify

Your subscription level governs the number of platforms you can connect to:

>> **Simple Start:** One sales channel

>> **Essentials:** Three sales channels

>> **Plus and Advanced:** Unlimited sales channels

You're probably thinking, hmmm, there are only three channels listed, so why did he write that Plus and Advanced users get unlimited sales channels? Simply put, Intuit is working on additional connections, so Essentials users will be able to choose up to three e-commerce channels, whereas Plus and Advanced users will have access to all added channels.

WARNING

The QuickBooks documentation states that you cannot enable the Multicurrency feature that I discuss in Chapter 8 for Essentials, Plus, and Advanced companies if you connect one or more sales channels in QuickBooks Commerce. Nonetheless, my technical editor Dan has a client that *is* using Multicurrency and Commerce together, so your mileage may vary.

Here's how to get started with QuickBooks Commerce:

1. **Choose Commerce from the sidebar menu.**

   Three submenus are available — Overview, Orders, and Payouts — but you won't see any data here until you connect to a platform.

2. Click Connect Sales Channel.

3. Choose a channel and then click Next.

From there you're prompted to provide your sales channel credentials and then configure how you want the information to flow into your books.

WARNING

If you click I Don't See My Channel, you'll be presented with a selection of other platforms, but none of these connections is actually available. Following the prompts simply provides Intuit with some feedback that their marketing and product development teams may find useful.

Intuit offers the following caveats for its Commerce offering:

» Your products and services are only sold in the United States and in United States dollars.

» You don't use a third-party payment processor, like PayPal, Affirm, or Authorize.net.

» You don't need to bring in customer, product, or inventory data from your sales channels.

If you encounter one or more dealbreakers on this list, read on to see how you can import data into QuickBooks.

Implementing Rules for Downloaded Activities

In Chapter 5, I discuss how you can automatically or manually import bank and credit card transactions with your books. In turn, the Rules feature instructs QuickBooks how to categorize and record such transactions automatically. Let's say that you often buy gas for your business vehicles at Shell stations. You can either manually categorize such transactions as Fuel Expense, or you can set up a rule to automate the process going forward. Rules are applied based upon the accounts, transaction types (money in or money out), and criteria that you specify. Rules can assign categories (meaning income/expense accounts) and modify other fields as well. This means that you can create a rule that updates one or more fields and then leave the transaction on the For Review screen. Or, you can create a rule that updates one or more fields and accepts the transaction, which means it posts to your books and then is displayed on the Categorized screen. Either way, you can always amend a transaction by choosing it from the Categorized screen, using the Search feature to locate the transaction, or by clicking on the transaction within a report.

REMEMBER

You can create up to 2,000 rules within a QuickBooks company.

Creating rules

QuickBooks may prompt you to create a rule when you are manually reviewing imported or synced transactions. Or you can create a rule directly by following these steps:

1. **Choose Transactions ⇨ Rules.**

2. **Click New Rule to display the Create Rule task pane shown in Figure 7-1.**

3. **Assign a meaningful name to the rule.**

   You can't use special characters like the apostrophe (') in a rule name.

4. **Indicate whether the rule applies to money coming in or money going out and select the account(s) to which you want the rule to apply.**

REMEMBER

QuickBooks Simple Start users can only create rules for connected bank accounts that synchronize automatically. Essentials, Plus, and Advanced users can also create rules for transactions that are manually uploaded.

5. **Set the transaction criteria for the rule by using the fields in the Include the Following section.**

   Use the Add a Condition link to set additional criteria and to specify if a transaction should meet all or any of the criteria. Specifying All is more stringent and makes QuickBooks more selective about applying the rule.

TIP

The first field in the section enables you to specify whether QuickBooks should compare the transaction description, the bank text, or the transaction amount with a condition you set. For those inquiring minds out there, *Description* (the transaction description) refers to the text that is displayed in the Description column of the Bank and Credit Cards screen. The *Bank Text* option refers to the Bank Detail description the bank downloads; you can view the Bank Detail description if you click any downloaded transaction. The Bank Detail description is displayed in the bottom-left corner of the transactions being edited. *Amount* is the dollar amount of an individual transaction.

For the Description and Bank Text, enter the text you want to scan for and specify that you want the rule to apply if the text you enter matches one of these criteria:

- Contains
- Doesn't Contain
- Is Exactly

For the Amount, you need to enter a value and specify one of these criteria:

- Doesn't Equal
- Equals
- Is Greater Than
- Is Less Than

6. Click Test Rule to determine how many unreviewed transactions the rule will apply to.

QuickBooks won't show you the actual transactions, but you'll at least know that you've specified the criteria correctly to match one or more transactions.

7. Specify one or more actions that you want apply to transactions that match the criteria that you've set.

Available actions include:

- Assign a transaction type, payee, and/or tags.
- Assign a single category or split the transaction between two or more categories. Splits can be based on percentages or dollar amounts.
- Assign a memo. Click Assign More to display the corresponding field.

TIP

See the "The Memo field and rules" sidebar for more ways to leverage the Memo field.

REMEMBER

- Disable automatic posting to your books by toggling the Automatically Confirm Transactions This Rule Applies To setting off.

When enabled, this setting causes transactions to post directly to your book and appear on the Categorized screen. If you encounter an unexpected outcome with a rule, you can still make changes later.

8. Click Save to finalize the rule setup.

The rule appears on the Rules screen and will act on any matching transactions that are synced or imported into QuickBooks.

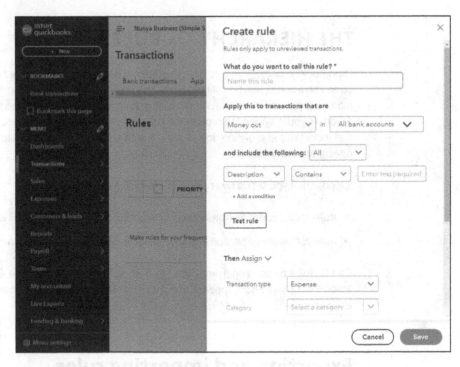

FIGURE 7-1:
The Create Rule
task pane.

REMEMBER

Rules in QuickBooks Online can only be triggered automatically when new transactions are synced or imported; they cannot be manually run on existing transactions.

TIP

Choose Copy in the Action column of the Rules screen to replicate a rule to use as a starting point (instead of starting from scratch). You can also edit, disable, or delete rules.

THE MEMO FIELD AND RULES

QuickBooks uses special icons in the register to identify transactions posted automatically with rules, but you can't filter a register to see only transactions that were added via a rule. You can, however, add a search term, such as "Added by Rule" to the Memo field, which you can then use to filter an account register.

THE HIERARCHY OF RULES

QuickBooks processes your rules in the order in which they are displayed on the Rules screen on a first come, first served basis. This means the first rule with criteria that match a given transaction gets applied, and no other rules are processed for that transaction, so you may need to reorder the rules in certain instances. To do so, drag the icon that looks like a grid of nine dots to the left of the rule on the Rules screen to move a rule up or down in the list.

Suppose that you set up two rules in the following order:

- **Rule 1:** Categorize all transactions of less than $10 as Miscellaneous Expenses.
- **Rule 2:** Categorize all Shake Shack transactions as Meals & Entertainment.

If a $12 dollar transaction from Shake Shack appears, Rule 2 applies. But if a $7.50 transaction from Shake Shack appears, Rule 1 applies. Mmm, Shake Shack. Is anyone else hungry?

Exporting and importing rules

Rules can be exported from one QuickBooks company and then imported into another. This is helpful when you have multiple entities that use the same conventions and chart of accounts. You can also create a set of generic rules to use as a starting point for crafting rules in other companies. Here's how to transfer rules from one company to another:

1. **Choose Transactions ⇨ Rules in the company that has the rules that you want to transfer.**

   The Rules screen opens.

2. **Choose Export Rules from the New Rule drop-down menu.**

   QuickBooks stores an Excel file containing the rules in your Downloads folder. The name of the file includes the QuickBooks company name whose rules you exported and the words Bank_Feed_Rules.

REMEMBER

   The Export Rules command is disabled if a given company doesn't have any rules established.

3. **Click Close.**

4. **Switch to the company into which you want to import the rules.**

   If you use the same Intuit account to access more than one QuickBooks Online company then choose the Gear icon ⇨ Switch Companies. Alternatively, in Chapter 18, I discuss how Accountant version users can toggle between sets of books.

5. **Choose Transactions ⇨ Rules.**

   The Rules screen opens.

6. **Choose Import Rules from the New Rule drop-down menu.**

   The first screen of the Import Rules wizard opens.

7. **Select the file you created in Step 2 and then click Next.**

8. **On the second wizard screen, select the rules you want to import and then click Next.**

9. **Optional: On the third wizard screen, select categories for the rules that match the current company's chart of accounts and make changes as needed.**

10. **Click Import.**

    A message tells you how many rules imported successfully.

11. **Click Finish.**

    The Rules screen opens.

12. **Review the rules.**

    You can edit or delete the rules in the same way as if you had created them by hand.

Correcting uploaded or downloaded transactions

Whether you're accepting transactions manually or on autopilot with rules, sometimes mistakes or mispostings can happen. There's no need to worry; you can use the same steps in either case.

REMEMBER

QuickBooks marks downloaded transactions as having cleared your bank so be sure to edit — as opposed to delete — transactions that have been accepted or confirmed.

Follow these steps to undo an accept transaction:

1. **Choose Transactions ⇨ Bank Transactions.**

2. **Select the bank or credit card that the transaction posted to.**

   QuickBooks maintains separate transaction lists for each account.

3. **Click the Categorized tab on the Bank Transactions screen.**

4. **Locate the transaction and click Undo in the Action column to send the transaction back to the For Review screen.**

   Alternatively, click on the category name in the Added or Matched column to display the corresponding transaction screen and make your edits there.

5. **Switch to the For Review tab, edit the transaction as needed, and then accept (confirm) or exclude the transaction.**

   If necessary, you can delete transactions from the Excluded tab. To do so, select one or more transactions and then click Delete. Keep in mind that QuickBooks will not prompt you for confirmation, so proceed carefully.

Converting Paper and Electronic Documents into Transactions

QuickBooks enables you to convert paper or electronic receipts or bills to transactions without having to key in all the details. To get started, choose Transactions ⇨ Receipts. You can capture receipts in four ways:

» Upload files from your computer.

» Upload files from Google Drive.

» Forward from email, which means establishing a special @qbodocs.com email address. The benefit of forwarding is that you can establish a filter in your email to automatically forward receipts that you receive by email for automatic posting to QuickBooks.

» Take pictures of receipts onscreen or on paper with the QuickBooks Online Mobile app.

TIP

To create an email address for forwarding receipts, click Manage Forwarding Email on the Receipts screen. You'll be prompted to create a special @qbodocs.com email address with up to 25 letters to the left of the @ symbol. Click Next ⇨ Looks Good ⇨ Done. Next, click Manage Forwarding Email and then specify one or more users assigned to your company in the Manage Receipt Senders section to finalize the setup process. Going forward, any emailed receipts will appear on the For Review screen.

After you click the Review link, you're prompted to review the following information:

1. **Specify a document type.**

   Choose Receipt or Bill.

2. **Select from the Payee field or leave the field blank.**

3. **Select from the Bank or Credit Card field.**

4. **Confirm the payment date.**

   The date from your receipt or bill should appear, but you can override this setting if necessary.

5. **Accept the default category or select from the Category field.**

   QuickBooks attempts to classify the transaction for you, but you can change the default value if necessary.

6. **Accept the default description or enter replacement text.**

7. **Accept the default value in the Total Amount (Inclusive of Tax) field or enter a new amount.**

   QuickBooks attempts to capture this amount for you, but you can correct the amount if necessary.

8. **To describe the transaction further, enter up to 4,000 characters in the Memo field.**

9. **If you plan for a customer to reimburse you, complete the following:**

   - Turn the Make Expense and Items Billable checkbox on.

   - Select from the Customer field.

   - If applicable, fill in the Reference Number field with information such as an invoice number or transaction identifier.

10. **Click Save and Next to post the transaction and review the next transaction in the queue.**

Transferring Data Between QuickBooks and External Sources

In addition to importing bank data, which I discuss in Chapter 5, you can import the following types of lists and transactions:

>> Customers

>> Vendors

>> Chart of accounts

>> Products and services

>> Journal entries

>> Invoices (Plus and Advanced Only)

WARNING

Although an Invoices option is displayed for Simple Start and Essentials users, you'll likely immediately run into a message that says `Import invoices isn't quite ready to support sales tax.`

Depending on what you're importing, you may not be able to import every field that you want to. For instance, you can import only some of the customer and vendor fields that you see onscreen when manually creating such records, so be prepared to fill in some gaps by hand.

If your company has an Advanced subscription, see Chapter 16, where I discuss how you can use Spreadsheet Sync to import and export data between Excel and QuickBooks Online.

The Apps screen within QuickBooks includes subscription options for several apps that allow you to import and export lists and transactions.

Exporting lists to Excel or Google Sheets

You can export customer, vendor, or product lists to Excel or Google Sheets by doing the following:

1. **Click the appropriate link on the side menu:**

   - Customers & Leads ⇨ Customers
   - Expenses ⇨ Vendors
   - The Gear icon ⇨ Products and Services

2. **Click the Export to Excel button just above the Action column.**

   An Excel spreadsheet will appear in your Downloads folder for customers or vendors, while a comma-separated value (CSV) file will appear for products and services.

3. **Double-click on the resulting file in your Downloads folder to open it in Excel, or in Google Sheets choose File ⇨ Import ⇨ Upload to import the workbook.**

4. **If you're using Microsoft Excel, you may have to click Enable Editing to exit Protected View.**

   I talk about how to disable Protected View and streamline opening Excel files exported from QuickBooks in Chapter 20.

Exporting lists from QuickBooks gives you the option to fill any gaps in the records by way of using a spreadsheet. You can then transfer the resulting records to the corresponding import file template.

Utilizing the import file templates

You can download template files that you can edit in Microsoft Excel or Google Sheets and then import them back into QuickBooks:

1. **Choose the Gear icon ⇨ Import Data.**

2. **Choose the type of import you want to perform.**

3. **Click Download a Sample File if you're using Excel or Preview a Sample for Google Sheets.**

   The sample file appears in your Downloads folder if you're using Excel.

4. **If you're using Microsoft Excel, double-click the file in your Downloads folder and then click Enable Editing.**

   In Excel or Google Sheets, examine the file's contents by scrolling to the right to see the information stored in each column.

5. **Create your own file, modeling it on the sample file.**

REMEMBER

Your import file can't contain more than 1,000 rows or exceed 2MB. You can save your file as an Excel workbook, as a CSV file, or as a Google Sheets workbook.

TIP

Dates that you import must be in yyyy-mm-dd format. If you have a date entered in cell A1 of an Excel worksheet, you can use this formula to transform a date such as 2/15/2025 into 2025-02-15:

```
=TEXT(A1,"yyyy-mm-dd")
```

Copy the formula down the column, and then select all the cells that contain the formula and choose Home ⇨ Copy or press Ctrl+C (Cmd+C in macOS). Next, choose Home ⇨ Paste ⇨ Paste Values to convert the formulas to static values in the yyyy-mm-dd format.

TIP

Microsoft 365 Excel for Windows users can press Ctrl+Shift+V to paste as values.

Importing lists and transactions

Here's how to import supported lists or transactions into QuickBooks:

1. **Make sure your spreadsheet or CSV file isn't open in Excel or Google Sheets.**

2. Choose the Gear icon ⇨ Import Data.

3. Choose the type of data you want to import.

4. Click Browse for an Excel or CSV file or Connect for a Google Sheet.

5. Navigate to the folder where you saved the file containing your import file.

6. Specify the file and click Open for an Excel or CSV file or click Select for a Google Sheet.

   The Import screen displays the name of the file you selected.

7. Click Next to upload your file to a staging area.

8. Map the fields in your data file to the corresponding QuickBooks fields.

   Select from the Your Field inputs to match the columns in your file with the import files.

9. Click Next to display the final screen of the wizard.

   A confirmation screen displays the records to be imported. You can widen the columns as needed.

10. Review the records to make sure that the information is correct.

    You can change the information in any field by clicking that field and typing. You can also deselect any rows that you've decided you don't want to import.

11. When you're satisfied that the information is correct, click the Import button.

    A status message briefly flashes on the screen to tell you how many records were imported.

TIP

I tried to trip up the process with two opening balance dates that were in *mm-dd-yyyy* format instead of *yyyy-mm-dd*, but the records were still imported. QuickBooks simply ignored the invalid input but imported the valid fields.

WARNING

If the Import button is disabled, some portion of the data can't be imported. Look for a field highlighted in red to identify information that can't be imported. If the problem isn't apparent, contact Intuit support for help, or set up the records manually.

2

QuickBooks Online Essentials Features

IN THIS PART . . .

Manage user access and implement the Multicurrency feature.

Work with product/service bundles, and efficiently track time and billable expenses.

Chapter **8**

Managing Users, Multicurrency, and Custom Fields

I n this chapter I show you how to control the amount of access that you can grant to users in Essentials or Plus companies. Simple Start companies only have a single user, so that means there's no access to manage. Conversely, in Chapter 13, I cover the additional security controls that administrators within Advanced companies can employ.

I also explain how the Multicurrency feature allows Essentials, Plus, and Advanced users to denominate transactions and bank accounts in over 150 global and digital currencies. As you'll see, this feature cannot be disabled after it is activated, nor can you change the home currency. Users must manage currency settings carefully to ensure accurate financial tracking and reporting.

Managing User Rights

QuickBooks allows you to limit a user's access to different areas of your books based upon their role in Essentials and Plus companies. In Chapter 13, I discuss the more granular security options available in Advanced companies. Depending on your subscription level, you can add up to four types of users to your company.

REMEMBER

Simple Start companies have only a single user who has access to all parts of the company.

Exploring the types of users

QuickBooks Online offers four user levels, with the number you can assign depending on your subscription level. The four levels are:

>> **Standard:** Each standard user is assigned a role that determines their level of access to your accounting records. I discuss the roles you can assign to each user later in this section.

>> **Accountant:** All subscription levels are allowed two accountant users who have full access to almost every aspect of your company by way of the QuickBooks Online Accountant platform, which I discuss in Part 5.

REMEMBER

The number of standard and accountant users is fixed for each company. You can add more standard users by upgrading to the next subscription level, but you can't add additional accountant users.

>> **Track Time Only:** Essentials, Plus, and Advanced companies can have unlimited time tracking users who have access only to time-related features (or QuickBooks Time, if available).

>> **View Company Reports:** Plus and Advanced companies are allowed unlimited View Company Reports users who can view all reports in your company except for those that show payroll or time-tracking contact information.

Table 8-1 shows the number of users that are available at each subscription level.

Reviewing QuickBooks feature areas

QuickBooks Online groups features by the major categories shown in Table 8-2. With the exception of payroll, reports, and lists, Essentials and Plus users have all-or-nothing access to these categories. In Chapter 13, I discuss how granular access to individual features can be granted in Advanced companies.

TABLE 8-1   **QuickBooks User Types Listed by Subscription Level**

Subscription Level	Standard User Limit	Time Tracking Users	View Company Reports Users
Simple Start	1	None	None
Essentials	3	Unlimited	None
Plus	5	Unlimited	Unlimited
Advanced	25	Unlimited	Unlimited

TABLE 8-2   **QuickBooks Feature Areas**

Area	Features
Sales	Invoices
	Estimates
	Sales receipt
	Receive payments
	Credit memo
	Refund receipt
	Delayed credit
	Delayed charge
Expenses	Bills
	Checks
	Bill payments
	Print checks
Products and Services	Products and services
Lists	Employees
	Vendors
	Customers
	Currencies

(continued)

TABLE 8-2 *(continued)*

Area	Features
Bookkeeping	Bank deposit
	Transfers
	Bank transactions
	Rules
	Tags
	Receipts
Accounting	Chart of Accounts
	Registers
	Reconciliation
	Journal entries
Reports	Payroll reports
	Sales reports
	Expense reports
	Management reports
	Custom reports
Time Tracking	Time tracking
Account Management	Access subscription
	Manage users
	Company info
Payroll	Payroll
	Workers compensation
	Benefits

Reviewing standard user roles

If you have an Essentials or Plus subscription, your ability to regulate access to the major feature areas is controlled by assigning users to one of the following roles:

>> **Primary Admin:** Whoever initiates a QuickBooks Online subscription becomes the primary admin, but you can reassign the primary admin as needed. Think of this as a superuser with unlimited rights to change any aspect of your accounting records, including adding and removing users.

- **Company Admin:** A company admin has all the rights of the primary admin, except company admins can't edit or remove the primary admin's access.

- **Standard All Access:** This role gives users access to all areas, plus payroll if the feature is enabled. Such users can also carry out these activities:

  - View and optionally edit company information, including preferences and subscriptions

  - View but not edit the user screen

- **In-House Accountant:** Previously known as Standard All Access Without Payroll, such users can access all reports as well as bookkeeping and accounting tools, but cannot access payroll or carry out administrative tasks such as managing users or changing settings.

- **Accounts Receivable Manager:** Previously known as Standard Limited Customers Only, this role has access to the following feature areas:

  - Sales, the Customers screen, and bank deposits

  - Products and Services, except for item quantities

  - Sales tax rates and authorities

  - Customer and Accounts Receivable reports

  - Time tracking

  - Multicurrency, including exchange rates

- **Accounts Payable Manager:** Previously known as Standard Limited Vendors Only. This role has access to the following feature areas:

  - Expenses as well as Products and Services

  - Vendor and Accounts Payable reports

  - Time tracking

  - Run and file sales tax returns

  - Multicurrency, including exchange rates

- **Standard No Access:** This billable role has access to the following feature areas:

  - Time tracking

- **Track Time Only:** If you have a Premium or Elite Payroll or Time subscription, choosing this option directs you to QuickBooks Time to manage the user's privileges. Otherwise, this non-billable role has access to the basic Timekeeping feature. Timekeeping users do not count toward your subscription limit, so you can create as many timekeeping users as you want.

REMEMBER

Track Time Only users cannot be vendors that track payments using 1099 forms. Such timesheets must be entered by another user.

➤ **View Company Reports:** Plus subscribers can assign this non-billable role to users that you want to view all reports except payroll and reports that contain contact information, such as customer and vendor lists.

TIP

The support documentation for QuickBooks Online states that the Standard Limited Customers and Vendors role has been discontinued and cannot be assigned to users after May 2024. This role functions as a combination of Accounts Payable and Accounts Receivable Manager. If it is still displayed on your roles list, as it is for me at the time of writing, you can continue to assign it. Any users already assigned to this role will retain their privileges even if the role is eventually removed from the roles list.

Managing users

Users with permission to view or edit users can choose Settings ➪ Manage Users to open the Manage Users screen. Those with edit privileges can add, edit, and delete users.

Adding users

Carry out the following steps to add users:

1. **Click Add User.**

   The Add a New User screen opens.

2. **Fill in the First Name, Last Name, and Email fields.**

3. **Choose a role from the Roles list.**

4. **If you want to control access to company information, subscriptions, and the user list, carry out these steps:**

   a. *Expand View All Permissions.*

   b. *Scroll down and expand Account Management.*

   c. *The Company Info checkbox defaults to a minus sign, indicating that the user has view-only access. Clicking the minus sign changes it to a checkbox, granting the user to edit company information. You can click the checkbox again to toggle it back to the minus sign.*

d. *The Access Subscription and Manage Users checkboxes are even more nuanced. Click the left-most checkbox to grant view and edit access or leave it blank and click the View checkbox to limit the user to view-only access.*

5. **Scroll to the bottom of the screen and click Send Invitation.**

QuickBooks emails the user an invitation to join your team.

Editing users

Here's how to edit a user's profile:

1. **Choose a user from the list.**

The Edit User screen opens.

2. **Update the First Name, Last Name, and Email fields if needed, or modify the user's role and optional privileges.**

TIP

Changing the user's email address on the user list doesn't affect their access to your company. The user can still log in using the email address they provided when they set up their email account.

REMEMBER

You can't change your own role or security settings unless you're the primary admin for a company,

3. **Click Save and then click Yes to confirm that you want to save the changes.**

Deleting users

You can delete users in the following fashion:

1. **Choose a user from the list.**

The Edit User screen opens.

2. **Scroll down and click Delete.**

The Are You Sure You Want to Delete This User? prompt appears.

3. **Click Delete User.**

4. **The User List screen opens.**

The user you deleted no longer displayed on the list.

TIP

You can't make a user inactive, but you can change their status to Standard No Access. Such users still count against the user limits predicated by your subscription level, but this does enable you to limit access while an employee is away on vacation or an extended absence.

Reassigning the primary admin role

The primary admin role is exclusive to a single user, and each QuickBooks company is required to have a primary admin user. The primary admin user can relinquish their rights and designate another user as the primary admin in the following fashion:

TIP

1. **Log in to your company as the primary admin user.**

   If you're unable to log in as the primary admin user, visit https://quickbooks.intuit.com/learn-support/ and search for *Request to be the primary admin or contact* to request that Intuit make this change for you. You're required to provide documentation that you have rightful ownership or access privileges.

2. **Choose Settings ⇨ Manage Users.**

3. **Confirm that the user you want to designate as the primary admin is already configured as a company admin. If necessary, click Edit adjacent to that user, change their role to Company Admin, and then click Save.**

4. **Click the arrow in the Action column and choose Make Primary Admin.**

REMEMBER

In Chapter 17, I discuss how you can assign the primary admin role to your accountant, and how your accountant can return the primary admin role back to you.

Working with Multiple Currencies

The Multicurrency feature — available to Essentials, Plus, and Advanced users — enables you to generate customer and vendor transactions denominated in currencies other than your home currency. You can also track bank accounts in other currencies. This includes the cryptocurrencies Bitcoin and Litecoin, as well as more than 150 global currencies. Use the search term **list of supported currencies** at https://quickbooks.intuit.com/learn-support/en-us to see the list of supported currencies. Multicurrency doesn't support customer- or currency-specific pricing, but QuickBooks Desktop does. Accordingly, converting from QuickBooks Desktop to QuickBooks Online can be problematic if you're currently using the Multicurrency feature in QuickBooks Desktop.

WARNING

A word of caution before you go further: You cannot turn the Multicurrency feature off after you enable it. You also cannot change your home currency because the Multicurrency feature affects many accounts and balances. In short, don't turn Multicurrency on unless you need to record transactions in other currencies or have bank accounts denominated in foreign currency, which includes cryptocurrency wallets.

Going forward, you will be required to specify a currency whenever you add an account to your chart of accounts or create a new customer or vendor record. You can assign only one currency to each account, customer, or vendor. QuickBooks automatically creates a new accounts receivable or accounts payable account when you create sales or expense transactions in a given currency.

REMEMBER

You can't change the currency for a customer, vendor, or account once you've posted a transaction to it. If such a need arises, you must deactivate the current record and then create a new customer, vendor, or account for which you can specify the new currency.

WARNING

Certain financial add-ons such as QuickBooks Payroll and QuickBooks Payments require your home currency to be U.S. dollars. Otherwise (as is the case with QuickBooks Commerce), the Multicurrency feature will not work or be enabled. You'll also want to confirm that any apps that you install work with the Multicurrency feature. I discuss apps for QuickBooks Online in Chapter 7.

Do you need Multicurrency?

The decision for using Multicurrency comes down to your base currency:

>> **U.S. dollars:** You need to enable the Multicurrency feature if you need to enter customer or vendor transactions denominated in any other currency.

>> **Any other currency:** You need the Global version of QuickBooks Online (https://quickbooks.intuit.com/global/) instead of the Multicurrency feature. This version only offers subscriptions for Simple Start, Essentials, or Plus.

REMEMBER

Income and expense accounts continue to use your home currency — the currency of the country where your business is physically located. You can specify the currency used for asset or liability accounts.

Enabling Multicurrency

Follow these steps to enable Multicurrency:

1. **Choose Settings ⇨ Account and Settings ⇨ Advanced.**

2. **Click the Edit icon in the Currency section.**

3. **Choose your home currency from the Home Currency drop-down list.**

Choose the currency of your country, meaning don't select USD – United States Dollar as your home currency if your business is based in Canada.

4. **Toggle Multicurrency on to activate the feature.**

QuickBooks warns you that

- You can't turn Multicurrency off.

- You can't change your home currency.

- Extra fields and columns will appear.

- Some features may be disabled.

5. **Select the checkbox labeled I Understand I Can't Undo Multicurrency.**

6. **Click Save.**

7. **Click Manage Currencies if you want to add one or more currencies now, or click Done if you plan to do that later.**

Setting up currencies

A Currencies option is displayed on your Settings menu once you've enabled Multicurrency. You can then establish the currencies that you accept:

1. **Choose Settings ⇨ Currencies to display the Currencies screen.**

CAD – Canadian Dollar and EUR – Euro may be automatically established as currencies for you by default.

2. **Click Add Currency.**

3. **Make a selection from the Add Currency list.**

4. **Click Add.**

The Currencies screen opens and the new currency is displayed.

Revaluing currencies

QuickBooks always records exchange rates, shown on the Currencies screen, as the number of home currency units needed to equal one foreign currency unit. QuickBooks downloads exchange rates every four hours from Wall Street on Demand, which is owned by S&P Global, but you can override this with your own exchange rates:

1. Choose Settings ⇨ Currencies to display the Currencies screen.

2. Choose Revalue from the Actions column for the currency that you want to revalue.

   The Revalue screen opens and indicates the currency that you are revaluing against your home currency.

3. Edit the Revalue Date if needed.

4. Choose Custom Rate.

5. Enter the exchange rate.

6. Deselect any accounts that you do not want to revalue, if appropriate.

7. Click Revalue and Save.

Removing currencies

Unlike all other lists in QuickBooks, you can delete currencies, as opposed to simply making them inactive:

1. Choose Settings ⇨ Currencies to display the Currencies screen.

2. Choose Revalue from the Actions column for the currency that you want to delete.

3. Click Yes to confirm you want to delete the currency.

   The Currencies screen opens and the deleted currency is no longer displayed.

Noticing how the Multicurrency feature changes QuickBooks

Several things change about QuickBooks after you turn on Multicurrency:

» A Currencies option is displayed on your Settings menu.

» A Currency column displayed on your chart of accounts screen reflects the currency assigned to each account.

» An Other Expense account named Exchange Gain or Loss is automatically added to your chart of accounts.

» Currency-specific accounts receivable (A/R) and accounts payable (A/P) accounts are automatically added to your chart of accounts the first time you create a related transaction.

>> Your bank and credit card registers reflect the currency of each transaction (in parentheses) adjacent to any columns that reflect dollar amounts, along with a separate Foreign Currency Exchange Rate column.

>> Sales and purchase forms that display your home currency allow you to specify a foreign currency for each transaction. QuickBooks then does all the conversions for you onscreen.

>> All foreign currency amounts are converted to home currency amounts on your reports.

Using multiple currencies

This section examines the effects of creating a bill transaction that uses a global or digital currency. Creating a sales transaction for a denomination in an alternative currency works in a similar fashion. You can also record journal entries in such currencies. However, payroll and other types of transactions must be processed using your home currency. For clarity, I refer to global, digital, and foreign currencies collectively as "alternative currencies" throughout the rest of this section.

REMEMBER

Time entries cannot be associated with a customer that has been assigned a global or digital currency.

This may sound loony, but let's suppose that you have a vendor whose base currency is the Canadian dollar, while your home currency is the U.S. dollar. In this context, when I refer to the "alternative currency," I am specifically talking about the Canadian dollar — affectionately known as the "loonie." Here's how to set the currency denomination for a new vendor:

1. Choose Expenses ⇨ Vendors.

The Vendor screen opens.

2. Click New Vendor.

3. Select the vendor's currency from the Currency field at the top of the task pane, as shown in Figure 8-1.

You'll see similar settings when you create a new customer or bank account.

TIP

4. Click Got It when the Currency Can't Be Changed prompt is displayed.

Optionally, click Don't Show This Again if you don't want to be reminded again.

REMEMBER

You cannot change the currency for a saved vendor. However, you can mark the saved vendor as inactive and create a new vendor record with the desired currency instead.

5. **Enter the information for the Vendor Display Name field, along with any other fields you want to complete.**

6. **Click Save.**

The Currency column on the vendor screen shows the currency assigned to each vendor. If you don't see the Currency column, click the Vendor List Settings button, click the Currency checkbox, and then click the Vendor List settings button again.

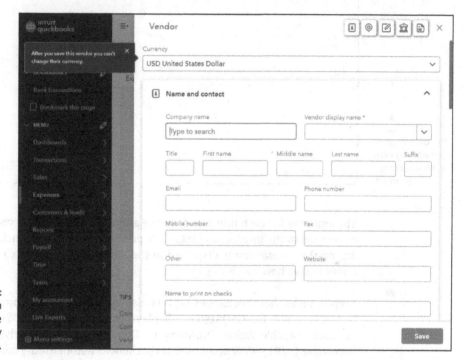

FIGURE 8-1:
Assigning an
alternative
currency
to a vendor.

To enter a bill denominated in a global or digital currency, choose Expenses ⇨ Bills and then choose Add Bill ⇨ Create Bill. After you select your vendor, the two currencies (first the alternative currency and then your home currency) associated with the transaction appear, as shown in Figure 8-2. Notice that you can override the exchange rate for this transaction if you want.

WARNING

The exchange rate field is erased when you enter a date beyond today. This makes sense because, well, you can't know the exchange rate until you get to that day. If you enter an exchange rate, QuickBooks asks if you want to apply it to that specific transaction or to all transactions on that date.

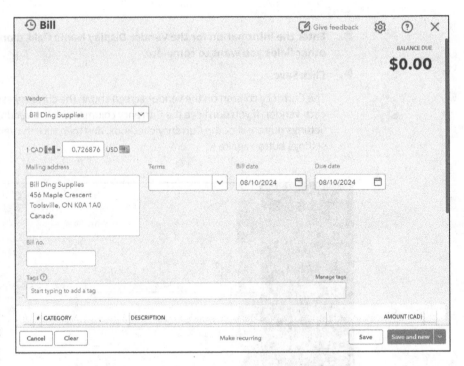

FIGURE 8-2:
The Bill screen in
a company with
Multicurrency
enabled.

The amounts for each line appear in the alternative currency as you add products or services to the invoice, and totals are presented in both currencies. The balance due on the transaction is displayed in the alternative currency so that your customer knows how much to pay.

Keep in mind that QuickBooks reports display values in your home currency. For instance, a bill for CAD$150.00 displays something like USD$109.03 on your Accounts Payable Aging Summary or Detail reports. Similarly, the Accounts Receivable (A/R) – CAD account that QuickBooks automatically adds to your chart of accounts reflects a balance of USD$109.03 on the Balance Sheet report.

Activating Custom Fields

Essentials users can add up to three custom fields to sales forms, while Plus users can add up to three custom fields to both sales forms and purchase orders. In Chapter 15, I discuss how Advanced users can add up to 48 custom fields to customer, vendor, and project records, as well as many more transaction forms. I also discuss how to manage the Custom Fields screen there, so in this chapter I stick to showing how to add custom fields in an Essentials or Plus company:

1. **Choose the Gear icon ➪ Custom Fields.**

   The Custom Fields screen opens.

2. **Click Add Custom Field.**

   The Add Custom Fields task pane opens.

3. **Fill in the Name field.**

   Custom field names can be edited at any time.

4. **Select All Sales Forms and/or Purchase Orders, depending upon your subscription level, and toggle Print on Forms On if you want the field to appear onscreen and in print.**

   I discuss how to enable the Purchase Orders features in Plus companies in Chapter 10.

5. **Click Save to close the Add Custom Field task pane.**

IN THIS CHAPTER

» **Enabling recurring transactions**

» **Working with bundles**

» **Implementing time tracking**

» **Applying billable time to invoices**

» **Recording billable expense entries**

Chapter **9**

Working with Recurring Transactions, Bundles, and Time Tracking

Essentials, Plus, and Advanced subscriptions unlock additional features and functionality, some of which I discuss in Chapter 8. I begin the chapter by exploring how recurring transactions can eliminate repetitive data entry. Next, I explain how the Bundle item type streamlines your invoicing process by being able to add two or more products and/or services to an invoice with a single selection. From there, I show how the Time Tracking feature can help streamline payroll- and invoicing-related tasks. Time tracking enables you to create billable time entries, which I demonstrate how to apply to invoices, along with billable expenses.

Establishing Recurring Transactions

Have you ever had that dream where you keep doing the same task over and over again? For some of us, it's more of a real-life nightmare. Fortunately, recurring transactions can eliminate some of the repetitive nature of your accounting transactions in Essentials, Plus, and Advanced companies. Just about every transaction is fair game, except for bill payments, customer payments, and time activities. Here are the types of recurring transactions you can create:

>> **Scheduled:** These types of recurring transactions post automatically to your books based on the schedule you establish. They're ideal for transactions with fixed amounts that rarely change, such as monthly rent payments. For instance, recurring bills scheduled for the first of the month post to your books automatically without any intervention from you and are even emailed automatically if you choose.

>> **Reminder:** This type of recurring transaction prompts you when the scheduled date comes around on the calendar. You can edit the transaction details before posting. This is well suited to transactions where the amount varies from month to month, such as a utility bill.

>> **Unscheduled:** This type of transaction hangs out in the background and doesn't remind you or post to your books but is available for use at any time in posting new transactions. Payroll journal entries or year-end closing transactions are ideal candidates for unscheduled recurring transactions.

With that background in mind, read on to learn how to create a recurring transaction. I find it easiest to click Make Recurring at the bottom of the screen when creating a transaction that you'd like to recur. However, I'll also show you how to create recurring transactions from scratch.

Generating impromptu recurring transactions

QuickBooks allows you to set most first-stage transactions as recurring, such as invoices, bills, sales receipts, expenses, and so on. Conversely, transactions such as Receive Payment and Bill Pay are second-stage transactions because they offset first-stage transactions, and thus cannot be set to recur.

Follow these steps to make a recurring version of an existing transaction:

1. Click Save to preserve the transaction that you have onscreen.

2. Click Make Recurring to display the recurring version of the transaction type you started with.

   Make Recurring is only displayed after a transaction has been saved.

3. Accept the default Template Name or enter a new name.

4. Select Scheduled, Reminder, or Unscheduled from the Type field.

5. Fill in the number of days in advance that a scheduled transaction should be created or the number of days before the transaction date that you want to be reminded.

6. Ensure that the vendor (or customer) and corresponding email address(es) are correct.

7. Customize the transaction further by enabling one or more options: Automatically Send Emails, Print Later, and Include Options.

8. Select the frequency for scheduled or reminder transactions, along with the time frame.

   - **Daily:** Specify the number of days between when this transaction should post.

   - **Weekly:** Specify the number of weeks between when this transaction should post and the day of the week that you want it to post.

   - **Monthly:** Specify the interval in months and the day of the month to pay the bill. For instance, you can schedule a transaction to post on a specific day each month or, say, on the last Tuesday of each month.

   - **Yearly:** Specify the month and day for the transaction to post each year.

   - **Start Date:** Indicate the first date when QuickBooks should post the transaction, along with an end date if appropriate. For instance, you might set an end date for a rent bill to coincide with the end of your lease.

9. Confirm that the mailing address and terms are correct, scroll down the screen to confirm that the detail section(s) of the transaction are correct, and add any memo information or attachments to the transaction.

   Any lines in the Category Detail or Item Detail sections that have a value of $0 aren't saved.

10. Click Save Template in the bottom-right corner of the screen.

Updating the Recurring Transaction screen

You can also add new transactions directly to the Recurring Transactions screen by following these steps:

1. Choose the Gear icon ⇨ Recurring Transactions.

   The Recurring Transaction screen opens.

2. **Click New to display the Select Transaction Type dialog box, choose a transaction type, and then click OK.**

   Depending upon your subscription level, available choices include the following: Bill, Non-Posting Charge, Check, Non-Posting Credit, Credit Card Credit, Credit Memo, Deposit, Estimate, Expense, Invoice, Journal Entry, Refund, Sales Receipt, Transfer, Vendor Credit, and Purchase Order.

3. **Complete the recurring transaction screen in the same fashion as described in the preceding section and then click Save.**

Editing recurring transactions

To work with existing recurring transactions, choose the Gear icon ⇨ Recurring Transactions to display the Recurring Transactions screen. Click Edit in the Action column to modify a recurring transaction. Any changes you make in recurring-transaction templates affect only future transactions. You have to manually edit any existing transactions that have been posted to your books.

REMEMBER

QuickBooks automatically updates recurring transactions when you modify a customer or vendor record, such as recording a change of address.

The Action column also includes the following options:

➤➤ **Use:** Enables you to record a Reminder or Unscheduled transaction to your books.

➤➤ **Duplicate:** Creates additional recurring-transaction templates from existing recurring-transaction templates. You might use the template for your rent to create another template to pay monthly insurance, for example. You can also use this option to create backup copies of complex transactions, such as a detailed payroll journal entry.

➤➤ **Delete:** Removes unwanted recurring-transaction templates.

REMEMBER

In many areas, deleting a record in QuickBooks translates to making a record inactive. Recurring transactions are deleted, and QuickBooks doesn't offer an undo capability, so think twice before deleting recurring transactions.

Finally, you can print a report of your existing recurring transaction templates. Choose Reports on the left menu bar, type **recu** in the Search box (that's all you need to type to find the Recurring Template List report), and click the report name to display the Recurring Template List report.

Bundling Products and Services

Essentials, Plus, or Advanced subscribers can group two or more items into a bundle, meaning a collection of products or services that a customer buys from you in a single transaction. For example, a company selling fruit baskets might create one or more bundles to simplify sales transactions. Instead of adding items one by one, they could offer a bundle known as *The Juice & Jam Pack*, comprising two products: *Orange You Glad Juice* and *Berry Good Jam*.

TIP

Bundles in QuickBooks Online are similar to *group items* in QuickBooks Desktop.

REMEMBER

QuickBooks Online does not track physical inventory for bundles, and you cannot establish a custom price for a bundle. Bundles are best thought of as a convenient way to sell two or more individual goods or services. The price for the bundle is automatically calculated as the sum of the individual line items multiplied by their respective quantities.

Follow these steps to create a bundle:

1. **Choose the Gear icon ⇨ Products and Services.**

   The Products & Services screen opens.

2. **Choose New ⇨ Bundle.**

   The Create a Bundle task pane opens.

3. **Fill in the Name field, which is required to identify the bundle.**

4. **To upload a picture of the item, click Add an Image, select a .JPEG, .JPG, or .PNG file, and then click Open.**

TIP

   Hover over the picture to display the Replace and Delete buttons, allowing you to choose another image or remove the picture, respectively.

5. **To assign a stockkeeping unit, complete the SKU field.**

6. **Enter up to 4,000 characters in the Sales Description field to describe the bundle.**

   This description is displayed on sales forms, including invoices, estimates, credit memos, and sales receipts unless you tell QuickBooks that you want to display the bundle components in Step 7.

7. **To display the individual line items on your sales forms, enable the Display Bundle Components When Printing or Sending Transactions option.**

This will show each item in the bundle separately instead of combining them into a single line with the description you entered in Step 6.

REMEMBER

A bundle is *not* an assembly, which in QuickBooks Desktop refers to a group of inventory items and/or non-inventory items combined to create a finished product with a tracked bill of materials. QuickBooks Online does not create a bill of materials or track bundles as separate items with quantities or cost. The price for a bundle is the sum of the prices for the individual components, which Plus and Advanced users can automatically modify by way of price rules, which I discuss in more detail in Chapter 10. To be clear, price rules can only adjust the price for individual items and services, and cannot be applied to bundles.

8. **Use the table in the Items Included in the Bundle section to specify the products and/or services and quantities that will comprise the bundle.**

9. **Click Save and Close, or choose Save and New if you want to create another bundle.**

Enabling Time Tracking

Time tracking is already enabled if you have a QuickBooks Time Premium or Elite payroll subscription or a Premium or Elite time tracking subscription. Here's how to tell if you have any of these plans:

1. **Choose the Gear icon ⇨ Account and Settings ⇨ Billing & Subscription.**

   The Billing & Subscription screen opens.

2. **If both the QuickBooks Online Payroll and QuickBooks Time sections display Learn More, you don't currently have a payroll or time tracking subscription; otherwise, the name of your plan is listed in the corresponding section.**

REMEMBER

The QuickBooks Core payroll subscription doesn't include the additional time tracking features that the Premium and Elite payroll subscriptions provide.

If you have a payroll or time tracking subscription, you can skip this section and move on to the following section of this chapter, "Creating employees and contractors." Otherwise, you need to enable the time tracking feature. The process for enabling most optional features, such as time tracking, starts with choosing the Gear icon ⇨ Account and Settings, but time tracking is an exception to this rule. Use these steps instead:

1. **Choose Time ➪ Overview.**

   A Supercharge Your Time overview screen opens.

2. **Click Check Out Pricing.**

   A sales screen opens for the QuickBooks Time Premium and Elite subscription plans.

TIP

The Premium and Elite payroll and time tracking enable your employees to track their time on a mobile device or via a time kiosk (a tablet computer running QuickBooks Time). You can also establish geo-fencing to remind employees to sign in or out as they enter or leave a job site or location and create customizable reports beyond what's offered in QuickBooks.

3. **Click Sign Up to subscribe to the corresponding plan or scroll down to the bottom of the screen and click the Use Basic Time Tracking (Included in Your Current Plan) link.**

   Intuit wants you to think that you have to pay for time tracking, and you may need to in order to get certain features, but a free option exists if you're still figuring out what your time tracking needs are.

WARNING

If you choose Use Basic Time Tracking, an Overview screen opens with a misleading checklist suggesting that the next step is to add a time entry. If you haven't set up employees or contractors yet, you're prompted to add an employee. To add a contractor instead, click Cancel on this screen and follow the instructions in the next section.

Creating employees and contractors

I cover creating employees and contractors in detail in Chapter 4, so I provide only a quick overview here. You can set up an employee as follows:

1. **Choose Payroll ➪ Employees.**

   If you haven't opted into a payroll plan and haven't created employees yet, you're presented with a screen extolling the benefits of the QuickBooks Payroll subscription plans. Otherwise, you see the Employees screen.

2. **The next step depends on the following variables:**

   - *You have an existing QuickBooks Payroll or Time subscription but haven't yet created an employee:* Expand the Get Ready to Pay Your Team section and then click Finish Up.

- *You want to purchase a QuickBooks Time Premium or Elite subscription:* Click Sign Up for the corresponding plan, and then follow the onscreen prompts.

- *You have a Time Tracking subscription or are using the Basic Time Tracking and want to add an employee:* Click Add Employee on the Employees screen.

- *You want to add a contractor:* Click the Contractor tab and then click Add Your First Contractor.

TIP

Depending on the approach you take, you may see a variety of different screens. See Chapter 4 for a more detailed discussion of adding employees and contractors.

REMEMBER

You need to set yourself up as an employee or contractor if you want to track your own time.

Establishing time tracking users

Earlier in this chapter, I mentioned that you can have unlimited time tracking users. Rest assured, time tracking users only see screens related to recording time and don't have any access to the rest of your accounting records. Once you have created an employee or contractor, you can give them time tracking privileges. The steps vary depending on your situation.

QuickBooks Payroll Premium or Elite subscription

If you have a QuickBooks Payroll Premium or Elite subscription, and you want an employee to track their time, follow these steps:

1. Choose Payroll ⇨ Employees.

2. Click the employee's name.

3. Click the Send Invite link for QuickBooks Time.

If you want a contractor to track their time, use these steps:

1. Choose Payroll ⇨ Contractors.

2. Click on the contractor's name.

3. Click Send Invite.

QuickBooks Time Premium or Elite subscription

If you have a QuickBooks Time Premium or Elite subscription and you want an employee or contractor to track their time, use these steps:

1. **Choose Time ⇨ Time Team.**

2. **Enable the Access toggle for the team member.**

If you are using the basic time tracking feature, and you want an employee or contractor to track their time, use these steps:

1. **Choose the Gear icon ⇨ Manage Users ⇨ Add User.**

2. **Complete the First Name, Last Name, and Email fields.**

3. **Choose Track Time Only from the Roles list.**

   If you choose any role other than Track Time Only the user counts toward the billable user limit for your subscription level.

REMEMBER

4. **Click View All Permissions.**

5. **Click Sync Team Member.**

6. **Choose an employee or vendor from the list or click Add New.**

   When you click Add New, a Vendor task pane opens, through which you can add a contractor. QuickBooks moves the vendor to your Contractor list even though you are setting them up as a vendor.

7. **Click Sync.**

8. **Click Send Invitation.**

   Your employees (or vendors) are notified by email and will be prompted to create a QuickBooks Online account if necessary.

Once a timekeeper logs in, they're presented with a summary screen of their hours for the current week and month. Three options are displayed when a timekeeper clicks Add Time:

>> **Weekly:** Enables employees to complete or add to a weekly time sheet.

>> **Single Activity:** Enables employees to record a single time-related activity.

>> **Go To Report:** Displays the Time Activities by Employee Detail report.

TIP

See Chapter 11 if you want to use the Project feature to track time and other transactions in a QuickBooks Online Plus or Advanced subscription.

You can also add time entries directly by choosing + New ⇨ Time Entry in an Essentials or Plus company or + New ⇨ Single Time Activity or Weekly Timesheet in an Advanced company. To run the Time Activity by Employee report, choose the Reports link on the left menu bar and enter the word **Time** in the Find a Report By Name search box. You can customize the report to display any time frame that you want. I cover reports in more detail in Chapter 6.

Creating Billable Time Entries

Your employees may complete activities required to run your company (such as preparing customer invoices or entering accounting information), and they may perform work related directly to your customers. In the latter case, you may want to track the time that employees spend on client-related projects so you can bill your customers for your employees' time. This section focuses on the time-tracking tools native to QuickBooks Online.

Enabling billable time entries

Once you've set up one or more employees or contractors who will be tracking time, you must turn on two options:

1. **Choose the Gear icon ⇨ Account and Settings ⇨ Time.**

   The General section indicates how many employees or contractors are set up for time tracking.

TIP

Click the Team Members link in the General section to display a task pane that shows the list of time tracking employees and contractors. You can then enable or disable time tracking on a case-by-case basis.

2. **Click the pencil icon in the Timesheet section.**
3. **Toggle the Show Service field on.**
4. **Toggle Allow Time to be Billable on.**
5. **Click Save and then Done.**

TIP

If your business has time-tracking needs that go beyond the basics, click See Plans to check out QuickBooks Time. This is one of several timekeeping apps that fully integrate with QuickBooks Online to enable your employees to track time on their mobile devices. Time entries that they record sync automatically with your books, with all the appropriate customer, job, and employee information.

Entering time activities

Perhaps you want to record two hours that an employee worked on a consulting project. Follow these steps to open the Add Time For screen if you're using Basic Time Tracking:

1. **Choose + New ⇨ Time Entry.**

   The Add Time For task pane is displayed.

REMEMBER

   QuickBooks Time users will have Single Time Activity and Weekly Timesheet options in lieu of Time Entry and similar, but somewhat different, forms to fill out.

   If you're working with a project, you can choose Projects (Business Overview ⇨ Projects), select the project, and click Add to Project.

REMEMBER

2. **Choose an employee from the Add Time task pane.**

3. **Choose the date when the work was performed.**

4. **Click Add Work Details.**

   The Add Work Details pane opens.

5. **Enter a time amount in the Duration field, such as 2 for two hours.**

   Alternatively, you can enter start and end times by toggling the Start/End Times option.

6. **Select the customer for which the work was performed.**

7. **Select the service that was performed.**

REMEMBER

   You can't add new services on the fly from the Add Work Details screen, so make sure to set up any new services before you try to create time entries.

8. **Toggle the Billable (/hr) option if applicable.**

9. **Enter any notes, such as a description of the work.**

   You can change the description after adding the time entry to the invoice.

10. **Click Done to save the entry, or click Delete to discard the entry.**

Adding billable time and expenses to an invoice

You can add billable time entries and expenses to an invoice in a couple of ways.

From the Customers screen

Use the following steps to add billable time through the Customers screen:

1. **Choose Sales or Customers & Leads ⇨ Customers.**

   The Customers & Leads screen opens.

2. **Click any customer's name.**

   The customer's record opens and displays a list of transactions.

3. **Choose Action ⇨ Create Invoice for any Time Charge transaction that hasn't been invoiced yet.**

   If you have multiple time charges you want to invoice, simply click Create Invoice for any one of the charges. The Invoice screen that opens enables you to add the other time entries to the invoice.

TIP

I discuss how to indicate that an expense is billable in Chapter 3.

From the Invoices screen

Use the following steps to add billable time through the Invoices screen:

1. **Choose +New ⇨ Invoice.**

   The Invoice screen opens.

2. **Choose a customer's name.**

   Any unbilled time entries or expenses are displayed on the right side of the screen.

3. **Click Add for any individual time or expenses you want to bill, or click Add All.**

   Each billable time entry's information is added to the invoice as a line with the service, description, quantity, rate, and total amount filled in. By default, time entries are listed individually in the invoice, but you can opt to group time entries by service type. You can edit any information as needed. Fill in the rest of the invoice as described in Chapter 2 to add other lines that don't pertain to time entries.

QUICKBOOKS ONLINE AND GOOGLE CALENDAR

If you use Google Calendar to track your time, you can install an app that enables you to pull event details into an invoice. This app is free if you have a Gmail account or a Google Workplace subscription (formerly known as G Suite). Choose Apps ⇨ Find Apps and then search for *Invoice with Google Calendar*. Click Get App Now and then follow the prompts.

When the app is installed, you can click the Google Calendar icon that is displayed on the invoice form. A task pane enables you to set search parameters, such as choosing a Google Calendar, specifying a time frame, and entering any keywords to search on. You can choose events to add to the invoice from the search results, which records the title, description, hours worked, and date from Google Calendar.

TIP

Don't forget that you can add a subtotal for time entries, or any group of line items on an invoice by clicking Add Subtotal.

3

QuickBooks Online Plus Features

Chapter **10**

Monitoring Inventory and Managing Purchase Orders

I n Chapter 2, I discuss how to create service items and non-inventory items in any QuickBooks company. In this chapter, I show you how to track physical inventory items in a Plus or Advanced company. I then discuss purchase orders, which are non-posting transactions that document requests for goods and services you've placed with a vendor.

Keep in mind that inventory tracking in QuickBooks Online is rather simplistic. My technical editor Dan DeLong sums it up as "I buy some stuff, and then I sell that stuff." If your business involves purchasing products like shoes from a wholesaler and selling them without modifications, QuickBooks' physical inventory tracking will likely meet your needs. However, if your operations involve manufacturing or transforming raw materials into finished goods, you may find QuickBooks Online's inventory tracking insufficient. In such cases, consider exploring the QuickBooks Online App Store, which I discuss in Chapter 7. There, you can find add-ons that may better suit your complex inventory requirements.

Working with Physical Inventory Items

QuickBooks Online requires you to use the first in, first out (FIFO) inventory valuation method. This means that the first items you purchase are the first ones you sell. This doesn't mean you need to physically keep track of the sequence in which items arrived in your storeroom or warehouse; rather, just know that QuickBooks associates the cost of the first items you purchase with the first items you sell.

WARNING

You must file Form 3115, Application for Change in Accounting Method (https://irs.gov/forms-pubs/about-form-3115), with the Internal Revenue Service if you're based in the United States and currently using another accounting method, such as last in, first out (LIFO) or average cost for valuing your inventory.

TIP

QuickBooks Desktop Enterprise offers more robust, advanced inventory capabilities, including support for manufacturing. Users can choose between the average cost and first-in-first-out (FIFO) valuation methods, offering greater flexibility in managing inventory.

Enabling the inventory feature

You can't track physical items in QuickBooks until you enable the Track Inventory Quantity setting by carrying out these steps:

1. **Choose the Gear icon ⇨ Account and Settings ⇨ Sales.**

2. **Click on the Products and Services section, and then enable the Track Inventory Quantity on Hand setting.**

3. **Click Yes to confirm your understanding of your inventory costing method becoming FIFO.**

4. **Click Save and then click Done.**

REMEMBER

Inventory items are always valued and reported on using your home currency. Enabling the Multicurrency feature has no effect on inventory item valuations, even if you buy or sell items in a global or digital currency. I discuss the Multicurrency feature in more detail in Chapter 8.

Adding inventory items

The steps for adding inventory items are similar to creating service and non-inventory items but with some additional fields:

DISPLAYING SKUS IN LISTS AND ON FORMS

 A SKU column is displayed by default on the Products and Services screen. To hide it, click the Gear icon just above the list and then uncheck the SKU checkbox. To display the SKU field on sales forms, choose the Gear icon ⇨ Account and Settings ⇨ Sales. In the Products and Services section, toggle the Show SKU Column on and then click Save and Done.

 1. **Choose the Gear icon ⇨ Products and Services or Sales ⇨ Products & Services.**

The Products and Services list opens.

2. **Click New ⇨ Inventory or Add Item if you haven't created a product or service yet.**

The Product/Service Information task pane shown in Figure 10-1 opens.

 If you didn't click Save when you enabled inventory tracking, you can click Turn On Inventory Tracking, and then click Turn On.

TIP

3. **Enter up to 100 characters in the Name field, which is the first of three required fields.**

4. **To assign a stock-keeping unit, enter up to 60 characters in the SKU field.**

A SKU is typically a part number or other identifier for your products and services.

 5. **To assign a picture, click Edit and then select an image.**

To remove an uploaded picture, click Delete, adjacent to Edit.

 6. **To categorize the item, select from the Category field.**

Assigning items to categories enables you to group related items, which I discuss in more detail in Chapter 2.

7. **To track this item by class, select from the Class field if displayed.**

Assigning items to classes in QuickBooks Online allows you to categorize and track income and expenses by different segments of your business, such as departments, locations, or product lines. I discuss the Class feature in more detail in Chapter 11.

8. **Enter an amount in the Initial Quantity On Hand field, which is the second required field.**

This amount is the starting inventory count you want to record in your books. Enter zero if you haven't yet procured or produced this item.

9. **Enter a date in the As of Date field, which is the third required field.**

Typically, you'll want to use the first day of your fiscal year for the As of Date. Enter this date in mm/dd/yyyy format, or make a choice from the calendar that is displayed when you click in the field.

REMEMBER

You cannot record transactions before the As of Date, which also should not be earlier than the start date of your QuickBooks company. However, start dates can vary by item, allowing you to track when you first started buying and selling specific items.

10. **To be notified when it's time to replenish an item, enter an amount in the Reorder Point field.**

QuickBooks will alert you when the quantity on hand for an item reaches or drops below the amount you indicate here.

11. **Confirm the Inventory Asset account.**

The Inventory Asset account field should be prefilled, but if you need to, you can select a different account from the drop-down menu or create a new asset account by clicking Add Account.

12. **Enter the details in the Description field to specify how the item should be displayed on sales forms.**

Sales forms include invoices, estimates, sales receipts, credit memos, and refund receipts.

13. **Fill in the Sales Price/Rate field.**

Consider this to be the base price for your product. You can override the price manually on transaction forms or employ pricing rules in the upcoming "Perfecting Price Rules" section.

14. **Confirm the Income Account.**

The Income Account should be prefilled, but if needed, you can select a different income account from the drop-down menu or create a new account by clicking Add Account.

TIP

In QuickBooks Online, accounts are sometimes referred to as "categories" on screens like sales forms for simplicity. However, in more detailed areas like the Add a New Product task pane, the term "account" is used.

15. **A Sales Tax section will display if you've enabled the sales tax feature, and you can optionally click Edit Sales Tax to override the default location-based sales tax calculations for this product.**

A Describe This Product or Service task pane opens, prompting you to choose a sales tax category. Alternatively, you can choose Taxable or Non-Taxable beneath the category list. Click Done to confirm your selection.

16. Enter the details in the Purchase Description field to specify how the item should be displayed on purchasing forms.

This purchase description will appear on purchase orders, bills, expenses, checks, and vendor credits.

17. To display a default price on purchasing forms, complete the Purchase Cost field.

18. If you typically procure this item from a specific vendor, select from the Preferred Vendor field.

Making a choice in this field does not prevent you from buying the item from other vendors when needed.

WARNING

As of this writing, the Preferred Vendor field can only be accessed by viewing an individual item record. You cannot filter your Products and Services list by vendor, nor can you include the Preferred Vendor field on any report. You can, however, filter by Category, so you may want to create categories that correspond with preferred vendor names.

19. Click Save and Close.

The Products and Services list opens, showing your newly added item.

Click the Gear icon above the Action column and then choose Compact to fit more products and services on the screen.

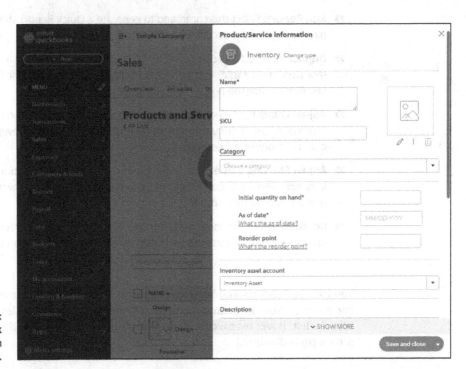

FIGURE 10-1:
Use this task pane to create an inventory item.

Editing inventory items

The Products and Services screen shows all your active inventory items, as well as services, non-inventory items, and bundles. To view inactive items, click Filter and set the Status field to either All or Inactive.

TIP

Bundles are combinations of inventory items, services, and non-inventory items you can add to an invoice as a single item or a collection of items. I discuss how to create bundles in more detail in Chapter 9.

The following commands in the Action column on the Products and Services screens are specific to inventory items:

>> **Edit:** This command is displayed in the Action column next to every item. Use it to make changes to an item's details.

>> **Make Inactive:** Select this command to deactivate an item. Once the item is inactive, this command changes to Make Active.

WARNING

When you make an item inactive in QuickBooks with a non-zero quantity on hand, QuickBooks automatically creates an inventory adjustment to reduce the quantity to zero. This adjustment is recorded in your inventory asset account. If you reactivate the item, the previous quantity is not restored, and you'll need to manually adjust the quantity if necessary.

>> **Run Report:** Select this command to generate a Quick Report showing the past 90 days of transactions for this item.

>> **Duplicate:** Select this command to display the Product/Service Information task pane used earlier in the chapter to create a new item. Some fields will be prefilled to ease the process of setting up similar items.

>> **Adjust Quantity:** Select this command to adjust the quantity on hand of Inventory items. I discuss this in more detail in the "Adjusting inventory quantities or values" section.

>> **Adjust Starting Value:** Select this command to adjust the starting value of Inventory items. I discuss this in more detail in the "Adjusting inventory quantities or values" section.

>> **Reorder:** Select this command to create a purchase order for reordering an inventory item. I discuss this in more detail in the "Reordering inventory items" section.

You use the Products and Services list similarly to the Customer and Vendor lists. For instance, you can search for an item by its name, SKU, or sales description. To sort the list, hover over a column heading and then click when the Toggle Sort By screen tip is displayed.

Perfecting Price Rules

As I discuss in Chapter 7, rules in QuickBooks generally refer to automation guidelines for categorizing and managing transactions. Price rules, on the other hand, allow you to set custom pricing for specific customers, items, or date ranges, as well as which employee completed the work. The Price Rules feature seems to be in perpetual beta testing, and Intuit recommends that you do not create more than 10,000 price rules. If you're willing to work within those limitations, here's how to enable the feature:

1. **Choose the Gear icon ⇨ Account and Settings ⇨ Sales.**

2. **Click in the Products and Services section and toggle on the Turn on Price Rules.**

3. **Click Save and then Done.**

Once you've enabled Price Rules, follow these steps to create one or more rules:

1. **Click the Gear icon ⇨ All Lists ⇨ Price Rules.**

   Price Rules should now appear near Products and Services on the All Lists screen.

TIP

   Choose the Gear icon ⇨ Switch to Accountant View if you do not see Price Rules on the All Lists screen after you have enabled the feature, or log out of your QuickBooks company and log back in again.

2. **Click Create a Rule to display the Create a Price Rule screen.**

3. **Assign a name to your rule.**

4. **To choose which customers the price rule will apply to, select All Customers, Select Individually, or Customer Type from the Customer list.**

   I discuss in more detail how to create and edit customer records, as well as how to establish customer types, in Chapter 2.

WARNING

   You may encounter one of the rough edges of this beta feature when you choose Select Individually: Checkboxes are supposed to appear to the left of each customer name for selection. However, in my experience, QuickBooks displays a prompt saying "What's up? You haven't added any customers yet." This suggests that you may need to assign a customer type to each customer that you want to apply a price rule to. The Products and Services list behaves similarly when you choose Select Individually.

5. To choose which items the price rule will apply to, select **All Products and Services, All Services, All Inventory, All Non-Inventory,** or **Select Individually.** Or choose a product category from the Products and Services list.

I discuss how to create and edit non-inventory and service items, as well as how to establish customer types, in Chapter 2, and how to manage inventory items in the "Working with Physical Inventory Items" section earlier in this chapter.

6. To choose a basis for the price rule, select **Percentage, Fixed Amount,** or **Custom Price Per Item** from the **Price Adjustment Method** list and then carry out the corresponding steps:

   - **Percentage:** Select Increase By or Decrease By from the Percentage list, enter an amount, and then choose an option from the Rounding drop-down menu.

   - **Fixed Amount:** Select Increase By or Decrease By from the Fixed Amount list, enter an amount, and then choose an option from the Rounding drop-down menu.

   - **Custom Price Per Item:** Activate the Products and Services tab and complete the Adjusted Price column.

7. To set a specific time period for the price rule, fill in the start date and end date fields.

8. Click Apply Rule to calculate the adjusted price for percentage or fixed amount rules on the Products and Services tab.

9. Click Save and Close, or choose Save and New if you want to create another price rule.

REMEMBER

You can't assign a price rule to a bundle, which is a group of inventory items, services, and/or non-inventory items combined and sold as a single unit. However, you can assign price rules to the individual items within a bundle to adjust their prices according to specific conditions. I discuss bundles in more detail in Chapter 9.

Recording Inventory Transactions

The most common inventory-related transaction that you'll likely carry out is reordering inventory, particularly if you purchase products for resale. However, when managing physical goods, discrepancies in the quantity on hand can occur or products may get damaged, requiring you to adjust inventory quantities or valuations.

Reordering inventory items

Running out of products that you offer can result in lost revenue, so QuickBooks Online offers two ways to easily identify items that have low stock or that are sold out. You can then optionally create a purchase order, as I describe in this section and in the "Procuring with Purchase Orders" section later in this chapter. Here's how to identify items that have low or no stock on hand:

1. **Choose the Gear icon ⇨ Products and Services or Sales ⇨ Products & Services.**

The Products and Services screen is displayed.

2. **Click either graphic at the top of the list:**

- **Low Stock:** This option filters your Products and Services list to show you items that have a quantity on hand either at or below their reorder level, or that have a quantity of 1.

- **Out of Stock:** This option filters your Products and Services list to show you items that have a quantity on hand of zero or below.

You can filter the list for Low Stock or Out of Stock items, but not both simultaneously.

You can also click Filter and then make a selection from the Stock Status field.

3. **You can create a purchase order to reorder inventory items in two ways:**

- Choose Reorder from the drop-down menu in the Action column to add a single item to a new purchase order.

- Select the checkbox to the left of two or more item names you're ordering from a single vendor, and then choose Batch Actions ⇨ Reorder to add multiple items to a new purchase order.

You cannot filter the Products and Service list by vendor, and you can only specify one vendor per purchase order.

The Reorder command will be disabled if you choose one or more non-inventory, service, or bundle items. You must manually create purchase orders for Non-Inventory and Service items you purchase.

4. **Click the X adjacent to either graphic, or click Clear Filter to display all items on the Products and Services list.**

5. **Complete the purchase order and then send it to your supplier.**

You can only create one purchase order at a time, so you'll need to repeat the steps for each vendor that you want to order from.

The Reorder option is only available in the Action column for Inventory items.

Adjusting inventory quantities or values

On occasion, you may need to adjust inventory item quantities on hand or starting values, particularly after performing a physical inventory count. You can print the Physical Inventory Worksheet report by choosing Reports and then typing the word **Physical** in the Search field. The resulting report enables you to record item quantities on hand as you count inventory. You can then compare the report to your accounting records and make adjustments as needed.

Adjusting inventory quantities

If your physical count results in a discrepancy from your accounting records, you need to create an adjustment to reconcile your books with the reality in your warehouse. Follow these steps to create an inventory adjustment:

1. **Choose + New ⇨ Inventory Qty Adjustment to display the Inventory Quantity Adjustment screen.**

   Click Show More if you don't see the Inventory Adjustment command on the + New menu. Alternatively, you can click the drop-down menu in the Action column for any item on your Products and Services screen and then choose Adjust Quantity.

2. **Update the Adjustment Date field if necessary.**

3. **Select another account from the Inventory Adjustment Account field if necessary, or click Add New to create a new expense account.**

4. **Update the Reference No. field if desired.**

5. **Choose an inventory item from the Product drop-down menu in row 1.**

   The Description field is populated, along with the current quantity on hand. The New Qty field defaults to the current quantity on hand.

   Class and/or location fields will be displayed on the Inventory Quantity Adjustment screen if you have enabled either or both features. I discuss these features in more detail in Chapter 11.

6. **Enter an amount in either the New Qty or Change in Qty fields.**

   If the Qty on Hand field indicates that you should have 345 left-handed wrenches, but you counted only 330 of them in your warehouse, you need to reduce the quantity on hand in QuickBooks by 15. You can do either of the following:

   - Enter **330** in the New Qty field.

   - Enter **–15** in the Change in Qty field.

7. **Repeat Steps 5 and 6 for each inventory item you need to adjust.**

   Click Add Lines if you want to add more rows to the table.

WARNING

   QuickBooks does not prompt you for confirmation when you click Clear All Lines, which erases the entire Inventory Quantity Adjustment table. To avoid accidentally losing your work, click Save periodically. In contrast, Cancel and Clear do prompt you to confirm your action.

8. **Enter a description in the Memo field to explain why you made this adjustment.**

   Your accountant, or perhaps your future self, will thank you for being diligent in documenting the reasons for the adjustments.

9. **Click Save and Close.**

TIP

   To prefill the inventory adjustment screen, select one or more inventory items from your Products and Services list then choose Batch Actions ⇨ Adjust Quantity.

Entering inventory quantity adjustments

You can review or amend inventory adjustment transactions by carrying out these steps:

1. **Choose + New ⇨ Inventory Qty Adjustment or select the Change Quantity command from the drop-down menu in the Action column of the Products and Services screen.**

   This will display the Inventory Quantity Adjustment screen.

2. **Click Recent Transactions.**

3. **Select an adjustment from the list or click View More to display the Search screen, where you can provide additional criteria and select a transaction.**

4. **Edit or delete the transaction.**

   Click Delete on the right side of a row to remove a line item, or click the Delete command at the bottom of the screen to remove the entire transaction.

5. **Click Save and Close.**

Adjusting an inventory item's starting value

If you find an incorrect starting value for an inventory item, you can edit the starting value for any inventory item after November 2015.

Changing an item's starting value can have wide-ranging effects, and a note to this effect is displayed when QuickBooks senses you're trying to edit an inventory item's starting value. If you're not sure what you're doing, ask your accountant. Please. They won't mind.

To adjust an inventory item's starting value, follow these steps:

1. **Choose the Gear icon ⇨ Products and Services or Sales ⇨ Products & Services.**

2. **Select Adjust Starting Value from the drop-down menu in the Action column adjacent to the item that you want to modify.**

   A warning is displayed, explaining that changing an inventory item's starting value may impact the initial value of your inventory.

3. **Assuming that you heeded the preceding warning and know what you're doing, click Got It!**

   The Inventory Starting Value screen opens.

   Class and/or location fields will be displayed on the Inventory Quantity Adjustment screen if you have enabled either or both features. I discuss these features in more detail in Chapter 11.

4. **Modify the Initial Quantity on Hand if needed.**

5. **Update the Adjustment Date field if necessary.**

6. **Enter an amount in the Initial Cost field if applicable.**

   Change the Inventory Adjustment Account only if you want to *really* get under your accountant's skin and complicate your books.

   If you're trying to change the inventory asset account, you're in the wrong place. Select Edit from the drop-down menu in the Action column of the Products and Services screen for the item you want to modify and then make the change in the Product/Service Information task pane.

7. **Click Save and Close.**

Procuring with Purchase Orders

Purchase orders are optional, non-posting transactions that are not recorded in your company's general ledger, nor do they affect your financial statements — they simply help you keep track of unfulfilled orders you've placed. Once the goods or services have been provided, you compare the packing slip or other documentation to the purchase order and then convert the purchase order to a bill to be paid or to a check or expense transaction. At this point your books will be affected as follows:

>> Bills that you create increase the balance of your accounts payable account. Checks reduce the corresponding bank account balance, whereas expenses may reduce your bank account balance or increase a credit card account balance.

>> If the purchase order includes one or more inventory items, your inventory account balance increases by the cost of the items received.

>> Any other line items on the purchase order typically increase the balance of corresponding expense accounts.

Configuring purchase order settings

Following are the purchase order–related settings you may need to enable or adjust:

1. Choose the Gear icon ⇨ Account and Settings ⇨ Expenses.

2. Toggle Show Items Table on Expense and Purchase Forms option on in the Bills and Expenses section.

3. Click Save.

4. Toggle the Use Purchase Orders option on in the Purchase Orders section.

5. If you want to manually enter the transaction numbers assigned to your purchase orders, toggle the Custom Transaction Numbers option on in the Purchase Orders section.

   Enable this setting if you want to assign your own transaction numbers to purchase orders; otherwise, purchase order numbers are automatically assigned to your transactions.

6. If you have boilerplate language that you would like to display on every purchase order, complete the Default Message on Purchase Orders field.

7. Click Save.

8. Click Edit in the Messages section if you want to customize the outgoing email messages that accompany purchase orders that you send.

9. Click Save.

10. Click Done to close the Account and Settings screen.

Now you're good to go and ready to start creating purchase orders.

NON-POSTING TRANSACTIONS

Purchase orders and estimates are two examples of non-posting transactions. Non-posting transactions don't affect your accounting records, but they're helpful because they enable you to track potential transaction information you don't want to forget. Other non-posting transactions include delayed charges and delayed credits.

Delayed charges record potential future revenue, much like estimates. In fact, you can convert a delayed charge to an invoice in the same way that you convert an estimate to an invoice. For details, see the section "Converting an estimate to an invoice," in Chapter 2.

Conversely, if you want to stage a credit memo to be posted against an invoice later, you can create a delayed credit. Unlike Credit Memo transactions that affect your books upon entry, Delayed Credit transactions affect your books only when they're applied to an invoice. This is helpful when you want to post a credit to a customer's account on a contingent basis, such as a credit to be applied to a future order.

Creating either transaction is much like creating an invoice, which I discuss in detail in Chapter 2.

Creating purchase orders

Follow these steps to create a purchase order from scratch:

1. **Choose + New ⇨ Purchase Order from the sidebar menu.**

The Purchase Order screen opens.

2. **Select from the Vendor field or click Add New to create a new vendor.**

The vendor's mailing is displayed onscreen.

3. **If you want to have the goods or services delivered to a customer, select from the Ship To field or click Add New to create a new customer record.**

This enables you to instruct the vendor to deliver the goods or services directly to your customer.

4. **To override the default date, enter a date in the Purchase Order Date field, or click the Calendar icon.**

Dates must be entered in mm/dd/yyyy format, although you can enter a month and day, such as 7/1 for the first day of July, and then press Tab to autocomplete the year.

5. **Enter up to 31 characters in the Ship Via field if applicable.**

Unfortunately this is a free-text field that you will need to complete manually on each purchase order, as opposed to a drop-down menu where you can make a selection.

6. **Add at least one line item either to the Category Details or the Item Details section.**

Use the Category Details section to order goods or services without specifying an item; otherwise, select items from your Products and Services list in the Item Details section.

7. **Use the Your Message to Vendor field to provide external documentation that your vendor will see on the purchase order. Likewise, use the Memo field to create internal documentation that only you and your team can view.**

8. **Use the Attachments field to attach an unlimited number of supporting files related to this transaction.**

I discuss the Attachments feature in detail in Chapter 1.

9. **At the bottom of the screen, you can choose any of the following options:**

- Cancel to close the screen and discard the purchased order.
- Print to display a preview of the purchase order, from which you can print a paper copy or download a PDF version.
- Make Recurring to schedule the transaction as a recurring purchase order.
- More to copy, delete, or view the audit history of the transaction.

TIP

More does not appear onscreen until you've saved the purchase order or clicked Print to display the print preview.

- Save to assign a purchase order number and save the transaction.
- Save and New to save your transaction and create a new purchase order.
- Save and Close to save the transaction and exit the Purchase Order screen.
- Save and Send to assign a purchase order number and save the transaction, after which you can edit the default email message, preview the purchase order, and then email a copy to the vendor.

TIP

Toggle between Save and New, Save and Close, and Save and Send by clicking the arrow on the button. The option you choose becomes the default behavior for purchase orders until you make a different selection in the future.

Converting estimates to purchase orders

In addition to creating purchase orders from scratch, you can also convert estimates into purchase orders. Estimates, which I discuss in Chapter 2, can be considered pre-invoices; they document what a customer has agreed to purchase from you. Once the customer approves the estimate, you may want to convert the estimate to a purchase order. Doing so doesn't close out the estimate because you also likely want to eventually convert the estimate into an invoice. However, this process minimizes data entry and helps ensure that the purchase order is accurate.

WARNING

You can only convert estimates with a Pending or Accepted status to purchase orders or invoices. Converting an estimate to an invoice sets its status to Closed, so convert estimates to purchase orders first if you need both.

Here's how to convert an estimate to a purchase order:

1. **Create and save a new estimate, select an estimate from a customer's transaction list, or use the Search command at the top of every QuickBooks screen.**

   Alternatively, choose + New ⇨ Estimates, and click Recent Transactions to display a list of recent estimates.

2. **Choose More Actions ⇨ Copy to Purchase Order.**

   A message informing you that some items on the estimate won't carry over to the purchase order is displayed when one or more non-inventory or service items in the estimate don't have the I Purchase This Product/Service from a Vendor option enabled within the corresponding item record.

   REMEMBER

   More Actions only appears onscreen after you click Save or Print and Download. So, if you can't find the command, rest assured — you're not going crazy.

3. **Click OK if a prompt indicates that some items may not carry over to a purchase order.**

4. **Edit the purchase order as necessary, selecting a vendor and adding any more items you want to the purchase order.**

5. **Choose Save and Send, Save and New, or Save and Closed, as appropriate.**

Duplicating existing purchase orders

The Copy command on the Purchase Order screen enables you to replicate an existing purchase order. This is helpful if you want to reorder a set of items you've ordered before, or you've converted an estimate to a purchase order but need to order items from more than one vendor. Here are the steps:

1. **Click Recent Transactions on the Purchase Order screen to view recent purchase orders, select a purchase order from a vendor's transaction list, or use the Search command.**

   Click the Copy command at the bottom of the Purchase Order screen.

2. **Edit the purchase order as needed and then save it.**

Receiving items against purchase orders

You can apply all or part of a purchase order to a Bill, Check, or Expense transaction. You record what you've received and later add the remaining items to another transaction as needed until the entire purchase order is fulfilled. QuickBooks can link multiple transactions to the purchase order and automatically close the purchase order when you've received everything or you've clicked the Closed checkbox for any line items that you won't receive in full.

Perhaps you have a purchase order with three items, and you receive one of the three items. Here's how to receive the items against the purchase order:

1. **Choose + New ⇨ Bill, Check, or Expense.**

   For this example, I'm using a check.

REMEMBER

   Purchase orders cannot be directly applied to credit card transactions, so you must first convert the purchase order into an expense or bill. You can then select the credit card as the payment method.

2. **Select from the Vendor or Payee field.**

   Open purchase orders for the vendor are shown in a task pane that displays a portion of the line items, as well as its original amount and current balance.

3. **Click Add for the corresponding purchase order.**

   This action adds all the lines on the purchase order to the Item Details or Category Details section, starting at the first available line in the appropriate section.

4. **Adjust the quantity or amount for each line to reflect the portion you want to record as partially received or paid.**

REMEMBER

   To partially pay a line on the purchase order, adjust the quantities on that line from the original number on the purchase order to the quantity you actually receive.

5. **Click Save.**

If you reopen the purchase order, you see that QuickBooks has kept track of the status of the items on the individual lines of the purchase. The purchase order itself remains open and shows any linked transactions. Repeat these steps as needed until you receive all the items or decide to close the purchase order, which I discuss in the next section.

TIP

Clicking Linked Transactions below the purchase order's status in the top-right corner of the Purchase Order screen displays any linked transaction types. Click the linked transaction prompt to display the related transaction(s).

Closing purchase orders

If your best laid plans don't work out, you can easily close an entire purchase order at any time by changing its status from Open to Closed:

1. **Choose Expenses ⇨ Vendors.**

   The Vendor List screen opens.

2. **Select the vendor to whom you issued the purchase order.**

   The vendor's transaction screen opens.

3. **Click Filter, choose Purchase Orders from the Type list, optionally set a Date filter, and then click Apply.**

4. **Select the purchase order from the transaction list or choose View/Edit from the drop-down menu in the Action column.**

   The Purchase Order screen opens, displaying the transaction that you selected.

5. **To mark the purchase order as closed, select Closed from the Purchase Order Status field, which currently displays Open, and then click anywhere on the screen to close the list.**

6. **Click Save and Close.**

TIP

Rest assured that you can always open a closed purchase order and change its status back to Open. So, no need to worry if you accidentally close out the wrong PO.

Tracking open purchase orders

The Open Purchase Order Detail enables you to keep tabs on the status of your pending purchase orders. To access it, choose Reports ⇨ Reports and start entering **Open Purchase Orders** in the Find Report by Name field. Select the report name from the resulting list. You can also use the Open Purchase Order List report. I discuss reports in more detail in Chapter 7, as well as custom reports for Advanced subscribers in Chapter 14.

Chapter **11**

Employing Classes, Locations/Departments, and Projects

You must have a Plus or Advanced subscription to use the features I discuss in this chapter. Class tracking enables you to categorize transactions into major segments, such as department or product line. Conversely, the Departments feature (previously known as the Locations feature) enables you to categorize transactions by department, office, state, region, and so on. Further, you can configure unique sales form titles and company contact information for each location.

I also show you how to use the Projects feature to group revenue and expenses for undertakings that you carry out on a customer's behalf. QuickBooks offers a single Project Profitability Summary report, but you can also use the Projects screen to monitor how a project is performing. The Tags feature that I discuss in Chapter 6 is an alternative, especially if you have a Simple Start or Essentials subscription.

Tracking Transactions with Classes

Class tracking is helpful whenever you need to isolate a subset of sales or expenses. For instance, a law firm might create a class for each partner, whereas a medical practice might create a class for each doctor. Classes can be assigned at departmental levels or by service line, such as commercial versus residential. You can then run reports such as Profit and Loss by Class, Sales by Class Summary, and Sales by Class Detail.

Enabling class tracking

The Class feature is turned off by default, but you can enable it as follows:

1. **Choose the Gear icon ⇨ Account and Settings ⇨ Advanced.**

2. **Click Edit in the Categories section.**

3. **Toggle on Track Classes.**

4. **If you want to ensure that every transaction is assigned to a class, turn the Warn Me When a Transaction Isn't Assigned to a Class checkbox on.**

5. **Specify how granular you want your class tracking to be by selecting an option from the Assign Class list:**

   - **One to Entire Transaction:** This option adds a Class field at the top of most transaction forms, allowing you to assign the entire transaction to a single class.

REMEMBER

   Classes apply to the income and expense categories (accounts) that you assign in the detail section of the transaction but not to balance sheet accounts, such as bank accounts, accounts payable, or accounts receivable. Thus, a check for $300 that allocates $100 each to three different categories will post four different line item entries in your books: one to record the expenditure to your bank account and three to categorize the expenses paid. The three expense items will be associated with the class, but the reduction in your bank account will not.

   - **One to Each Row in Transaction:** This option adds a Class column to the details section of most transaction forms so that you can individually assign a class to each row of a transaction.

6. **Click Save and then Done.**

You can also enable class tracking for payroll if you have a QuickBooks Payroll subscription:

1. **Choose the Gear icon ⇨ Account and Settings ⇨ Payroll Settings.**

2. **Click Edit in the Accounting section.**

3. **Click Edit in the Class Tracking section.**

4. **Choose how you want to track classes for payroll.**

5. **Assign a class to each employee or assign a single class for all employees.**

6. **Click Continue and then Done.**

Creating classes

You can add or remove classes from your company's class list once you've enabled class tracking. Here's how to add classes to the list:

1. **Choose the Gear icon ⇨ All Lists.**

2. **Choose Classes.**

   The Classes command is not displayed on the All Lists screen until you enable the feature.

3. **Click New.**

   The Class dialog box appears.

4. **Enter a name for the class.**

   It isn't apparent based on the size of the Name field that class names can be up to 60 characters long, including spaces.

5. **If you want to create a sub-class, click Is Sub-Class and then make a selection from the Enter Parent Class field.**

   Sub-classes are used to further categorize and track financial data within a main class, allowing for more detailed reporting. They enable you to break down a broader category into more specific segments, providing deeper insights into your business activities.

6. **Click Save.**

Plus subscriptions allow you to create up to 40 combined classes and locations, while Advanced subscriptions can create unlimited classes and locations.

Editing classes

You can rename classes or change their sub-class status by following these steps:

1. **Choose the Gear icon ⇨ All Lists.**
2. **Choose Classes.**
3. **Select Edit from the drop-down menu in the Action column.**
   The Class dialog box appears.
4. **Revise the class settings as needed.**
5. **Click Save.**

Deleting classes

A tricky aspect of QuickBooks is that most lists don't allow you to physically delete items, so you must mark them inactive instead. This applies to classes as well:

1. **Choose the Gear icon ⇨ All Lists.**
2. **Choose Classes.**
3. **From the Action column, select Make Inactive (Reduces Usage) in Plus companies, or Make Inactive in Advanced companies.**

   Or you can enable the checkbox for one or more classes on the class list and then choose Batch Actions ⇨ Make Inactive.

4. **Click Yes to confirm that you want to deactivate the class(es).**

You can reactivate a class at any time by carrying out these steps on the class list:

1. **Choose List Settings ⇨ Include Inactive and then click anywhere on the Classes screen to close the Settings list.**
2. **Click Make Inactive next to the class you want to activate.**

Looking at Track Locations/Departments

As of this writing, the Track Locations feature seems to be amidst an identity crisis. In some companies, QuickBooks refers to this feature as Track Locations on the Settings screen, and as Departments everywhere else. In other companies, it's labeled as Locations everywhere. I sincerely hope that Intuit will choose a single term across the board in the future. Nonetheless, the Track Locations/Departments feature provides an additional dimension for categorizing and tracking transactions. While reporting by location isn't as robust as class tracking is, there are a couple of hidden benefits. As you'll see later in this section, you can create a bank deposit for all payments from a specific location/department at once, and theoretically customize your sales forms by location/department as well. I explain the theoretical part later in this section.

REMEMBER

Plus subscriptions are limited to 40 combined locations and classes, while Advanced subscriptions can create unlimited locations and classes.

Enabling the Track Locations/Departments feature

Here's how to enable the Track Locations/Departments feature:

1. **Choose the Gear icon ⇨ Account and Settings ⇨ Advanced.**

2. **Click Edit in the Categories section.**

3. **Toggle the Track Locations option on.**

   Given that this feature is in flux, you may see some variation of Track Departments instead of Track Locations.

4. **Make a choice from the Location Label list: Business, Department, Division, Location, Property, Store, or Territory.**

5. **Click Save and then Done.**

Going forward, a field with the label that you choose will be displayed on most transaction forms.

Creating locations/departments

Here's how to add a location/department to the list:

1. **Choose the Gear icon ⇨ All Lists.**

2. **Choose Locations or Departments.**

3. **Click New.**

   The corresponding Information dialog box appears.

4. **Fill in the Location or Department field.**

It isn't immediately obvious based on the size of the Name field, but location/department names can be up to 40 characters long, including spaces.

5. **If you want to create a sub-location or sub-department, click Is Sub-Location or Is Sub-Department and then make a selection from the Enter Parent Location or Enter Parent Department field.**

TIP

Sub-locations/sub-departments are a way to further categorize and track financial data within a main location, like how sub-classes work with classes. Sub-locations/sub-departments allow you to break down a primary location/department into more specific locations or departments locations, providing detailed reporting and management of smaller segments of your business.

6. **Select any or all of the remaining checkboxes in the corresponding Information dialog box, and then hope for the best.**

Yes, I am being facetious here regarding the following options:

- This Location/Department Has a Different Title for Sales Forms.

- This Location/Department Has a Different Company Name When Communicating with Customers.

- This Location/Department Has a Different Address Where Customers Contact Me or Send Payments.

- This Location/Department Has a Different Address Where Customers Contact Me or Send Payments.

- This Location/Department Has a Different Phone Number Where Customers Phone Me.

Each option has a corresponding field that enables you to purportedly customize the information that is displayed on sales forms. Your mileage may vary here, and will hopefully be better than mine, because I found that the customizations appeared most reliably on Estimates, and not so much on other sales forms.

7. **Click Save.**

REMEMBER

Plus subscriptions allow you to create up to 40 combined locations and classes, while Advanced subscriptions can create unlimited locations and classes.

Editing locations/departments

You can rename locations/departments or change their settings by following these steps:

1. **Choose the Gear icon ⇨ All Lists.**

2. **Choose Locations or Departments.**

3. **Select Edit from the drop-down menu in the Action column.**

   The corresponding Information dialog box appears.

4. **Revise the settings as needed.**

5. **Click Save.**

Deleting locations/departments

Any locations/departments that you save become permanent additions to Quick-Books because you can't delete them. You can, however, make them inactive:

1. **Choose the Gear icon ⇨ All Lists.**

2. **Choose Locations or Departments.**

3. **From the drop-down menu in the Action column, select Make Inactive (Reduces Usage) in Plus companies or Make Inactive in Advanced companies.**

   Or you can enable the checkbox for one or more classes on the class list and then choose Batch Actions ⇨ Make Inactive.

4. **Click Yes to confirm that you want to mark the locations/departments(s) as inactive.**

REMEMBER

Transactions associated with an inactive location/department will continue to display the corresponding name on reports, with *(Deleted)* appended to indicate that the location/department is no longer active

You can reactivate locations/departments by carrying out these steps:

1. **Choose the Gear icon ⇨ All Lists.**

2. **Choose Locations or Departments.**

3. **Choose List Settings ⇨ Include Inactive and then close the List Settings window.**

4. **Select Make Active from the drop-down menu in the Actions column.**

Running location/department-based reports

You won't find location or department-specific reports on the Reports screen in QuickBooks. However, you can run a QuickReport:

1. **Choose the Gear icon ⇨ All Lists.**

2. **Choose Locations or Departments.**

3. **Select Run Report from the Actions column.**

   The QuickReport screen opens.

You can customize the QuickReport just the same as most other reports. The Location/Department Full Name column is displayed by default on most transaction reports that have been converted to Modern View, and that column can be added to many other reports. I discuss customizing reports in more detail in Chapter 6.

Grouping bank deposits by location/department

In Chapter 5 I discuss the process of recording bank deposits, which entails moving payments from the Undeposited Funds account into a bank account. A special technique becomes available when the Track Locations/Departments is enabled. A Show Payments for This Location/Department field is displayed above the Add Funds to This Deposit section. Selecting from this list filters the bank deposit transaction down to payments for the specified department. This filtering simplifies the recording process, as it allows for accurate deposits by location.

For instance, the team at the Peoria, Illinois location of the fictional company that I've created is assuredly dropping off their deposits at a different bank than the team in Peoria, Indiana — where I had the memorable experience of watching the 2024 eclipse with my son.

Managing Projects

The Projects feature can help you organize all related transactions, time spent, and necessary reports in one central location. This feature includes reports that help you determine each project's profitability, track unbilled and nonbillable time and expenses, and manage project details. You can still complete all the various sales transaction forms described in this chapter as usual, but you have the option to start from the Project tab instead of the Sales transaction list or + New menu. Establishing a new project in QuickBooks before entering the associated transactions provides a clearer picture of a project's profitability.

TIP

The Tags feature allows you to track revenues and expenses across multiple customers if needed. In fact, you can go wild and use projects and tags together if you need that level of tracking. I discuss the Tags feature in Chapter 6.

Turning on the Project feature

You must have a Plus or Advanced subscription to use the Projects feature, which means this feature isn't available to Simple Start or Essentials subscribers.

REMEMBER

The Projects feature is enabled by default in the Plus and Advanced editions of QuickBooks. You must manually enable it in QuickBooks Accountant.

Follow these steps to enable the Projects feature:

1. **Choose the Gear icon ⇨ Account and Settings ⇨ Advanced ⇨ Projects.**

2. **Toggle on the Organize All Job-Related Activity in One Place option.**

3. **Click Save and Done.**

   A Projects command now appears on the sidebar menu. Selecting this command will prompt you to create your first project.

TIP

The primary admin user can turn the Projects feature off by toggling off the Organize All Job-Related Activity in One Place option in Step 2.

Contrasting projects with sub-customers

Simple Start and Essentials subscribers can use sub-customers as a simplistic method of project tracking. (I say *simplistic* because you can only track invoices in this fashion.) Plus and Advanced subscribers create sub-customers as well, but can also use the Projects feature to track every transaction type. Each project's screen has five tabs:

>> **Overview:** Provides a bird's-eye view of income, costs, and profit margin.

>> **Transactions:** Shows every transaction assigned to the project.

>> **Time Activity:** Displays activity by period and then by employee or service.

>> **Project Reports:** Allows you to use three project-specific reports.

>> **Attachments:** Shows files that you've uploaded.

The Projects feature keeps all the information for each project in one place. Sub-customers don't offer this centralization — unless you convert them to projects.

>> Any sub-customers you want to convert to projects must be marked as billed to the parent customer. To confirm this setting, edit the sub-customer record and then ensure that Bill Parent Customer is enabled just below the Parent Customer field.

>> You can choose which sub-customers you want to convert to projects and which ones you don't.

>> You can't undo the conversion of a sub-customer to a project.

First I show you how to create a project, and then I show you how to convert sub-customers to projects.

Creating a new project

You can create projects by following steps that are similar to adding records to the other lists I've discussed in this chapter, or you can convert a sub-customer to a project. The steps for creating a project are similar to creating customers or vendors:

1. **Choose Projects on the sidebar menu.**

2. **Click Start a Project if you haven't created a project yet or click New Project.**

3. **At a minimum, fill in the Project Name and Customer fields on the New Project task pane.**

   You can optionally specify start and end dates as well as project status, and you can add notes. You can't add attachments to a project, but you can add attachments to customer records as well as customer-related transactions.

4. **Click Save to display the screen for your project.**

   Although you specified a customer, no transactions appear on the Projects screen. Newly created projects have no transactions, so there's nothing to see just yet.

To convert a sub-customer to a project, choose Sales ⇨ Customers. A message asks whether you want to convert the first level of sub-customers to projects. Click Convert Now in the message window and select the eligible sub-customers to convert.

TIP

If the Convert Sub-customers to Projects prompt doesn't appear on your Customers screen, choose Projects on the sidebar menu, and then choose Convert from Sub-customer from the New Project drop-down menu.

After you click Convert, a message explains that you're about to convert a sub-customer to a project — and that there's no going back. If you're sure you want to do this, click Continue to convert the sub-customer(s), set the status of the project(s) to "in progress," and then decide whether you want to go to the Projects Center or redisplay the Customer list. Any previous activity for the sub-customer is displayed on the corresponding Projects screen.

WARNING

If you're thinking about changing the customer name in existing transactions, ensure that those transactions are assigned to the corresponding project first. Changing the customer can have widespread effects throughout QuickBooks. For instance, if you try to change the customer assigned to a payment transaction that you've deposited, you need to remove the transaction from the deposit before making the change, potentially complicating the deposit if you forget to re-add the payment. Although a customer and sub-customer or project may be linked, each entry in the Customers list remains a unique element.

You can choose whether to show projects in your customer list alongside sub-customers. To do so, choose Sales ⇨ Customers to display the Customers screen. Choose the Gear icon ⇨ Include Projects. Going forward you will see projects on the Customers screen and in list boxes on transactions, as well as on the Projects Center screen.

Adding transactions to a project

You can assign transactions to projects in two ways. First, you can create sales transactions in the manner I discuss in Chapter 2, but you'll select the project name from the Customer drop-down list rather than choosing the customer name directly. Second, you can initiate estimates, invoices, purchase orders, bills, expenses, time entries, and payment receipts by selecting from the Add to Project drop-down menu on the Projects screen for a given project. The project name will appear automatically on the transaction.

TIP

You cannot create Sales Receipts via Add to Project, but you can choose + New ⇨ Sales Receipt instead.

Reporting on projects

The power of projects becomes apparent once a project accumulates some activity, such as invoices, time charges, and expenses. The Projects screen for a given project includes an Overview tab that serves as a dashboard, while Transactions and Time Activity provide instant access to underlying transactions. The Project Reports tab offers three reports:

>> **Project Profitability:** A Profit & Loss report for the project.

>> **Time Cost by Employee or Vendor:** Labor and external service fees posted to the job.

>> **Unbilled Time and Expenses:** Details any unbilled time and costs charged to the project.

Updating project status

You can change the status of a job from either the project list or the corresponding screen for a specific project. Select Options in the Action column on the Project list screen, or change the status by way of the drop-down menu adjacent to the customer name on a project's screen. You can change the status of any project to Not Started, In Progress, Completed, or Canceled. You can then filter the project list based upon any of these filters:

>> Status

>> Customer

>> End Date

The Search for Project field enables you to search by entering part of the project name. Finally, the See Info Based On field is used to filter and view project-related costs and expenses based on specific criteria:

>> **Hourly Costs:** This option displays information related to the costs associated with hourly labor or time entries logged against the project.

>> **Payroll Expenses:** This option shows payroll expenses tied to the project, reflecting the costs of wages and salaries paid to employees working on the project.

While they might seem unrelated, both options help you track different aspects of project costs, either from direct labor or payroll-related expenses.

Deleting projects

QuickBooks idiosyncratically pretends that you can delete a project as long as you haven't assigned transactions to it yet. In reality, you're simply marking the project as inactive, because deleted projects can be revived. Let's first wink, wink, "delete" a project:

1. **Click Projects from the sidebar menu.**

2. **Select Delete Project from the three-dot menu, known as More Actions, in the Action column.**

   Here you'll see yet another user interface inconsistency in QuickBooks Online; unlike most other lists where the most frequently used command appears at the top of the Action menu drop-down, the Projects list uses a More Actions icon instead.

3. **Click Delete to confirm that you (wink, wink) want to "permanently delete" the project.**

Now you can restore the permanently deleted project:

1. **Click the Gear icon just above your list of projects and then select Show Deleted Projects from the bottom of the menu.**

2. **Click the Options menu in the Action column for any deleted project, and then make a choice that will simultaneously undelete the project and set its status.**

3. **Click the Gear icon just above your list of projects and then clear the Show Deleted Projects checkbox.**

   You won't be able see your active projects again until you uncheck the Show Deleted Projects checkbox in the Project Settings menu.

WARNING

IN THIS CHAPTER

» **Basing a budget from actual results**

» **Editing your budget**

» **Uploading budgets from a spreadsheet template**

» **Running budget-related reports**

» **Projecting cash flow**

Chapter **12**

Formulating Budgets and Planning Cash Flow

I f you want to create a budget within QuickBooks, you need a Plus or Advanced subscription. Budgets are typically projections of revenues and expenses for the coming year. QuickBooks allows you to choose from that type of budget, known as a Profit and Loss budget, or you can forecast assets, liabilities, and cash flow by way of a Balance Sheet budget. As the year rolls on, actual results can be compared to a budget to monitor whether things are going as planned. Budgets can be based on current or prior fiscal year actual results or started from scratch. Budget numbers can be entered directly into QuickBooks or imported from a spreadsheet template. From there, the Budget Overview and Budgets vs. Actual reports enable you to keep tabs on your financial prognostication. In the final section of this chapter, I discuss how the Cash Flow Planner feature serves as a shorter-term forecasting tool.

TIP

In Chapter 16, I discuss how Advanced users can use the Spreadsheet Sync feature to create budgets.

Creating a Budget

You can create a budget at any time by using these steps:

1. **Sign in to your QuickBooks company as an admin or a user with correct permission to access budgets.**

   Here's how to determine if you have the proper rights:

   - **Simple Start:** You can't create budgets with this version.
   - **Essentials:** Unfortunately, you can't create budgets with this version either.
   - **Plus:** *Standard* users with *All Access* are able to create budgets.
   - **Advanced:** Users with *Standard All Access* rights or specific access to the budgeting feature can create budgets.

TECHNICAL STUFF

   Choose Settings ⇨ Manage Users to adjust the access rights for specific users. Admin users have complete access to every element of a QuickBooks company.

2. **Choose Settings ⇨ Account and Settings ⇨ Advanced ⇨ Accounting and confirm that the first month of your fiscal year is set correctly.**

   Click the section or Edit to modify the fiscal year if needed.

3. **Choose Settings ⇨ Budgeting.**

   The Budgets screen appears.

4. **The next step depends on whether you've created a budget:**

   - **You haven't created a budget yet:** Click Create a Budget at the bottom of the screen.
   - **You've created one or more budgets:** Click Create New at the top-right corner of the screen.

5. **The How Do You Want to Set Up Your Budget? screen appears, as shown in Figure 12-1.**

6. **Specify a Budget Type of Profit and Loss or Balance Sheet.**

   A profit and loss budget allows you to forecast income and expenses for a fiscal year, while a balance sheet budget enables you to project assets, liabilities, and cash flow.

7. Choose a fiscal year from the Period list.

QuickBooks allows you to create a budget for the current year, four subsequent years, and two prior years.

8. Choose Consolidated or Subdivided budget.

A consolidated budget is created at the organization level, whereas subdivided budgets can be created by location, class, or customer.

As I discuss in Chapter 11, the Track Locations feature may be referred to as the Department feature in your QuickBooks company.

9. If you want to base your budget on prior activity, select from the Pre-Fill Data list.

You can prefill your budget based upon year-to-date actuals for the current year, up to four prior years, or any existing budgets.

10. Click Next to create your budget.

Depending upon your choice in Step 8, a blank or prefilled budget appears. Figure 12-2 shows a blank version.

If you change your mind about creating a budget, simply click the X in the upper-right corner or press Escape. Click Yes to indicate that you want to leave without saving.

11. To rename a budget, click Edit next to the budget name at the top-left corner.

12. To display a column with actual amounts for a prior period, make a selection from the Reference Data list.

You can choose actuals from the current year or any of the four prior years.

13. To display monthly columns with actual amounts for a prior period, click Show All Reference Data.

Initially your reference data appears in a single column, as shown in Figure 12-2. The Show All Reference Data button shows your reference data on a monthly basis (see Figure 12-3).

To hide all reference data columns, click Hide All Reference Data or toggle Compare Reference Data off. You can then selectively unhide any reference data columns by clicking the right arrow column in the budget column heading.

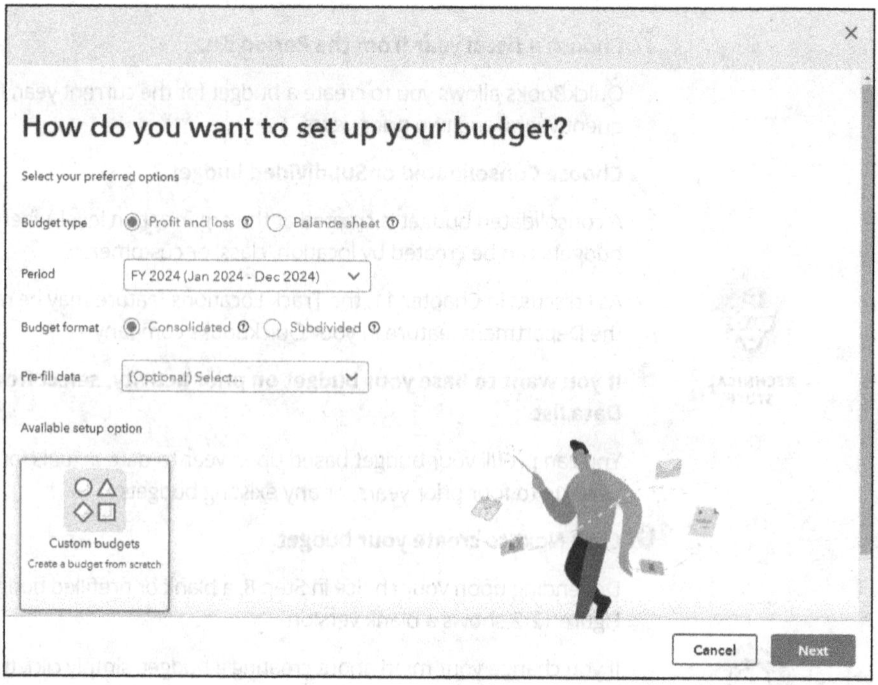

FIGURE 12-1:
The New
Budget screen.

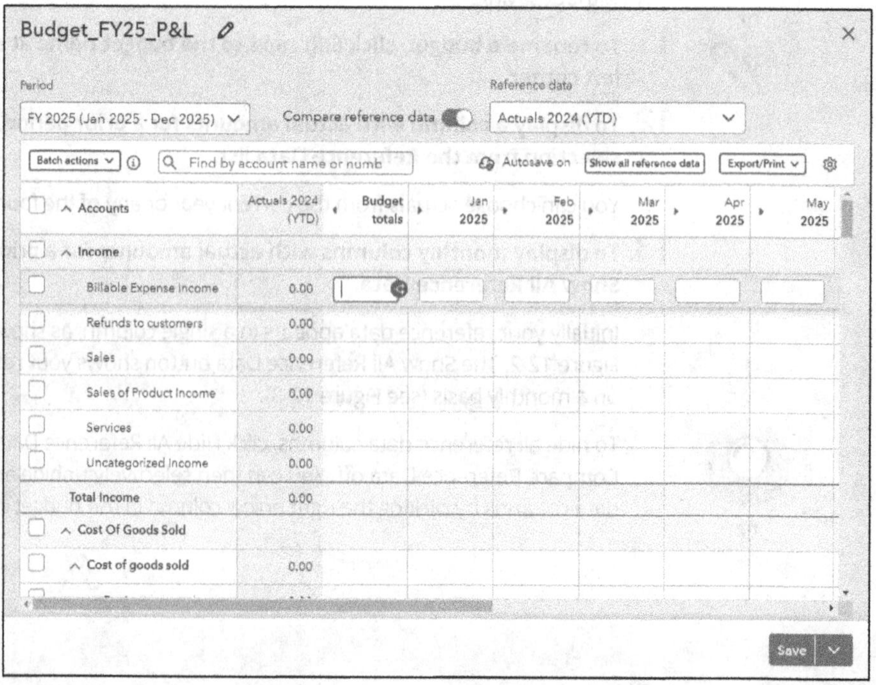

FIGURE 12-2:
The Budget input
screen with a
single reference
data column.

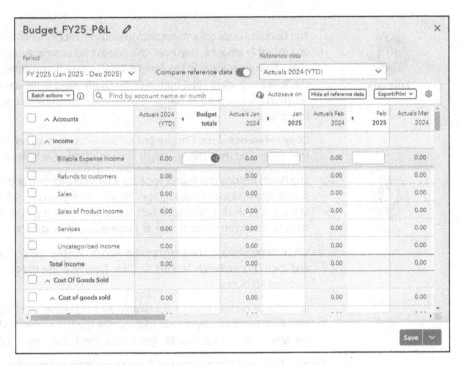

Populating a Budget

Figures 12-2 and 12-3 give the impression that you need to type amounts into each budget field, but that's not at all the case.

1. **Populate your budget in one of the following ways:**

   - **Manually type amounts in each field:** Use this approach when the amounts differ from the reference data amounts and vary from month to month.

   - **Enter a calculation in a field:** Type basic mathematic formulas into the amount fields, such as 100*1.05, 1200/100, 100+200, or 300–75.

   - **Copy an amount or calculation to the right:** Click the blue arrow within the active budget field to copy amounts or calculations to any remaining months.

   - **Split the Budget Total across all 12 months:** Enter an amount or calculation in the Budget Totals column and then click the blue button with two arrows to divide the amount by 12 and copy it across all 12 months. The Split icon appears in the Budget Totals column for the Billable Expense Income account in Figure 12-2.

The Budget Totals column recalculates automatically whenever you change any monthly amount. However, this doesn't automatically work in reverse. If you type an amount in the Budget Totals column, you either need to use the Split the Budget Total button or manually allocate the amount across the months. The Budget Totals field turns red whenever a discrepancy like this arises.

- **Copy reference data:** Choose one or more checkboxes on the left side of the screen and then choose Batch Actions ⇨ Copy Reference Data.

The Batch Actions command appears after you click one or more checkboxes. In addition to choosing specific accounts, you can click the checkbox at the top of the list to select all accounts, or choose a group checkbox, such as for Income to populate all income accounts at once.

- **Clear data:** Choose one or more checkboxes on the left side of the screen and then choose Batch Actions ⇨ Clear Data to erase the activity for selected accounts.

No undo or restore feature is available for the budget, but the AutoSave feature is turned on by default to minimize the risk of data loss. Choose the Gear icon ⇨ Autosave Budget to turn this feature off or back on.

2. **Choose Save and Close from the Save drop-down menu when you're ready to leave the budget.**

Importing a Budget

If you need more flexibility than the budget screen in QuickBooks offers, you can import a budget by way of a spreadsheet template that you download, edit, and then upload. You must adhere to the format that QuickBooks Online generates for you from a column and row standpoint. As of this writing, you can import profit and loss budgets, but not balance sheet budgets.

Make sure that you add any new accounts to your chart of accounts before starting the import process. You can't add new accounts to the chart of accounts by importing a budget template.

Here's how to import a budget:

1. **Choose Settings ⇨ Budgeting.**

   The Budgets screen appears.

2. Click Import Budget.

The All Your Budgets in One Place screen appears.

REMEMBER

Advanced users will also see a Create In Spreadsheet button, which initiates the Spreadsheet Sync process that I discuss in Chapter 16.

3. Choose a fiscal year from the Period list.

QuickBooks allows you to create a budget for the current year, four subsequent years, and two prior years.

4. Choose Consolidated or Subdivided budget.

A consolidated budget is created at the organization level, whereas subdivided budgets can be created by location, class, or customer.

5. Click Next.

6. Click the P&L Budget_template.xlsx link.

A workbook named P&L Budget_sample.xlsx appears in your Downloads folder.

7. Open the budget template in Microsoft Excel or Google Sheets, complete your budget, and then save and close the workbook.

8. Click Upload Budget and then select your template.

TIP

Hold on, hold on, I know you're thinking, "I need more time to build out my budget spreadsheet!" I get it — the Import process skips over that part. If you're not ready to upload, simply Close the All Your Budgets In One Place page, carry out your spreadsheet work, and then repeat Steps 1 through 5, skip Steps 6 and 7, and resume with Step 8.

9. Click Next.

A progress indicator dialog box appears while your budget is being imported.

10. Close the Start Creating a Budget dialog box and then click View Budget to accept the import or click Cancel Import if you change your mind.

Your imported budget appears on the same screen that you would have used to create your budget within QuickBooks.

REMEMBER

You can freely modify imported budgets by using the techniques I discussed in the "Populating a budget" section earlier in this chapter.

Maintaining and Reporting on Budgets

All your active and archived budgets appear on the Budgets screen. You then have several options regarding managing budgets and generating budget-related reports:

1. **Choose Settings ⇨ Budgeting.**

   The Budgets screen appears and displays a list of your budgets.

2. **Choose a command from the drop-down menu in the Action column:**

   - **View/Edit** displays the budget screen shown in Figure 12-2 so that you can continue working on the budget or make other changes.

   - **Run Reports in Spreadsheet Sync** launches the Spreadsheet Sync feature in Advanced companies, as I discuss in Chapter 16.

   - **Run Budgets vs. Actuals Report** generates a report that compares your actual results against your monthly budget.

   - **Run Budget Overview Report** generates a report that details your budget.

TIP

   Type the word **Budget** in the Find Report by Name field on the Reports screen to view additional budget-related reports.

   - **Archive** enables you to deactivate a budget. To reactivate a budget, toggle the Hide Archive Budgets command on and then choose Options ⇨ Unarchive within an archived budget.

   - **Duplicate** enables you to make a copy of a budget.

   - **Delete** removes a budget from the list. To delete two or more budgets at once, make two or more selections and choose Batch Actions ⇨ Delete.

Estimating Future Cash Flow

The Cash Flow Planner feature allows you to create a financial forecast based upon historical data and your future expectations without affecting your accounting records. The planner incorporates transactions from linked bank and credit card accounts into a projection that you can modify by adding or removing items. I discuss how to link your bank and credit card accounts to QuickBooks in Chapter 5.

REMEMBER

The Cash Flow Planner is unavailable if your company has Multicurrency enabled. Additionally, this feature is not included in the Accountant version.

Chapter 14 outlines the Forecasts feature, exclusive to Advanced companies, which offers more sophisticated planning tools than the rudimentary Cash Flow Planner.

Here's how to use the Cash Flow Planner feature:

1. **Choose Dashboards ⇨ Planner.**

2. **If prompted, choose Start Planning and then Let's Go.**

   These commands appear the first time that you use the Cash Flow Planner.

3. **Review the Money In/Out tab to view your income and expenses on a bar chart or choose Cash Balance to see your past and projected cash balances.**

4. **Use the Upcoming section to add new items, or modify transactions derived from your books:**

   - **Edit existing transactions:** Click on any bill or invoice transaction to reveal Date and Amount fields that you can use to override default values derived from the transaction.

     If the Overdue Transactions section appears on screen, you can click update to adjust the dates and amounts for any past due transactions.

   - **Add new items:** Click Add Item and then fill in the Date, Description, and Amount fields. Specify whether it's Money In or Money Out, toggle the Repeating setting on if applicable, fill in the corresponding fields, and then click Save.

5. **Choose In the Past from the Upcoming drop-down menu to see a list of transactions that have already occurred but are still impacting your cash flow projection.**

   These are typically past due invoices and unpaid bills.

6. **If you want to view or adjust the assumptions and transaction types used, click Filters.**

   You can include or exclude transactions from your books, as well as items that you have manually added.

7. **If you want to save a copy of your cash flow plan, click Download Report, and then choose Export as CSV, Save as PDF, or Export to Excel.**

4

QuickBooks Online Advanced Features

IN THIS PART . . .

Utilize the Desktop app and customize user access.

Create and analyze custom reports and visual charts.

Streamline your operations by managing tasks and workflows.

Integrate and sync your accounting data with Microsoft Excel.

Chapter **13**

Administering the Desktop App, Backups, and Customizable Security

I n this chapter, I cover some features that are specific to the Advanced version of QuickBooks, including the desktop app that offers a number of benefits over accessing your books via a web browser. I then cover how to back up and restore your company, as opposed to trusting that it will be backed up in the cloud. Granted, Intuit is basing its reputation on keeping everyone's accounting data safe, but you can never have too many backups. I close the chapter with a discussion of how you can somewhat customize the access that users have to features and reports, including limited access to certain features by location.

Installing the Desktop App

The QuickBooks Online desktop app is simply an optional user interface for Quick-Books Online that you can install on your macOS or Windows computer. It is not related to QuickBooks Enterprise Desktop, which is a separate accounting software offered by Intuit. The desktop app for QuickBooks Online offers the following benefits compared to accessing your books via a web browser:

>> You can stay signed in for up to six months, rather than having to log in to the QuickBooks website multiple times a day when your web browser session expires.

>> The app offers a navigation map and drop-down menus that will feel familiar to QuickBooks Desktop users who have migrated to QuickBooks Online.

>> You can open and access multiple QuickBooks companies without having to sign in and out. You can only download the app if you have a QuickBooks Online Advanced subscription, but you can access Simple Start, Essentials, Plus, or Advanced companies within the app.

REMEMBER

You can open multiple companies at once in the desktop app, but all companies have to be tied to the same Intuit account email address.

Here's how to download and install the QuickBooks Online desktop app:

1. **Choose the Gear icon ⇨ Get the Desktop App.**

2. **Scroll down and choose Download for Windows or Download for Mac.**

3. **Double-click the installation file in your Downloads folder and then follow the onscreen instructions.**

TIP

I discuss how to download and install the QuickBooks Mobile app for use on a mobile device in Chapter 7.

4. **Sign into the app in the same way that you log into QuickBooks Online via your web browser.**

5. **Choose a company to open if you have multiple entities associated with your Intuit account.**

   You aren't prompted to choose a company if you only have access to a single QuickBooks company. Your company is displayed in the first tab of the app.

6. **To display two screens within your company side-by-side, toggle Desktop View on and then click Split Screen.**

   This can be helpful if you're working on a bank reconciliation and want to view an underlying transaction at the same time.

7. To open an additional tab, click +. You then have the following options:

- Navigate to a different screen within your company than you're using on the first tab.

- Display another company by making a choice from the You're Viewing list at the top-right side of the screen.

You can add as many additional tabs as you want. Although you can't tell from the tab names, in Figure 13-1, I'm accessing two different QuickBooks Online companies at the same time.

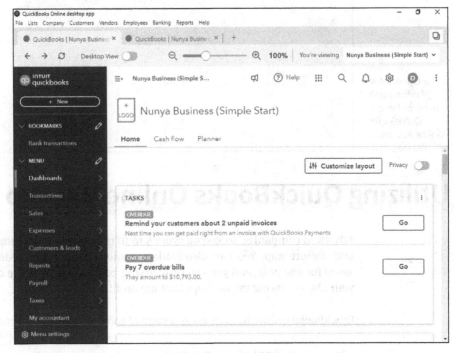

FIGURE 13-1:
Each tab in the QuickBooks Online desktop app can display a different company, or different screens within the same company.

8. To display the Open Tabs/Windows task pane shown in Figure 13-2, click Open Tabs/Windows.

A preview of the tab appears in the task pane when you hover your mouse over a tab name. Click the Open Tabs/Windows button again to hide the task pane.

REMEMBER

The QuickBooks Online desktop app keeps you logged into your companies, so when you launch the app you have immediate access without signing in. Choose File ➪ Sign-Out if you don't want anyone to be able to access your books by simply launching the desktop app.

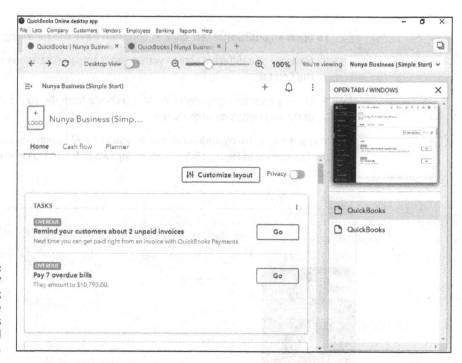

FIGURE 13-2:
The Open Tabs/
Windows task
pane within the
QuickBooks
Online Advanced
desktop app.

Utilizing QuickBooks Online Backup

Advanced companies backed up every 5 to 10 minutes by way of the Online Backup and Restore app. You can also initiate manual backups if needed. Backups are saved for one year, and you can restore your company back to the date and time of your choice among the backups that are on file.

QuickBooks Online Backup saves a copy of most of your data. Exceptions include

>> Account-based billable expenses

>> Audit log entries

>> Bank feeds and their links to transactions and bank rules

>> Custom form templates

>> Custom reports

>> Customer types

>> Employee Social Security Numbers

>> Delayed credits and charges

- » Item-based billable expenses with markup
- » Pricing rules
- » QuickBooks Online Payments information
- » Reconciliation reports
- » Recurring transactions
- » Vendor tax fields

In addition, Intuit Payroll transactions and inventory adjustments are backed up as journal entries. If you allow me a moment of personal commentary, given that all your data is being stored in a database, how on earth can Intuit not create a backup that grabs everything? Regardless, this is a constraint you have to work within.

Manually backing up your QuickBooks company

You can initiate an on-demand backup by using these steps:

1. **In QuickBooks, choose the Gear icon ⇨ Back Up Company.**

   The Home screen of the Online Backup & Restore app opens.

2. **Choose Backup ⇨ Run Manual Backup.**

   The Run Manual Backup task pane opens.

3. **Make a choice from the Select Company to Backup field.**

4. **Choose a type of backup:**

   - **Incremental:** Backs up only the data that has changed since the last backup and is the fastest option.

   - **Full:** Backs up any data flagged as changed and takes less time than a Complete backup.

   - **Complete:** Comprehensively searches your data for changes and takes the longest time to complete.

5. **Click Backup.**

   The Backup screen of the Online Backup & Restore app opens.

Your backup request will appear on the Restore screen. The Status column will initially show Queued. Once the backup has begun, an In-Progress indicator will appear, which will then be replaced by a status of Success once the backup has completed.

Restoring your QuickBooks company

If necessary, you can restore any previous backup you've made. Keep in mind the exceptions that I laid out at the beginning of this section, and remember that any transactions you've entered subsequent to the backup that you choose to restore are discarded. Here are the steps to restore a backup:

1. **Ensure that all other users are logged out of your company and remain logged out until the restore process is complete.**

2. **Choose the Gear icon ⇨ Back Up Company.**

   The Home screen of the Online Backup & Restore app opens.

3. **Choose Restore ⇨ Create Restore.**

   The Restore Company Data task pane opens. See Figure 13-3.

4. **Select the company you want to restore from the Source Company field.**

5. **Choose a company from the Source Company list.**

6. **Enter or choose a date from the Date field.**

7. **Select from the Time field.**

8. **Click Next.**

9. **Read the onscreen warnings and then turn on the checkbox.**

10. **Click Start Restore.**

    The Restore screen of the Online Backup & Restore app opens.

Your restore request will appear on the Restore screen. The Status column will initially show Queued. Once the restoration has begun, an In-Progress indicator will appear, which will then be replaced by a status of Success.

TIP The Backup & Restore app includes a Copy command that allows you to duplicate a QuickBooks Online Advanced company. However, as of this writing, Intuit has not updated their online documentation to explain how this process works. Therefore, I've chosen not to provide detailed instructions. Hopefully, by the time you read this, the documentation will be updated to match the app, and you'll be able to use this functionality if needed.

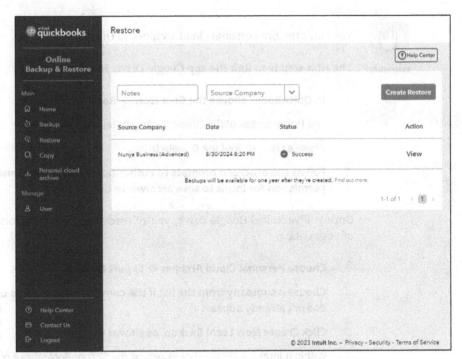

FIGURE 13-3:
The Restore
Company Data
task pane.

Creating personal cloud archives

This feature enables you to export much of the data in your QuickBooks company to a Google Drive folder. The archive is composed of a ZIP file that contains the following comma-separated value (.CSV) files:

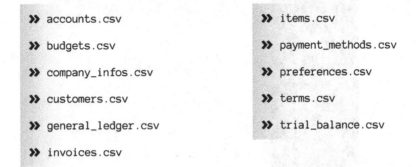

- accounts.csv
- budgets.csv
- company_infos.csv
- customers.csv
- general_ledger.csv
- invoices.csv

- items.csv
- payment_methods.csv
- preferences.csv
- terms.csv
- trial_balance.csv

This serves as a limited alternative to the Spreadsheet Sync feature I discuss in Chapter 16. In Chapter 21, I discuss how you can use Power Query to create links to CSV files to analyze your data.

REMEMBER

You can't restore personal cloud archives to QuickBooks Online.

The first step is to link the app Google Drive. Here's how:

1. **In QuickBooks choose the Gear icon ⇨ Back Up Company.**

   The Home screen of the Online Backup & Restore app opens.

2. **Choose User ⇨ Re-Link Google Drive.**

3. **Follow the onscreen prompts to authenticate with Google and grant permission for Intuit to save archives to Google Drive.**

Once you've linked Google Drive, you're ready to create a personal cloud archive of your data:

1. **Choose Personal Cloud Archive ⇨ Export Backup.**

2. **Choose a company from the list if the company you want to back up doesn't already appear.**

3. **Click Create New Local Backup, as shown in Figure 13-4.**

   Within minutes, a ZIP file should appear the ChronoBooks\[*your company name*] folder within your Google Drive account.

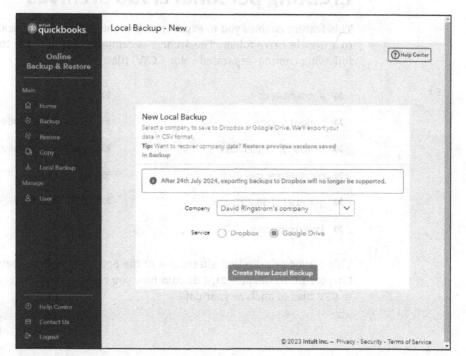

FIGURE 13-4:
The New Local
Backup screen.

TIP

Once you extract the CSV files, you can double-click any of them to open the file in Microsoft Excel, or in Excel choose File ⇨ Open ⇨ Browse, choose Text Files from the file type list, and then navigate to the ChronoBooks\[*your company name*] folder and open the file of your choice. In Chapter 21, I discuss how you can use Power Query to connect to CSV files.

Customizing User Security Privileges

Every user in QuickBooks must be assigned a role that determines their level of access to features and reports. In Chapter 9, I discuss how Essentials and Plus users can assign predetermined roles to users. An Advanced subscription offers the ability to somewhat edit the following additional roles:

>> **Expense Manager:** Such users have access to expense transactions, vendors, products and services, sales tax, and currencies.

>> **Expense Submitter:** These users can submit expense receipts, which I discuss in Chapter 15.

>> **Inventory Manager:** A user with this role can view and edit the products and services list and carry out inventory-related tasks.

>> **Payroll Manager:** This type of user can manage employee records, run payroll, and perform other payroll-related tasks.

>> **Sales Manager:** Assigning this role grants access to sales transactions, customers, products and services, sales tax, and currencies.

You can't customize the built-in roles I discussed in Chapter 9, but you can customize the roles in the preceding list and create new ones from scratch, albeit with major limitations on what you can and can't grant or prohibit access to. I first walk you through the Manage Users screen, which you can access by choosing the Gear icon ⇨ Manage Users. You then see three tabs:

>> **Users:** This list displays all the users assigned to the company. QuickBooks Online Advanced companies can have up to 25 billable users. In Chapter 9, I discuss how you can also have unlimited Time Tracking and View Company Reports users.

>> **Roles:** This tab shows the standard roles that are available in Essentials and Plus companies, along with the roles that I mentioned earlier. You can't customize the standard roles, but you can all other roles, and you can add new roles and tailor them to your exact specifications. The number of custom roles you can create is unlimited.

>> **Accountants:** This tab lists any accounting firms that have been invited to oversee your QuickBooks company. Advanced companies are permitted up to two accountant users.

Editing prebuilt roles

Here's how to edit a prebuilt customizable role:

1. **Choose the Gear icon ⇨ Manage Users.**

   The Manage Users screen opens.

2. **Activate the Roles tab.**

3. **Click the Edit link adjacent to a role, such as Expense Manager.**

4. **Click Yes when asked if you're sure you want to edit the role.**

   A screen opens, displaying the rights available to that role. You have a limited ability to edit the built-in roles.

5. **Make any adjustments as you see fit and then click Save Role.**

Establishing new roles

The limitations on the access that you can and can't grant for prebuilt roles extend to new roles as well. You may well find that you're simply unable to create a role that has the exact combination of characteristics you're seeking. Here's how to give it a try:

1. **Choose the Gear icon ⇨ Manage Users.**
   The Manage Users screen opens.

2. **Activate the Roles tab.**

3. **Click Add Role.**

   The Add a New Role screen opens, as shown in Figure 13-5.

4. **Fill in the Role Name field.**

5. **Recommended: Enter up to 150 characters to describe the role.**

   The description you provide here appears on the Roles tab of the Manage Users worksheet, which makes it easier to assign proper roles to your users.

6. **Expand the program area sections as needed and choose from the settings that are available for you to customize.**

The description that you provide here appears on the Roles tab of the Manage Users worksheet, which makes it easier to assign proper roles to your users.

You can limit sales transactions to specific locations, which are labeled as Departments. I discuss this feature in Chapter 11.

7. **Expand the sections and choose from the settings that are available for you to customize.**

All customizable options are turned off by default until you enable them when customizing a role.

8. **Click Save Role.**

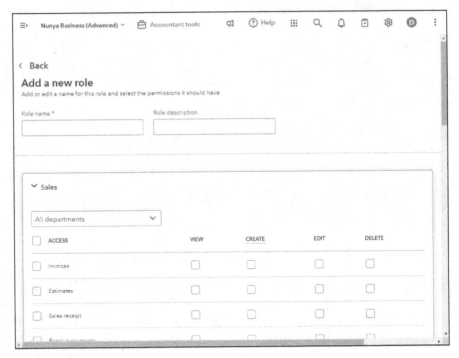

FIGURE 13-5:
You can only enable or disable certain features.

Once you've created or customized your roles, you manage the users in your company in the same fashion that I described in Chapter 9, albeit with additional role options that aren't available in Essentials and Plus companies.

Chapter **14**

Generating Custom Reports and Charts

I n this chapter, I show you the additional reporting capabilities available in QuickBooks Online Advanced. These include a custom report builder and the ability to add custom fields to records and transactions. If you don't have an Advanced subscription or haven't added enough transactions to generate meaningful reports, you can explore these features using the Advanced sample company at https://qbo.intuit.com/redir/testdrive_us_advanced.

TIP

Remember to log out of your QuickBooks company before trying to sign into the sample company. You can also open the sample company from an incognito page of your browser or use a different profile in your browser.

Introducing the Custom Report Builder

You can customize the built-in reports for every QuickBooks subscription level to a certain extent. This means that you can hide or display columns, control whether headers and footers are included in the report, and make other minor cosmetic changes. The Custom Report Builder lets you go far beyond what's possible with this basic functionality, as described here:

1. **Choose Reports ⇨ Reports.**

Scroll down the sidebar menu if you don't immediately see the Reports command.

2. **Click +Create New Report.**

3. **Make a choice from the Select the Report Type dialog box, and then click Create.**

The following options are available:

- Blank
- Invoice
- Expenses
- Sales
- Bills
- Journal Entry
- Banking Transactions
- Transactions List

Choose Invoice if you want to follow along with this example and then click Create. You may have to scroll down to see the Create button, which enables you to display an Invoice Report that has the following options:

- A blank My Custom Report appears with two buttons: Start by Report Creation Wizard or Start by Adding Data Columns.

- A default report format appears, such as Invoice Report.

The following commands are available within custom reports:

- **Table View:** This default view displays your report in list form.

- **Chart View:** This command is adjacent to Table View and presents your report in chart form.

- **More Actions:** The commands available vary based upon view.

Table View

- *Schedule Report:* This command creates a workflow, which I elaborate on in more detail in Chapter 15.

- *Email Report:* This command opens a Send dialog box, where you can compose an email by filling in the To, CC, Subject, Message, and File Name fields, as well as choose between Excel, CSV, and PDF formats.

- *Add to Management Reports:* This command displays a dialog box from which you can add the report to a new or existing management report.

TIP

I discuss management reports in more detail in Chapter 6.

Chart View

- *Add to Performance Center:* Adds the chart to a secondary dashboard that you can access by choosing Reports ⇨ Performance Center.

- *Add to Management Reports:* This command displays a dialog box from which you can add the chart to a new or existing management report.

- **Export/Print:** This command is available in Table View and offers the following options:

  - *Export to Excel:* Downloads the report to an Excel workbook on your computer.

  - *Run Report and Sync with Excel:* Creates a Spreadsheet Sync connection, which I discuss in more detail in Chapter 16.

  - *Export to CSV:* Downloads the report to a comma-separated value file on your computer.

  - *Print/Save as PDF:* Displays the Print or Save as PDF dialog box from which you can create a hard copy of a report or download a PDF version to your computer.

- **Export Chart:** This command is available in Chart View and offers the following options:

  - *Print/Save as PDF:* Displays the Print or Save as PDF dialog box from which you can create a hard copy of a chart or download a PDF version to your computer.

  - *Save as PNG:* Downloads the chart to a PNG file on your computer.

TIP

PNG stands for Portable Network Graphic and is like GIF and JPG files used for displaying images.

- **Report Period:** Select a period or custom date range from this field.

- **Accounting Method:** Select cash or accrual from this field.

- **View Options:** Select Normal View or Compact View, when available. Normal View uses a larger font, and when available Compact View fits more information onscreen and in print.

- **Pivot:** This command is enabled in Table View, allowing you to create a summary report from your data.

- **Group By:** This command is enabled in Table View, allowing you to group transactions on your report in various ways.

- **Filter:** This command enables you to narrow down your report by applying criteria that you specify.

- **General Options:** This command enables you customize number formatting and manage headers and footers, as shown in Figure 14-1.

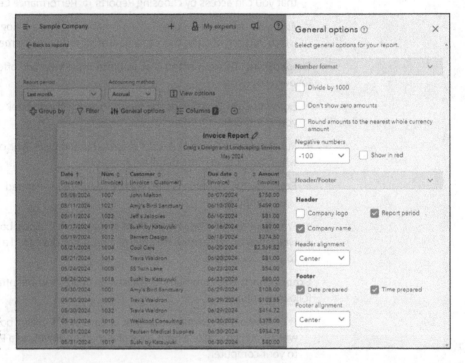

FIGURE 14-1:
General Options
task pane.

- **Columns:** This command displays a task pane that varies depending upon the current view:

  - *Table View:* Specify columns to display on the report.

  - *Chart View:* Choose a chart type, specify the horizontal (X) and vertical (Y) axes, and optionally split by transaction type or number, posting, or period type.

  - *Pivot View:* Arrange data fields, creating dynamic summaries and comparisons within your report.

- **Collapse:** Hides the row of buttons starting with Table View on the left and ending with Save on the right. Also toggles to an Expand button that redisplays the buttons.

The following commands are also available in Table View:

» **Report Name:** Click Edit to update the name of the report.

» **Refresh Report:** Include recent changes within your QuickBooks company.

REMEMBER

Custom reports cannot be exported directly to Google Sheets. Instead, you must first export your custom report as an Excel workbook, then create a blank Google Sheet and select File ⇨ Import ⇨ Upload.

TIP

The + Add New Chart button also launches the Custom Report Builder.

Now that you have the lay of the land, you're ready to delve deeper into what's possible with custom reports.

Utilizing Table View

Let's dig deeper into the Table View by way of the Invoice report:

1. **Choose Reports ⇨ Reports.**

2. **Click +Create New Report.**

3. **Select an option, such as Invoice, and then click Create.**

   From here, use the commands discussed in the previous section to customize your report. Use Table View to control the layout and data, and then adapt further using Chart View or Pivot.

Exploring Chart View

Chart View enables you to present the data you've assembled in Table view into chart form:

1. **Open any report in Table View, as discussed in the previous section.**

2. **Click the Chart View tab, which appears below the report title.**

   A Customize Chart task pane appears, as shown in Figure 14-2, enabling you to build one of four different types of charts:

   - **Vertical bar:** This is a standard bar chart similar to what you may have created in Microsoft Excel or Google sheets.

- **Trend line:** A trend line chart in QuickBooks is known as a line chart in Excel and Google Sheets.

- **Stacked bar:** In Excel or Google Sheets, a stacked bar chart has the bars broken down into segments, but in QuickBooks a stacked bar chart is pretty much indecipherable from a vertical bar chart.

- **KPI:** This type of chart allows you to specify a key performance indicator.

3. **To change how the data is grouped and displayed along the bottom of the chart, select from the Horizontal (x) Axis field.**

   Charts typically display a date field by default, but other options may be available. Any date field can be displayed by day, week, month, quarter, or year.

   You cannot change the horizontal (x) axis for KPI charts.

4. **To change the numeric basis for the chart, select from the Vertical (y) Axis drop-down menu.**

   Typically this is an amount, but you may have the option to choose a different metric based upon the fields you chose in Table View.

5. **To break data down into subcategories, select from the Split By list when the field is available.**

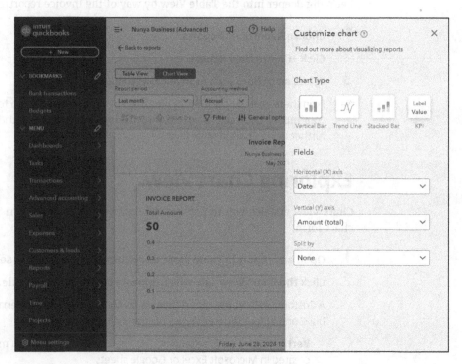

FIGURE 14-2:
Customize Chart task pane.

Pivoting a Report

Before we get started, I must mention the iconic *Friends* scene where Chandler and Rachel are trying to help Ross carry a new couch up the stairs to his apartment, with Ross repeatedly yelling "Pivot!" You don't have to yell "Pivot" when using this feature, but please feel free to do so — I won't judge.

TIP

QuickBooks-based pivot tables can only sum fields that contain numeric values, so you can't create reports within QuickBooks that count the number of invoices by customer. In Chapter 20, I show you how to use Microsoft Excel's PivotTable feature to create such reports.

Let's say you want to create a pivot report that summarizes your product sales by item and by customer. The Product/Service field is not part of the default custom Invoice report, so you need to add the field before you can pivot the data:

1. **Choose Reports ⇨ Reports.**

2. **Click +Create New Report.**

3. **Select Invoice and then click Create.**

4. **Click Columns.**

   The Columns task pane opens.

5. **Click More Columns.**

6. **Type Product/Service in the Search Columns field.**

7. **Choose Invoice ⇨ Line Items.**

8. **Click the Product/Service checkbox.**

9. **Click the Pivot button.**

   A Pivot task pane opens, as shown in Figure 14-3.

10. **Select the Product/Service from the Rows field.**

    Your report displays a row for each item that you choose, meaning that if you choose an invoice number, you see details on an invoice-number basis.

11. **Select the Customer Name from the Columns field.**

12. **Select the Amount from the Values field.**

    The pivot table report appears, as shown in Figure 14-4.

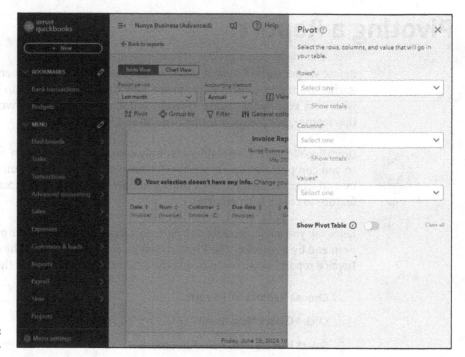

FIGURE 14-3:
Pivot task pane.

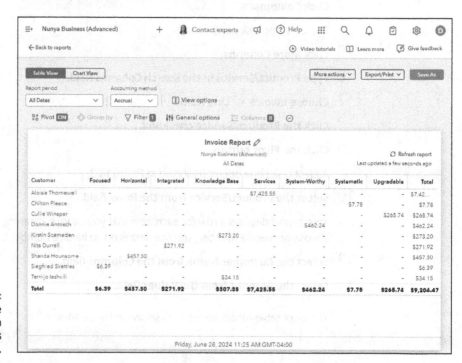

FIGURE 14-4:
A pivot table
report in
QuickBooks
Online Advanced.

CUSTOMIZING THE PERFORMANCE CENTER

The Performance Center in QuickBooks Online lets you monitor key financial metrics with customizable charts and reports. It provides real-time insights into your business's financial performance. To access the Performance Center, choose Reports ⇨ Performance Center. Click Quick Add Charts to add one or more of these charts to the dashboard:

- Expenses over time
- Revenue over time
- Gross profit over time
- Net profit over time
- Accounts receivable
- Accounts payable
- COGS over time
- Net cash flow
- NPM versus industry benchmarks (net profit margin)
- GPM versus industry benchmarks (gross profit margin)

REMEMBER

You must turn the pivot table off if you want to return to Table View. To do so, click Pivot and then toggle Show Pivot Table off, or click Clear All.

IN THIS CHAPTER

» Working with the Tasks feature

» Automating repetitive tasks with workflows

» Overseeing employee expense reports

» Creating, modifying, or deleting multiple transactions

» Automating revenue recognition and depreciation

Chapter **15**

Tailoring Tasks, Workflows, and Other Advanced Features

I n this chapter, I explore more things you can do only in a company that has an Advanced subscription. I start off by showing you how to use the Workflows feature to automate internal and external communication regarding transactions. From there, I show you how you can save time entering data into QuickBooks by using the Batch Transactions feature. I close out the chapter by examining the Revenue Recognition feature, which helps you stay compliant with generally accepted accounting principles (GAAP).

Exploring the Tasks Feature

Simple Start, Essentials, and Plus companies offer a vastly simplified version of the Tasks feature that is available to Advanced users. For those companies, tasks are limited to high-level notifications, such as "x invoices need to be sent."

Accessing the Tasks list

You can access the Tasks list, shown in Figure 15-1, by choosing from the sidebar menu. From there you can carry out a variety of activities:

>> Click the button in the Actions column for a task, such as clicking Send for a Review Invoice task. The button includes an arrow through which you can choose to mark the task as completed, edit it, or delete it.

>> Click the checkbox to the left of two or more tasks and then select Mark Completed or Delete in the Actions column.

FIGURE 15-1:
The Task screen in Advanced companies.

You can filter the Tasks list based on the following criteria:

>> All Open Tasks

>> Due Today

>> Overdue

>> Upcoming

>> Deleted

You can also click Filter to filter the Tasks list based on multiple criteria. You can optionally click Notification Settings and signify whether you want to receive an email when a task is assigned to you, when a task you assigned to someone else is completed, or when tasks you've created or assigned are updated.

Creating tasks manually

You can manually add a task that you assign to a single user in your company by following these steps:

1. **Choose Tasks.**

   The Tasks screen opens.

2. **Click Add Task.**

   The Add Task pane shown in Figure 15-2 opens.

3. **Complete the Task Name field.**

   Task names are limited to 50 characters.

4. **Choose a QuickBooks user from the Assign To list.**

5. **Enter a due date.**

6. **To create a recurring item, toggle Recurring Task on and then establish a schedule.**

7. **To describe the task in more detail, fill in the Notes field.**

   Notes are limited to 1,500 characters.

8. **To attach one or more documents to the task, use the Attachments field.**

TIP

   I discuss the specifics of attachments in the "Creating customer records" section of Chapter 2.

9. **Click Save to add the task to the user's task list.**

FIGURE 15-2:
The Add
Task pane.

Utilizing the Workflow Automation Feature

The Workflow Automation feature serves as an automated tickler and routing system that can create tasks, send emails, and update the Memo field of certain transactions. As of this writing, Advanced users can choose from around 40 different workflow templates. You can also create workflows for 17 different transaction types, lists, and reports.

Reviewing available actions

I walk you through creating a specific workflow in a moment, but at a high level, here are the types of activities a workflow can carry out:

>> **Reminder:** This type of workflow can add an item to your Task list, send an email externally — say, to a customer or vendor — send an internal email to one or more QuickBooks Online users, or send a push notification to one or more users.

Toggle the Send Consolidated Email option off under Send a Company Email if you want to customize the email message.

>> **Approval:** This type of workflow can route a transaction through up to four levels, based on conditions that you set, such as transaction amount, location, or customer or vendor name, among other criteria. The transaction doesn't post to your books until the approval process has been completed.

>> **Notification:** This is similar to the Send Reminder task, but it's more limited. Notifications are an email message you can customize, whereas Reminders give you additional communication options. You can't include CC or BCC email addresses on a notification.

>> **Send:** This workflow emails a transaction form and includes CC and BCC fields.

>> **Update:** This type of workflow can update the memo field of certain transactions.

>> **Scheduled Actions:** This type of workflow enables you to automatically create and send statements and generate email reports.

The Workflow Automation feature can only send statements and reports as PDF attachments.

Editing a workflow template

Let's say that you want to create a bank deposit reminder. This is a prebuilt task you can edit by carrying out these steps:

1. **Choose Workflow Automation ⇨ Templates.**

   The Workflow Automation screen opens, as shown in Figure 15-3.

2. **Click Set Bank Deposit Reminder in the Workflow Templates section.**

   The Set Bank Deposit Reminder screen opens.

3. **Update the Name field if needed.**

4. **Fill in the fields for Condition #1 to establish a trigger for the workflow.**

5. **Complete the customizable fields in the Actions section to indicate what you want the workflow to accomplish.**

6. **Click Save and Enable to activate the workflow; otherwise, click Save to keep your changes without activating the workflow.**

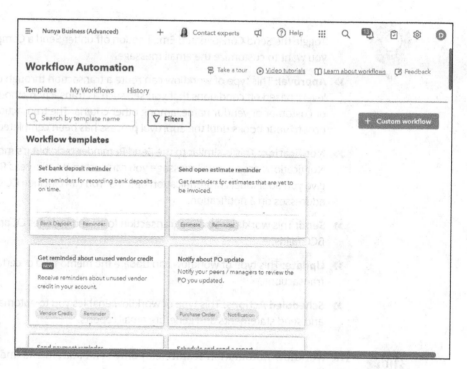

Nunya Business (Advanced)   +   Contact experts   Help

Workflow Automation   Take a tour   Video tutorials   Learn about workflows   Feedback

Templates   My Workflows   History

Search by template name   Filters   + Custom workflow

Workflow templates

Set bank deposit reminder
Set reminders for recording bank deposits on time.

Bank Deposit   Reminder

Send open estimate reminder
Get reminders for estimates that are yet to be invoiced.

Estimate   Reminder

Get reminded about unused vendor credit
NEW
Receive reminders about unused vendor credit in your account.

Vendor Credit   Reminder

Notify about PO update
Notify your peers / managers to review the PO you updated.

Purchase Order   Notification

Send payment reminder   Schedule and send a report

FIGURE 15-3:
The Workflow Automation screen.

REMEMBER

The workflow screens depend on the template that you choose, but all workflow screens have a fairly similar format. The one exception is the approval tasks workflow that presents a flowchart approach so that you can visually see how the approval process will work.

Creating a custom workflow

You're not limited to the built-in workflow templates. Use these steps to roll out your own workflow:

1. **Choose Workflow Automation.**

    The Workflow Automation screen opens.

2. **Click + Custom Workflow.**

    The first Create Custom Workflow screen opens, as shown in Figure 15-4.

3. **Make a selection from the Select Record for Workflow list.**

    The row of available actions changes to show you which action(s) can be carried out for a given record type.

TIP

4. **Select an action.**

   You must select an action even if only one is available.

5. **Click Next.**

   The second Create Custom Workflow screen opens, as shown in Figure 15-5.

6. **Fill in the Workflow Name field.**

7. **To modify the transaction type for this workflow, make a selection from the Source Transaction field.**

   This list is identical to the Select Record for Workflow list in Step 3.

8. **Fill out the fields shown onscreen, which vary depending on the type of record and action you've chosen.**

9. **Click Save and Turn On to activate the workflow; otherwise, click Save to keep your changes without activating the workflow.**

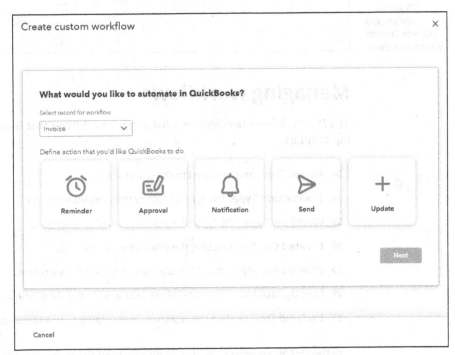

FIGURE 15-4:
The first
Create Custom
Workflow screen.

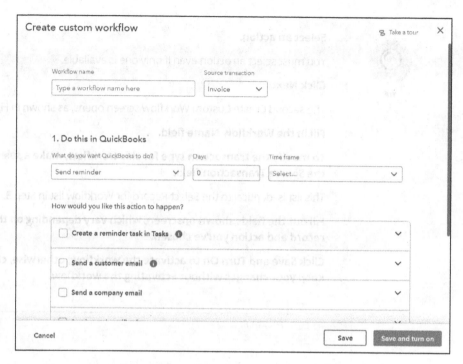

FIGURE 15-5:
The second
Create Custom
Workflow screen.

Managing workflows

The My Workflows tab displays a list of your workflows that includes the following columns:

- **Name:** The name assigned to the workflow.

- **Transaction Type:** The type of record the workflow acts on.

- **Workflow Type:** The type of action the workflow executes.

- **Created On:** The date that the workflow was created.

- **Created By:** The name of the user who initiated the workflow.

- **Last Updated By:** The name of the user who last updated the workflow.

- **Updated On:** The date the workflow was created or last updated.

Use the On/Off column to enable or disable workflows, or click the three-dot More Actions menu in the Actions column and then choose Edit, Copy, History, or Delete.

REMEMBER

The History command simply activates the History tab of the Workflows screen, as opposed to the history for a specific workflow.

Auditing workflows

The History tab provides an audit trail of all workflows, which you can access by choosing Workflow Automation ⇨ History. This screen displays the following columns:

>> **Record:** The transaction, report, or list item that the workflow is related to.

>> **Updated On:** The date and time that the workflow was last updated.

>> **Workflow Name:** The name assigned to the workflow.

>> **Workflow Status:** Started indicates that the workflow is active but may not have been completed, while Completed indicates that the workflow has finished.

>> **Action:** A View command displays a task pane that provides additional details.

Crafting Enhanced Custom Fields

Users in Advanced companies can add custom fields of the following types to customer, vendor, and project records, as well as certain transaction forms:

>> **Text and Number:** A free-form field that will accept up to 31 characters.

>> **Number:** A field that will accept up to 15 digits. You can enter periods but not commas in a number field.

>> **Date:** A field that will accept dates in mm/dd/yyyy format.

TIP

You can quickly enter dates within the current year by entering a month and a day, like 1/1 for New Year's Day, and then pressing the Tab key to automatically append the current year.

>> **Drop-down List:** A field that holds up to 100 predefined options.

You can assign up to 12 custom fields to each category — customer, vendor, transaction, or project — allowing for a total of 48 custom fields. Custom fields can be added to the following transaction forms, both onscreen and in print:

>> Sales Receipt

>> Invoice

>> Estimate

- » Credit Memo
- » Refund Receipt
- » Purchase Order

You can only designate up to three custom fields per form to be included in print. Additionally, custom fields can be displayed onscreen, but not in print, on the following forms:

- » Expense
- » Bill
- » Check
- » Vendor Credit
- » Credit Card Credit

Creating pre-defined custom fields

Here's how to create a pre-defined custom field:

1. **Choose the Gear icon ⇨ Custom Fields.**

   The Custom Fields screen opens.

2. **Click Add Field.**

   Add Custom Field task pane opens, as shown in Figure 15-6.

3. **Select from the Suggestion for You section, such as Sales Rep.**

   QuickBooks will preselect a data type, category, add the field to any applicable transaction, and toggle the Print On Form for selected forms. Two Dropdown List Item fields will appear when applicable; click Add Item as needed to add additional fields.

4. **Override the default settings and fill in any Dropdown lists if needed.**

5. **Click Save to close the Add Custom Field task pane and add the new field.**

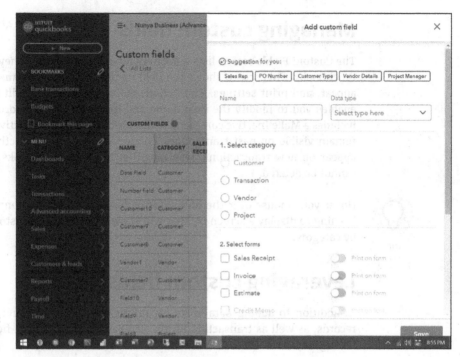

FIGURE 15-6:
The Add Custom
Field screen.

Defining custom fields manually

You can also add custom fields manually:

1. **Click Add Field on the Custom fields screen.**

   Add Custom Field task pane opens, as shown in Figure 15-6.

2. **Fill in the Name field.**

3. **Select from the Data Types field.**

4. **Make a choice from the Select Category section.**

   Choose Transaction if you only want the field to appear exclusively on transaction forms. Conversely, you can choose Customer, Vendor, or Project to have the custom field appear on the corresponding records, as well as optionally on transaction forms.

5. **Select the corresponding checkboxes if you want the field to appear on one or more transaction forms, and optionally choose Print On Form.**

   REMEMBER

   Custom field data types and categories cannot be modified once the field has been created, but all other settings, such as Name and Select Forms can be changed.

6. **Click Save to close the Create Custom Field task pane and create the new field.**

Managing custom fields

The Custom Fields screen lists custom fields in the order that they were added to QuickBooks. This screen shows the field names, categories, forms that the fields appear, and print settings. The Actions column features an Edit command that enables you to modify the field name and form settings. The drop-down menu includes a Make Inactive command to disable custom fields. Inactive custom fields remain visible on past transactions created when they were active but will not appear on new transactions. Like most list items in QuickBooks, custom fields cannot be deleted.

TIP

Hover your mouse over the blue information icon in the Custom Fields column heading to display a screen tip that will show the number of custom fields in use by category.

Leveraging custom fields

In addition to adding data entry capabilities to customer, vendor, and project records, as well as transaction forms, you can also use custom fields in the following ways:

- >> **Sort:** Add a custom field to a record or transaction list and then click the column heading.
- >> **Filter:** Click Search and then enter the custom field name in the Search field.
- >> **Report:** Custom fields can be used in the following fashion on reports:
  - *Column:* Expand reports by adding custom fields.
  - *Sort:* Sort reports based upon custom fields.
  - *Group:* Aggregate related items together on reports.
  - *Filter:* Use custom fields as report criteria.

Recording Expense Claims

The Expense Claims feature allows you to invite employees to submit expense reimbursement requests. Employees can upload a copy of their receipt or initiate an expense claim manually, and then in either case indicate whether they are requesting reimbursement. You must first invite one or more employees or vendors to use the feature, and then you can make some minor customizations. Going forward, expense claim requests will appear on the Expense Claims screen for approval. You can then convert the requests into Expense transactions.

Configuring expense claims

Carry out the following steps to invite one or more employees to use the Expense Claims feature and then tailor the feature to suit your needs:

1. **Log in to a QuickBooks Advanced company as an admin user.**

2. **Choose Expenses ⇨ Expense Claims.**

3. **Choose Manage Settings and then carry out these steps:**

    a. *Choose Manage Users and add one or more users or adjust their user rights to have access to expense claims.*

    I discuss managing user's roles and rights in Advanced companies in Chapter 13.

    b. *Choose Manage Categories and create nicknames for one or more categories that you want your employee to be able to code expenses to.*

REMEMBER

QuickBooks confusingly uses the term *category* in multiple contexts. Many transaction screens in QuickBooks use the word category as a euphemism for account, meaning an account on your chart of accounts.

    c. *Click Manage Expense Form to enable employees to code expenses to customers, projects, classes, and/or locations.*

REMEMBER

The Add Expense screen that your employees use to record expenses includes an optional Customer/Project field your employees can type free form text into, unless you enable the Customers list, which then allows employees to choose a customer from your customer list.

Entering an expense claim

Any employees with access to the Expense Claim feature can record expenditures by logging into QuickBooks Online via their computer or by using the QuickBooks Online mobile app, which I discuss in Chapter 7. Users can use the following steps to record expenses via their computer:

1. **Choose Expenses ⇨ Expense Claim.**

2. **Click New Expense Claim and then select Upload Receipt or Enter Expense Info Manually.**

    You will be prompted to select a .PDF, .JPG, .PNG, or .JPEG file if you choose Upload Receipt.

3. **Complete the Amount, Transaction Date, Vendor, and Business Purpose fields, along with any of the optional fields. Click I Need to Be Reimbursed, if applicable.**

If you specified one or more nicknames for categories, the optional Category field will show the nicknames you created. Otherwise, this field will not appear.

REMEMBER

The Vendor field is not tied to your list of vendors but rather is an input field that accepts up to 70 characters. If your company makes direct purchases from Amazon, any reports where Amazon is the vendor do not include expense claim transactions where an employee listed Amazon as the vendor as well.

4. **Click Submit for Review.**

The expense claim appears on the Expense Claims screen. Amounts shown don't appear in your general ledger or on your financial statements until the expense claim is approved.

Approving expense claims

Admin users can approve or delete expense claims by carrying out the following steps:

1. **Choose Expenses ⇨ Expense Claim.**

The For Review tab of the Expense Claims screen lists any expense claims that need to be processed.

2. **Click Review in the Action column for an expense claim.**

The Uploaded Receipt screen opens, no matter whether your employee actually uploaded a receipt or manually entered the expense claim.

3. **Choose Receipt or Bill from the Document Type field.**

Choose Receipt if you want to record an expense transaction to your books for a charge your employee made on a company credit or debit card. Otherwise, choose Bill if you need to reimburse your employee.

4. **Complete the required fields for the given transaction type.**

The required fields for Receipt transactions are Bank/Credit Card Account, Transaction Date, Account/Category, and Amount. Alternatively, you must complete the Payee, Transaction Date, Due Date, Category/Amount, and then Amount fields.

5. **Click Save and New.**

6. **If warranted, match the expense claim with an existing transaction in QuickBooks; otherwise, click Create Bill or Create Expense.**

REMEMBER

The Expense Claims feature confusingly uses the terms *Receipt* and *Expense* interchangeably, which can further be confused with Sales Receipt transactions, which I discuss in Chapter 2. A simple way to keep it straight is to think of an Expense Claim as attaching a purchase receipt to an expense or bill transaction.

You can pay any bills that you record via the Expense Claims feature in the manner described in Chapter 3.

Batching Transactions

The Simple Start, Essentials, and Plus versions of QuickBooks require you to enter, modify, or delete transactions one at a time. The Advanced version has all the same sales and expenses forms, but it also offers the Batch Transactions feature that enables you to create multiple transactions at once of the following types:

>> Invoices

>> Bank deposits

>> Sales receipts

>> Bills

>> Expenses

>> Checks

You can also import transactions from a CSV file created in Excel or Google Sheets.

TIP

You can also use the Batch Transactions feature to modify or delete existing invoices.

Creating transactions

Here are the steps for creating new transactions by way of the Batch Transactions feature:

1. **Choose +New ⇨ Batch Transactions.**

   The Batch Transactions screen shown in Figure 15-7 appears.

2. **Select a transaction type from the list, if necessary.**

3. **To turn columns on or off, click Customize Columns.**

You can choose to collapse or expand the Category Details and Item Details sections of the transaction grid by clicking the corresponding buttons in the title row of the grid.

4. **Select a transaction type from the list, if necessary.**

5. **Click the cell for the first column in row 1.**

Default values appear on certain fields, which you can then override.

Click Shortcuts to display a list of keyboard shortcuts you can use when working in the Batch Transactions grid.

6. **Complete the relevant columns.**

Calculated columns are shaded in gray and can't be modified.

7. **Right-click on any row number to reveal choices that vary based on transaction type but include variations on the following choices, among others:**

- **Duplicate Row:** A command generally appears that enables you to duplicate the given transaction type. Some transactions, such as invoices, have an additional command that allows you to duplicate the row for multiple customers.

- **Insert Row Below:** This command inserts a new row into the Batch Transactions grid.

- **Insert Line Item Below:** Batch transactions are assumed to have a single line item unless you use this command to add line items as needed.

- **Delete Row:** This removes the row from the Batch Transactions grid.

8. **Add transactions to the grid as needed.**

9. **Click Save to post the transaction(s) to your books.**

A second version of the Save command appears for some transaction types, enabling you to make choices such as Save and Send or Save and Print.

TIP

Import CSV/Excel on the Batch Transactions screen is a shortcut to the Import Transactions screen that I discuss in Chapter 7, which enables you to import transactions into QuickBooks from comma-separated value (CSV) files. Create in Spreadsheets enables you to use Spreadsheet Sync to create and edit transactions in Excel, which I discuss in Chapter 16.

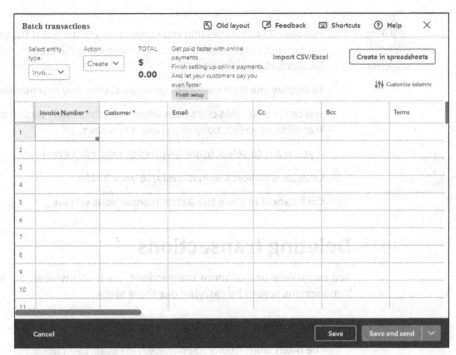

FIGURE 15-7:
The Batch
Transactions
screen.

Modifying transactions

You can use the Batch Transactions screen to edit multiple transactions, such as invoices, from a single screen:

1. **Choose +New ⇨ Batch Transactions.**

2. **Choose Invoice from the Select Entity Type field, if necessary.**

3. **Choose Modify from the Action menu.**

   Transactions dated within the past 30 days appear by default on a version of the Batch Transactions screen that includes selection checkboxes.

4. **To fine-tune the list of transactions, click Filter to display criteria options.**

5. **Click the checkboxes associated with the invoices you want to modify.**

   Click the checkbox in the header row of the Batch Transactions grid to select all invoices on the list at once.

TIP

6. **Click Edit to display a version of the Batch Transactions screen that shows all the invoice details, and then make changes to the invoices as needed.**

   Fields that you edit or that are affected by changes to other fields are marked with a red border so that you can keep track of the changes you've made.

REMEMBER

You can't undo changes that you made by way of the Batch Transactions screen, so consider making a backup before using this feature. I discuss the Backup feature in Chapter 13.

7. **To display the New Line Item command, click any row number.**

   You can't delete rows or invoices when using the Modify version of the Batch Transactions screen, but you can insert new rows.

8. **If you want to select other invoices to edit, click Previous.**

9. **Click Save to post the invoices(s) to your books.**

10. **Click Cancel to close the Batch Transactions screen.**

Deleting transactions

You can delete one or more transactions, such as invoices, by way of the Batch Transactions screen by carrying out these steps:

1. **Choose +New ⇨ Batch Transactions.**

   The Batch Transactions screen shown in Figure 15-7 opens.

2. **Choose Invoice from the Select Entity Type field, if necessary.**

3. **Choose Delete from the Action menu.**

   Invoices dated within the past 30 days appear by default.

4. **To fine-tune the list of transactions, click Filter and enter criteria.**

5. **Click the checkboxes associated with the invoices you want to delete.**

6. **Click Delete and then confirm the deletion.**

7. **Click Cancel to close the Batch Transactions screen.**

Recognizing Revenue

Accounting platforms such as QuickBooks Online Advanced can help ensure that your business follows generally accepted accounting principles, also known as GAAP. Think of these standards as being similar to the rules of the road when you're driving. When everyone follows agreed-upon and often legally mandated traffic rules and conventions, for the most part, we all stay safe and avoid crashes. Similarly, GAAP ensures that businesses are keeping their books in a similar fashion, which makes peer comparisons within an industry possible and facilitates the purchase and sale of businesses.

Some businesses, particularly public firms and large firms with more than $25 million in revenue, are required to follow additional standards, such as those promulgated by the Financial Accounting Standards Board (FASB). ASC 606 is one of many rules that FASB has issued. (ASC is short for accounting standards codification.) This rule specifically relates to revenue recognition, meaning that revenue should be posted to your books in a timeline commensurate to when the goods or services are being provided.

Maybe your customer pays you $36,000 upfront on July 1, 2025, for a three-year service contract. Both GAAP and ASC 606 direct that you don't recognize $36,000 in revenue in July 2025 and then zero revenue for August 2025 through June 2027. Instead, you record the $36,000 to a liability account, such as prepaid revenue, and move $1,000 of the contract per month to something like service revenue until the contract has been fulfilled.

The Revenue Recognition feature can automatically allocate service revenue evenly on a monthly basis over the entire contract. From a GAAP standpoint, this both smooths out spikes in revenue and matches revenue with ongoing expenses that are incurred to fulfill the contract.

Let me share some caveats before I show you how to enable this feature:

>> The Revenue Recognition feature cannot be turned off once it has been used to record a transaction.

>> You can only use Revenue Recognition with Service type items on your invoices.

>> The Service Dates listed on your invoices cannot be in the past.

>> You cannot preview or edit the journal entries that Revenue Recognition generates.

Phew! Writing all of that out made me feel like one of those voices at the end of a drug commercial that discloses all of the potential side effects.

Enabling revenue recognition

Oh, hi! You're still here? Great! Let's see how to turn on the Revenue Recognition feature:

1. **Choose the Gear icon ⇨ Account Setting ⇨ Sales.**

   The Account and Settings screen opens.

2. **Click Edit in the Products & Services section.**

3. **Toggle Revenue Recognition on.**

4. **Click Save and then Done.**

Enabling the feature here turns on the fields you need elsewhere to utilize revenue recognition.

REMEMBER

QuickBooks automatically posts revenue recognition entries at the end of each month.

Establishing a service with revenue recognition

The next step is to add a service item to your products and services list that utilizes revenue recognition. You need to create an item for each time span that revenue needs to be recognized over by following these steps:

1. **Choose the Gear icon ➪ Products and Services (or Sales or Sales & Expenses ➪ Products and Services).**

   The Products and Services screen opens.

2. **Choose New ➪ Service.**

   The Product/Service task pane opens.

3. **Fill in the requisite fields to create a service item.**

   I discuss creating service items in Chapter 2.

4. **Click the I Recognize Revenue for This Product Monthly checkbox shown in Figure 15-8.**

5. **Make a selection from the Liability Account list, such as Deferred Revenue, or create a new liability account where the revenue for the service will initially post.**

   Each month QuickBooks automatically moves a portion of the service into the income account that you specify for the service.

6. **Specify a service duration in months or years.**

7. **Complete any other fields needed and then click Save and Close.**

You can now use the service you created on invoices you generate for your customers.

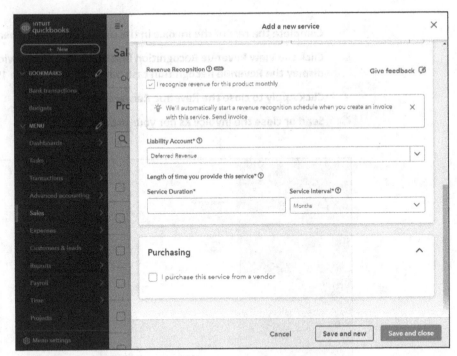

FIGURE 15-8:
Revenue
Recognition
option for
service items.

Creating invoices that use revenue recognition

QuickBooks automatically allocates the revenue for service items that are tagged as utilizing revenue recognition. I discuss creating invoices in more detail in Chapter 2, so I offer streamlined instructions here:

1. **Choose +New ⇨ Invoice.**

   The Invoice screen opens.

2. **Fill out the top portion of the invoice in the usual fashion.**

   See Chapter 2 for all of the gory details.

3. **Fill in the Service Date column on each row that includes a service entailing revenue recognition.**

REMEMBER

   QuickBooks won't carry out automatic revenue recognition if you leave this field blank or choose a service item that doesn't have the Revenue Recognition option enabled.

4. **Choose a revenue recognition-enabled service from the Product/Service list for that row.**

5. **Complete the rest of the invoice in the usual fashion and then click Save.**

6. **Click the View Revenue Recognition link in the Product/Service field to display the Revenue Recognition task pane shown in Figure 15-9.**

7. **Click Apply to close the Revenue Recognition task pane.**

8. **Send or close the invoice as per your usual steps.**

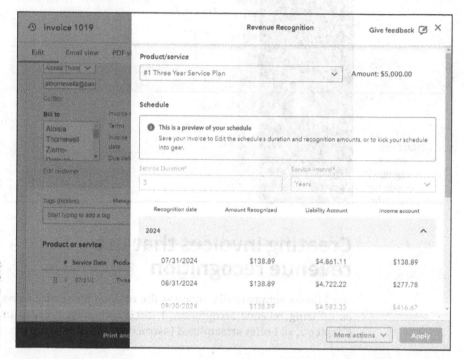

FIGURE 15-9:
Revenue
recognition
schedule for a
service item
that has been
invoiced.

Running the Revenue Recognition report

The Revenue Recognition report documents transactions where revenue has been allocated across two or more periods. QuickBooks automatically records revenue recognition entries at the end of each month, so if you enter an invoice that uses a revenue recognition–enabled service on August 1, the transaction won't appear on the Revenue Recognition report until September 1 because, until that date, there won't be anything to report. Here's how to run the Revenue Recognition report:

1. **Choose Reports (or Business Overview ⇨ Reports).**

   The Reports screen opens.

2. **Type** Rev **in the Find a Report by Name field and then choose Revenue Recognition Report.**

   Although you cannot customize it, the Revenue Recognition report also appears in the Custom Report Builder section of the Reports screen.

3. **Filter the report by date range if you want.**

   I discuss standard QuickBooks reports in Chapter 6 and the Custom Report Builder in Chapter 14.

Tracking Fixed Assets and Calculating Depreciation

Accountants refer to depreciation as a non-cash expense, namely because you do not write a check to anyone, and you can't put depreciation on your credit card. Depreciation is a means of both matching expenses with revenue and recognizing the diminishing value of an asset over time. Let's say that you buy a $12,000 piece of equipment you plan to use for five years and then sell for $2,000. Generally accepted accounting principles (GAAP) require you to record the equipment on your balance sheet as an asset. You may be able to take a Section 179 deduction on your tax return to record the $12,000 expense in the year of purchase, but GAAP prevents you from recording a $12,000 expense all in one year.

In this case, because you're expecting the asset in effect to lose $2,000 in value each year due to wear and tear, you'll need to record $2,000 in depreciation expense each year for five years. Of course, this is just for this one asset. You must perform similar calculations and entries for every depreciable asset your business purchases, which includes but is not limited to buildings, equipment, furniture, fixtures, vehicles, and so on.

REMEMBER

Land is not depreciable, so you must separate the value of any buildings from the value of the underlying land when computing depreciation.

As you can see from my brief example, fixed asset accounting can get tricky fast, which makes the Fixed Assets screen a welcome addition for companies with Advanced subscriptions. Unlike Revenue Recognition, you don't have to enable a feature and can instead jump right into depreciating your assets:

1. **Choose Advanced Accounting ⇨ Fixed Assets from the sidebar menu.**

   The Fixed Assets screen opens.

2. Click Add Asset.

The Add Fixed Asset task pane opens.

3. Enter the name of the asset.

This can be anything that helps you identify a specific asset.

4. Fill in the class, location, and/or description fields, if desired.

5. Enter an amount in the Purchase Price field.

This is the amount that you paid for the asset.

REMEMBER

You must still record the purchase of any assets directly in your books.

6. Enter an amount in the Salvage Value field that reflects your best estimate of what you can sell the asset for at the end of its useful life, if desired.

The salvage value defaults to zero if you leave this field blank.

7. Enter a number in the Useful Life field.

The useful life of depreciable assets is usually recorded in years.

8. Choose Straightline, Double Declining, or 150% Accelerated from the Depreciation Method list.

Consult your accountant or a tax professional if you're not sure which one to choose.

9. Enter the date that the asset first started depreciating in the Depreciation Start Date field.

You can enter any date in this field. An Accumulated Depreciation Amount field is displayed if you enter a prior date.

10. Click Calculate.

The Accumulated Depreciation Amount field reflects the current accumulated depreciation amount. The Calculate button doesn't work until you fill in the Purchase Price, Depreciation Method, and Depreciation Start Date fields.

REMEMBER

You cannot edit the accumulated depreciation amount, but you can record an adjusted entry to your books if the amount that QuickBooks computes differs from your current fixed asset accounting records.

11. Fill in the Asset, Depreciation Expense, and Accumulated Depreciation Account fields.

12. Click Save to save the record.

A depreciation schedule for the asset appears within the Add Fixed Asset task pane. Click any year to display the monthly depreciation for that year.

13. Click Close to return to the Fixed Assets screen.

The asset is displayed on the Fixed Assets screen.

The Actions column of the Fixed Assets screen contains commands to view or delete an asset. The View command displays a Fixed Assets Detail task pane that shows all of the inputs you provided, along with the depreciation schedule. At the time of writing, you are limited to viewing depreciation schedules online in Quick-Books because there is no provision for printing the schedules. QuickBooks does provide a Fixed Assets Detail report that provides an overview of your fixed asset accounting.

TIP

Click Add Multiple Assets to display a batch entry screen that works in a similar fashion to the Batch Transactions feature I discussed in the "Batching Transactions" section earlier in this chapter.

Chapter **16**

Synchronizing QuickBooks and Excel

The Spreadsheet Sync feature serves as a conduit between QuickBooks Online companies and Microsoft Excel. As you'll see in this chapter, once you install an add-in, you can create refreshable reports in Excel that are directly connected to your QuickBooks companies. Most Spreadsheet Sync features require an Advanced subscription, with one exception. You can create consolidated reports that combine results from Simple Start, Essentials, Plus, and/or Advanced companies when at least one company has an Advanced subscription. You can also use Spreadsheet Sync to add and edit list records and transactions as well as create or edit company-level budgets.

TIP

I discuss the QuickBooks App Store in Chapter 7, where you can find apps that allow you to import/export data into any subscription level, including Simple Start, Essentials, Plus, or Advanced companies. For example, check out Flash Reports for QuickBooks (www.finaticalsoftware.com).

Getting Started with Spreadsheet Sync

Spreadsheet Sync is a powerful feature that empowers you to make wholesale changes to lists and transactions in Advanced companies.

Users can carry out any of the following actions:

>> **Create a report:** This includes standard and custom reports.

>> **Add and edit data:** This includes adding and editing list entries for most QuickBooks lists. This capability is why only one user can have access to Spreadsheet Sync at a time; otherwise, one user could overwrite the changes that another user is making at the same time.

>> **Run multi-company reports:** This involves creating combined Profit & Loss, Balance Sheet, and Trial Balance reports for up to ten companies, including companies that have Simple Start, Essentials, or Plus subscriptions. All companies must use the same currency.

>> **Manage budgets:** Create and edit budgets in Excel that can be returned to QuickBooks.

Installing the Spreadsheet Sync Add-in

You must install a free Microsoft Excel add-in on any computer that you want to use Spreadsheet Sync with by carrying out these steps:

1. **In QuickBooks, choose the Gear icon ⇨ Spreadsheet Sync.**

   The instructions screen shown in Figure 16-1 appears.

2. **Click Let's Go to begin the installation process, and then, if prompted, choose Open Excel.**

   Your browser may ask you for permission to open Excel. Alternatively, a Spreadsheet Sync.xlsx workbook may simply appear in your Downloads folder. In that case, choose File ⇨ Open in Excel to open the workbook manually.

REMEMBER

   At this point, Excel for macOS users may encounter a warning that the file format and the extension for the filename Spreadsheet Sync.htm do not match and that the file might be corrupted or unstable. You can safely disregard this warning and click Yes to continue.

3. **Click Accept and Continue, as shown in Figure 16-2.**

   Excel add-ins enhance the application with additional functionality.

4. **Choose File ⇨ Close or press Ctrl+W (Cmd+W for Mac) to close the Spreadsheet Sync workbook. Then click Don't Save.**

   Spreadsheet Sync is now part of your Excel application.

5. **Choose File ⇨ New or press Ctrl+N (Cmd+N for Mac) to create a blank workbook.**

6. **Choose Home ⇨ Spreadsheet Sync to display the task pane shown in Figure 16-3.**

   All Spreadsheet Sync–related tasks are initiated by way of this task pane. Going forward, you can carry out tasks in the task pane or by way of the Spreadsheet Sync ribbon tab that appears within workbooks that have an established connection to QuickBooks.

The Spreadsheet Sync command should appear on the right side of the Home tab of Excel's ribbon. If you do not see the command, choose Home ⇨ Add-ins, search for Spreadsheet Sync, and then click Add.

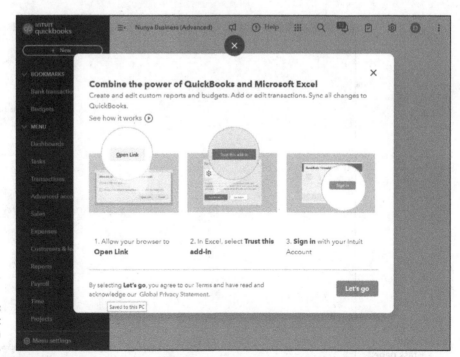

FIGURE 16-1:
Spreadsheet Sync installation instructions.

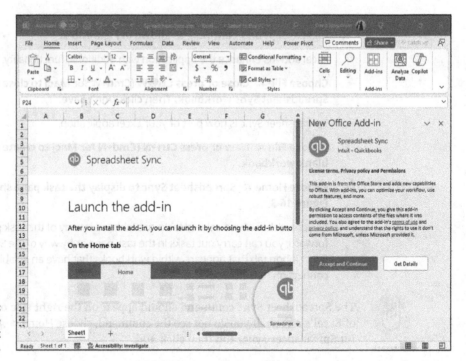

FIGURE 16-2:
Installing the
Spreadsheet
Sync add-in.

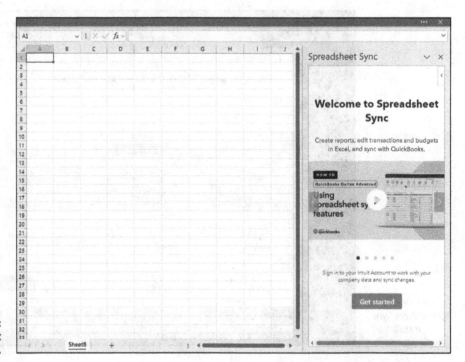

FIGURE 16-3:
Spreadsheet Sync
task pane.

Signing in to Spreadsheet Sync

Here's how to sign in to initiate a Spreadsheet Sync task or report with a new or existing Excel workbook:

1. **Activate the workbook and then the worksheet where you want to use Spreadsheet Sync.**

2. **Choose Home ⇨ Spreadsheet Sync if the Spreadsheet Sync task pane isn't currently displayed.**

3. **Scroll down the task pane and then click Get Started to display the login pane. Enter your QuickBooks Online credentials and then click Continue.**

   You remain logged in to Spreadsheet Sync until you close Excel. Accountant users will be prompted to choose their firm's name from a separate list.

4. **Select a QuickBooks company if prompted and then click Next.**

REMEMBER

The Search for a Company or Firm list shows all active QuickBooks subscriptions you have access to, including Simple Start, Essentials, or Plus companies that can only be accessed via Spreadsheet Sync when you're creating a multi-company report.

You see the What Do You Want to Do? pane shown in Figure 16-4. This is the starting point for initiating any new type of activity via Spreadsheet Sync.

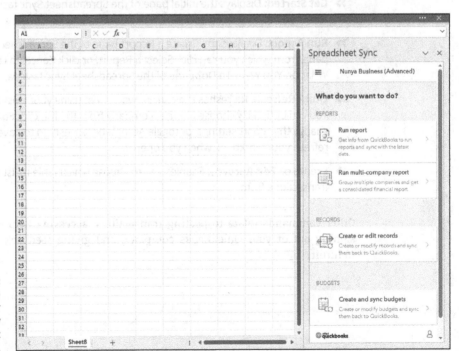

FIGURE 16-4:
This is the starting point for every new Spreadsheet Sync report or task.

You're logged out of Spreadsheet Sync in the same fashion that you're logged out of QuickBooks Online after a period of inactivity. If this happens, click Sign In, enter your credentials as prompted, and then click Sign In again.

Utilizing the Spreadsheet Sync ribbon tab

Although you may not see it in Excel yet, a Spreadsheet Sync tab appears in Excel's menu structure, known as the ribbon, whenever you utilize a Spreadsheet Sync feature or activate a workbook that contains data provided by Spreadsheet Sync. As shown in Figure 16-5, the tab contains the following major commands:

>> **Group:** Displays the Company tab of the Spreadsheet Sync task pane and allows you to add a company to your existing report group or to create a new group:

  • Click Group Multiple companies if you have not yet created a report group.

  • Click Add Company if you want to add a company to the report group.

  You must have the same user ID or email address in every QuickBooks Online company that you want to include in a report group. An easy way to see a list of which companies you can include is to choose the Gear icon ⇨ Switch Company within QuickBooks Online.

>> **Get Started:** Displays the initial pane of the Spreadsheet Sync task pane that allows you to choose an activity.

>> **Run Report:** Displays the Create a Report pane of the Spreadsheet Sync task pane, from which you can click Select a Report, or click Cancel to return to the What Do You Want To Do? pane of the Spreadsheet Sync task pane.

>> **Quick Refresh:** Refreshes the current worksheet using your existing filters. You can optionally choose another company from the list, click Edit Filters to change the report settings, or toggle Automatic Refresh on to have Excel refresh your workbook when you open it.

>> **Create or Edit Records:** Enables you to choose which table to list records or transactions from.

Other commands relate to posting transactions, accessing help documentation, signing out of your QuickBooks company, and giving feedback on the feature to Intuit.

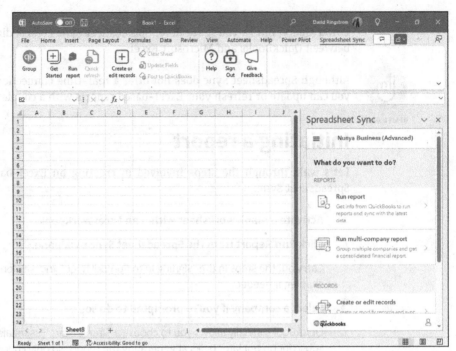

FIGURE 16-5:
The Spreadsheet
Sync ribbon tab
in Microsoft Excel.

Uninstalling Spreadsheet Sync

You'll most likely find Spreadsheet Sync to be a highly useful tool, but you can uninstall the add-in at any time. Keep in mind that doing so means that you will no longer be able to update any of your reports until you reinstall the add-in. Here's how to uninstall Spreadsheet Sync:

1. **Right-click on the Spreadsheet Sync command on the Home tab of the ribbon in Microsoft Excel and then choose Remove Add-In.**

2. **Click Yes when the Remove Add-In prompt appears.**

   Spreadsheet Sync no longer appears on the Home tab of the Excel ribbon.

Creating Refreshable Reports in Excel

As I discuss in Chapters 6 and 20, you can export most reports to Excel from QuickBooks, but each report is simply a snapshot in time. This means that you must manually export new versions of reports that you use in Excel on a repetitive basis. In Chapter 21, I discuss how you can partially automate this process with

Power Query, but as you'll see here, Spreadsheet Sync creates direct connections between QuickBooks and Microsoft Excel.

REMEMBER

Although Spreadsheet Sync does not offer a real-time connection to your books, you can update or refresh your Excel-based reports with a couple of mouse clicks.

Initiating a report

Let's walk through the steps involved in creating an Excel-based report with Spreadsheet Sync:

1. **Activate a blank worksheet within an Excel workbook.**

2. **Click Run Report from the Spreadsheet Sync task pane.**

   Carry out the steps in the "Signing in to Spreadsheet Sync" section earlier in this chapter, if needed.

3. **Select a company if you're prompted to do so.**

   QuickBooks initially allows you to choose a Simple Start, Essentials, or Plus subscription but later balks at generating the report, so only choose companies that have Advanced subscriptions.

4. **Make a choice from the Select Report list.**

5. **Choose a saved filter or make choices from the General and Filters sections, if desired.**

TIP

   Click Save New Filter to save your settings changes in the General and Filters section for use with other reports.

6. **Click Run Report**

   The report now appears in the active worksheet, along with a Spreadsheet Sync tab in Excel's ribbon, which I discuss in the "Utilizing the Spreadsheet Sync ribbon tab" section earlier in this chapter.

7. **Click Go Home to return to the main pane of the Spreadsheet Sync task pane.**

   You can now add reports to the workbook as needed, but make sure to add and then activate a blank worksheet before starting the process of adding another report.

Utilizing a template

As of this writing, Spreadsheet Sync offers a single Management Report template that you can use to create reports for two or more entities, including those that have Simple Start, Essentials, or Plus subscriptions. Here's how to use the Management Report template:

1. **Activate a blank worksheet within an Excel workbook.**

2. **Click Run a Report from the Spreadsheet Sync task pane.**

   Carry out the steps in the "Signing in to Spreadsheet Sync" section earlier in this chapter, if needed.

3. **Select a company if you're prompted to do so.**

   QuickBooks allows you to choose a Simple Start, Essentials, or Plus subscription but later balks at generating the report, so only choose companies that have Advanced subscriptions.

4. **Click Run Report.**

5. **Click the Template Gallery link beneath the Select Report list.**

6. **Click Management Report and then Get Template.**

   Four new worksheets that don't yet contain dates are added to your workbook:

   - **Notes and Controls:** This worksheet has parameters that control the output of your reports.

   - **Trial Balance — Multiple Period:** This worksheet initially displays an empty template for a multi-period trial balance report.

   - **Balance Sheet — Multiple Period:** This worksheet initially contains an empty multi-period balance sheet.

   - **Profit and Loss — Multiple Period:** You guessed it: A blank Profit and Loss template is hanging out here now.

7. **Set the parameters for your report by way of the Notes & Controls worksheet shown in Figure 16-6.**

8. **Select a company from each drop-down list and then click Quick Refresh for each sheet shown in Figure 16-7.**

REMEMBER

You must first create a report group that contains any Simple Start, Essentials, or Plus companies that you want to include before you can select them for use with this template. I show how to do this in the "Consolidating multiple companies" section later in this chapter.

TIP

If you accidentally overwrite a worksheet in Excel for Windows, choose File ⇨ Info. Click any time stamp in the Manage Workbook section — if available — to open a backup copy of your workbook alongside the live copy of the file to restore any overwritten data. Alternatively, if you save your files to OneDrive, click the filename at the top of the Excel workbook, choose Manage Versions, and choose an earlier version to open.

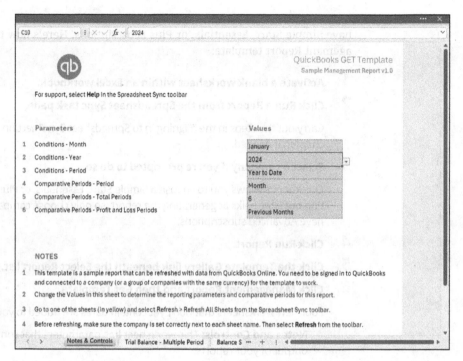

FIGURE 16-6:
Set the parameters for your management report template by way of the Notes & Controls worksheet.

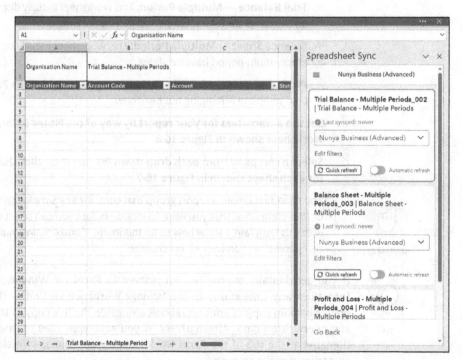

FIGURE 16-7:
You can choose which company to display on each Management Report worksheet.

TIP

Most Spreadsheet Sync reports have predetermined formats, but you can add or delete columns as needed once a report appears within an Excel worksheet. There are no restrictions on adding or removing worksheets within workbooks that utilize Spreadsheet Sync.

Consolidating multiple companies

You can combine the Profit and Loss and Balance Sheet reports for two or more QuickBooks Online companies. At least one company must have an Advanced subscription, but the other companies can be a mix of Simple Start, Essentials, or Plus subscriptions. Here's how to create a Multi-Company Report:

1. **Choose Run Multi-Company Report from the Spreadsheet Sync task pane.**

2. **Choose an existing group from the Select Group list. Then click Add New Group on the Select Group list or create a new group if prompted.**

   Here are the steps to add a new group:

   a. *Fill in the Group Name field.*

   b. *Choose a base currency for the reports.*

   Your spreadsheet is connected to a live foreign exchange (forex) feed if you choose one or more companies that have a different base currency.

TIP

   c. *Click the Add Companies to Group checkboxes for two or more companies.*

   Your user ID/email address must be the same across all the companies.

   d. *Click Save.*

REMEMBER

3. **Click Select Report.**

4. **Choose Balance Sheet – Multiple Periods, Profit and Loss by Class, Profit and Loss – Multiple Periods, or Trial Balance – Multiple Periods.**

5. **Change the report options if desired.**

6. **Click Run Report.**

   You can insert a new worksheet and add a different report by carrying out Steps 1 through 6 again. You can also add worksheets and create reports for different time periods.

7. **Choose New Sheet or Current Sheet from the Run Report in Current Sheet prompt.**

TIP

If the Spreadsheet Sync task pane starts reporting an error, saving, and closing your workbook, exiting Microsoft Excel and then opening your workbook again should clear up the issue. In the worst-case scenario, delete the affected worksheet(s) and create the reports again.

Refreshing reports

Spreadsheet Sync does not offer a real-time connection to your books, so changes that you make to your accounting records don't appear in any Excel-based reports until you initiate a refresh. You can initiate a refresh by way of the Spreadsheet Sync task pane or the Spreadsheet Sync ribbon tab. Use the following steps to initiate a refresh with the Spreadsheet Sync task pane:

1. **In Excel, choose Home ⇨ Spreadsheet Sync to display the Spreadsheet Sync task pane.**

2. **Sign in to Spreadsheet Sync if necessary. Choose a company and then click Next.**

3. **Activate an Excel worksheet that contains a Spreadsheet Sync report.**

4. **Click Run a Report in the Spreadsheet Sync task pane.**

5. **Click Refresh if displayed on the task pane. Otherwise, click Quick Refresh for each report that you want to update.**

WARNING

You cannot refresh multiple reports at once, but must instead click Quick Refresh for each individual report that appears within the Spreadsheet Sync task pane.

TIP

You can optionally click Automatic Refresh for each worksheet that you want to update each time you sign in to Spreadsheet Sync or open the workbook that contains the report(s) while you're signed in to Spreadsheet Sync.

Managing List Records with Spreadsheet Sync

You can add or edit the following types of list records with Spreadsheet Sync:

>> Vendors, Customers, and Projects

>> Chart of Accounts

>> Inventory Items, Non-Inventory Items, and Service Items

>> Employees

>> Classes and Departments

TIP

Spreadsheet Sync refers to the Locations list as *Departments*.

WARNING

You can't undo a sync within QuickBooks that adds to lists or edits existing records. However, you may be able to use the Undo command within Excel to undo changes to existing records that you've made, which you could then sync with QuickBooks.

REMEMBER

See Chapter 13 for instructions on creating a backup of your company that you can restore if you sync any data unintentionally.

You use the same initial steps whether you're crediting or editing records. An additional step is required to make the data from your lists appear in the worksheet:

1. **Choose Create or Edit Records from the Spreadsheet Sync task pane.**

2. **Choose a company from the Select Company list if you have more than one Advanced subscription.**

    This field isn't editable if you have just a single QuickBooks Online Advanced subscription.

3. **Make a selection, such as Vendors & Customers, from the Select Record Type list.**

4. **Choose Add New Records to QuickBooks or Edit QuickBooks Records and Sync Back.**

5. **Click Get Template.**

    A worksheet appears in the active workbook spreadsheet, as shown in Figure 16-8, along with a separate Notes & Controls worksheet that documents certain restrictions and procedures to use with Spreadsheet Sync.

6. **Add or change records as desired.**

    Whether you retrieve your records or not, you can use the template to post new customers, vendors, and projects to QuickBooks. Choose Yes in Column A for any rows where you edit an existing record or where you add new records. Choose a List Type, such as Customer, Vendor, or Project in Column B for new records, and at a minimum, enter a display name in Column C.

REMEMBER

Drop-down lists appear in certain columns, such as the Yes/No/Archive in the Post column. If you don't see the drop-down lists, move down one more row. The gray row below the column headings isn't editable, so start with the next row beneath that.

7. **Choose Yes or Archive in the Post column for any changes that you want to sync to QuickBooks.**

   The Archive option marks the list item as inactive.

8. **Click Sync to QuickBooks in the Spreadsheet Sync task pane.**

9. **Click Sync to confirm that you want to sync the data.**

   You can now close the Spreadsheet Sync task pane. You can display it when you need it by choosing Home ⇨ Spreadsheet Sync in Excel.

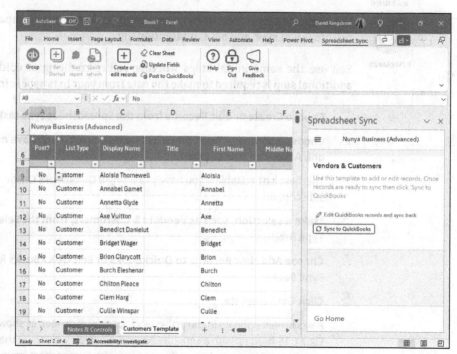

FIGURE 16-8:
Choose Yes, No, or Archive in the Post column when adding or updating records that you want to sync to QuickBooks.

Reviewing, Editing, and Creating Transactions

You can choose the following transaction templates from the Spreadsheet Sync task pane to create or edit the corresponding transaction types:

>> Invoices and Bills (includes Invoices, Bills, Credit Memos, and Vendor Credits)

>> Journal Entries

>> Purchase and Sales Receipts

>> Time Activities

>> Estimates

TIP

Transaction lists typically have multiple required fields. Be sure to pay close attention to the onscreen instructions.

WARNING

Be sure to choose a date range when you are editing transactions in companies that have been on QuickBooks Online for years or that have significant transaction volume, otherwise Spreadsheet Sync may become unresponsive.

WARNING

You can't undo a sync within QuickBooks that adds transactions, but you can do a second sync that voids unwanted transactions. You may be able to use the Undo command within Excel to undo changes to existing transactions that you've made, which you could then sync with QuickBooks.

See Chapter 13 for instructions on creating a backup of your company that you can restore if you sync any data unintentionally.

Here's how to use Spreadsheet Sync to edit or create transactions in QuickBooks. I walk you through customer- and vendor-related transactions specifically:

1. **Choose Create or Edit Records from the Spreadsheet Sync task pane or the Spreadsheet Sync ribbon tab.**

2. **Choose a company from the Select Company list if you have more than one Advanced subscription.**

This field isn't editable if you have just a single QuickBooks Online Advanced subscription.

3. **Make a selection from the Select a Record Type list, such as Invoices and Bills.**

A blank worksheet appears in your workbook, along with a separate Notes & Controls worksheet that documents certain restrictions and procedures to use with Spreadsheet Sync. The Notes & Controls worksheet also displays transaction counts and sometimes totals.

4. **Choose Add New Records to QuickBooks or Edit QuickBooks Records and Sync Back.**

5. **Add or change records as desired.**

Drop-down lists appear in certain columns, such as Yes/No/Void in the Post column. If you don't see the drop-down lists, move down one more row. The gray row below the column headings isn't an editable row, so start with the next row beneath that.

REMEMBER

You can use payment columns appearing to the right to record invoice payments and bill payments.

TIP

Templates that include an Upload Sheet column enable you to attach an Excel worksheet from the current workbook to the transaction in QuickBooks. Refer to the Notes & Controls worksheet for guidance. For instance, in the case of Invoices and Bills, the supporting worksheet name must be identical to the Invoice/Bill Number field in the template.

6. **Click Sync to QuickBooks in the Spreadsheet Sync task pane.**

7. **Click Sync to confirm that you want to sync the data.**

WARNING

Be mindful when editing transactions because you can easily solve one problem and create new ones, such as creating discrepancies between the payments posted against invoices or bills. Study the template carefully and read all notes and warnings. In Chapter 13, I discuss how you can back up and restore a QuickBooks Advanced company.

Creating or Editing Consolidated Budgets

Companies with QuickBooks Plus subscriptions or that want to create subdivided budgets are limited to the budget-creating techniques I discuss in Chapter 12. Subdivided budgets are broken down by customer, location, or class, as opposed to consolidated budgets that are company-wide. Here's how to create consolidated budgets in Excel:

1. **Choose Create and Sync Budgets from the Spreadsheet Sync task pane.**

2. **The next steps depend on the choice that you make:**

    Use the following steps to create a new budget:

    a. *Click Create New Budget.*

    b. *Select your company, if prompted.*

    c. *Fill in the Name Your Budget field.*

    d. *Choose a period.*

    Spreadsheet Sync enables you to create a budget for the previous year, current year, or any of the five subsequent years.

    e. *Click Set Up Budget.*

To edit an existing budget, follow these steps:

a. *Click Create New Budget.*

b. *Select your company, if prompted.*

c. *Choose a budget from the Select Budget list.*

d. *Click Next.*

A Notes & Controls worksheet and a Consolidated Budget worksheet appear in your workbook.

The Notes & Controls worksheet shows your total budgeted revenue and expenses and includes data entry notes to keep in mind when budgeting.

3. **Update the Consolidated Budget worksheet, and then click Sync to QuickBooks in the Spreadsheet Sync task pane.**

TIP

You can only send the budget back to QuickBooks by way of the Spreadsheet Sync task pane, which you will likely close so that you can see more columns within the spreadsheet. In that case, choose Home ⇨ Spreadsheet Sync to display the task pane again.

5

QuickBooks Online Accountant Features

Explore essential tools and features.

Review and manage financial records for multiple clients.

Streamline your practice management.

IN THIS CHAPTER

» Initializing QuickBooks Online
   Accountant

» Building out your client list

» Overseeing your clients' books

» Managing administrative rights for
   QuickBooks companies

» Establishing your team

Chapter **17**

Coordinating Client and Team Management

Q uickBooks Online Accountant is a free practice management platform that enables accountants and their authorized team members to easily access their clients' QuickBooks companies on the fly with a single sign-on. Accounting practice owners receive a free QuickBooks Online Advanced subscription and a free Payroll Elite subscription for use in managing the accounting records for their firm. The platform also enables accountants to access subscription discounts that can be retained or shared with their clients, depending on who is paying for the subscription. You can manage just about any type of QuickBooks Online subscription in the Accountant version, including Self-Employed, Schedule C, and ProConnect Tax Online clients, but not Solopreneur.

Getting Started with QuickBooks Online Accountant

The Accountant version of QuickBooks is free, and you're not required to provide any sort of proof that you're an accountant. Visit https://quickbooks.intuit.com/accountant and then click Sign Up for Free on the left side of the screen to get started. Your home screen will look like Figure 17-1 after you complete the registration process and sign in. Going forward, you'll sign in at https://qbo.intuit.com, just as your clients do.

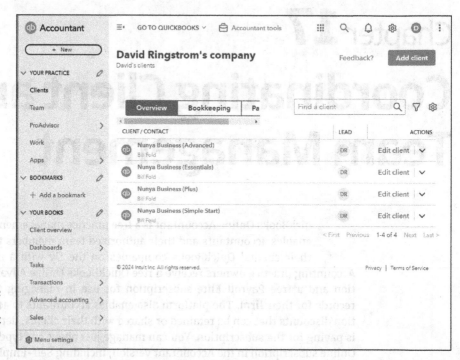

FIGURE 17-1: A typical Accountant version home screen.

TIP

Intuit's free ProAdvisor program entitles you to Online, Advanced Online, and Payroll Certified ProAdvisor designations at no cost. QuickBooks Desktop certification is available to those who purchase the desktop bundle add-on through the ProAdvisor program. Free continuing professional education (CPE) is offered to certified public accountants (CPAs) for completing any of the certifications, as well as for attending webinars, virtual conferences, and in-person events led by QuickBooks Accountant University.

Adding Companies to the Client List

You can add to your client list in three ways:

›› Establishing a new QuickBooks Online subscription for your client

›› Adding a client or prospective client to the list without a subscription

›› Accepting an accountant invitation from your client

Establishing new QuickBooks Online subscriptions

The Accountant version enables you to initiate Simple Start, Essentials, Plus, and Advanced subscriptions. Your clients need to initiate any other type of subscription, such as QuickBooks Self-Employed, and then invite you to be the accountant, as described in the section "Accepting client invitations" later in this chapter.

Follow these steps to start a QuickBooks subscription for a client:

1. **Choose Clients on the sidebar menu.**

2. **Click Add Client in the top-right corner.**

3. **Select Business or Individual, depending on whether you're adding a business or a self-employed individual.**

4. **Provide a name and an email address for the company.**

5. **Fill in the Display Name As and Mobile fields if desired.**

6. **Optional: Click Add More Info to provide billing and shipping addresses, as well as the company phone number and website address.**

7. **Click Show All Team Members to specify any additional team members who need to access the company.**

8. **Choose between Yes, Add a Subscription and No, No Subscription Needed.**

9. **Choose a billing option if you chose Yes, Add a Subscription:**

   • **ProAdvisor Discount:** This option provides a permanent 30 percent discount on QuickBooks Online in exchange for Intuit billing you directly. You can pass along or retain the discount when you invoice your client.

   • **Direct Discount:** Intuit bills your client directly. The subscription starts with a 30-day free trial, followed by a 30 percent discount for 12 months. Your client must provide their billing information during the trial period.

- **Revenue Share:** Intuit bills your client directly. The subscription starts with a free 30-day trial, followed by a 50 percent discount for three months. Intuit pays you 30 percent of the amounts billed to your client for 12 months, along with 15 percent of employee fees. You must opt into the free Revenue Share program to utilize this approach.

10. **Click Next.**

11. **Select a QuickBooks subscription level (Advanced, Plus, Essentials, Simple Start, or Ledger) and click Next.**

TIP

See the "Leveraging QuickBooks Ledger" section later in this chapter to learn about QuickBooks Ledger.

12. **Optional: Add Payroll, Contractor Payments, or Time subscriptions.**

13. **Optional: Click Make Me the Primary Admin.**

TIP

You can transfer primary admin rights between you and your client at any time.

The Make Me the Primary Admin checkbox doesn't appear on the screen until you select a subscription level.

14. **Click Place Order.**

The company is created and appears in the list of companies on your Clients screen, although you may need to refresh the browser page or log out and back into the Accountant version.

REMEMBER

You have up to 180 days to import your client's data from QuickBooks Desktop when you initiate a subscription in the Accountant version. Conversely, clients who initiate their own subscription have only a 60-day window. Data can be imported as many times as needed during the respective windows. Each new import replaces any existing QuickBooks Online data.

Adding a client or prospective client without a subscription

Your client list can include customers who don't have a subscription or haven't yet sent you an accountant invitation. You can add such clients to your list in this manner:

1. **Choose Clients on the sidebar.**

2. **Click Add Client in the top-right corner.**

3. **Select Business or Individual, depending on whether you're adding a business or a self-employed individual.**

4. **Provide a name and an email address for the company.**

5. **Choose No, No Subscription Needed.**

6. **Click Save.**

You can add a subscription at any time by carrying out these steps:

1. **Click the Edit Client link for your client.**

2. **Scroll down to the Product section and choose Subscription.**

3. **From there, carry out Steps 9 through 14 in the previous section, "Establishing new QuickBooks Online subscriptions."**

Accepting client invitations

Clients who want to grant an accountant access to their company can carry out the following steps:

1. **Choose Settings ⇨ Manage Users.**

2. **Click the Accounting Firms tab.**

3. **Provide an email address and then click Invite.**

   The Accounting Firms tab of the Manage Users screen reappears, showing the email address with a status of Invited. Your clients can click Resend Invite from this screen if needed.

In turn, you (the accountant) click Accept Invitation in the invitation email to open the Accountant version login screen, choose an accounting firm, and then click Continue. The new client then appears on the client list. Email confirmations are sent to the client and accountant confirming that the invitation was accepted.

Customizing the Client List

You can customize the client list by using the list box above the table to filter the list to show all clients, for example, or only the QuickBooks Payroll clients in your list. You can determine which columns appear on the screen, and you can hide or display inactive clients. Click Settings just above the list of clients and make choices from the Settings menu shown in Figure 17-2.

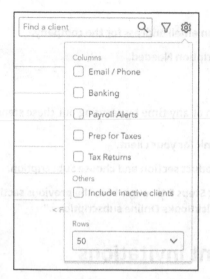

FIGURE 17-2:
Control the
appearance
of the client
list with the
Settings menu.

The company-level Gear icon appears at the top-right corner of every screen, whereas the screen-level Gear icon tends to appear lower down, such as just above the list of clients on the Clients screen.

Removing Clients from the Client List

You can choose to make a client inactive, or you can sever a relationship permanently by choosing to delete a client permanently. Let's first see how to keep one foot in the door with a client by marking them as inactive:

1. **Choose Clients from the sidebar.**

2. **Choose Make Inactive from the Action column drop-down list next to your former client's name.**

   A prompt asks whether you're sure you want to make the client inactive.

3. **Click Yes.**

It's likely that you'll no longer see this client on your list unless you choose to display inactive clients:

1. **Click the Gear icon above the Action column on the Clients screen.**

2. **Toggle the Include Inactive option on.**

   Alternatively, clear the Include Inactive checkbox if you want to hide such clients again.

At any point you can change a client's status back to Active with the following steps:

1. **Carry out the previous steps to display inactive clients if you don't see the client on your list.**

2. **Choose Make Active in the Action column next to the client's name.**

    You can then hide inactive clients again if you choose.

As the saying goes, all good things must come to an end, so let's say that you know that the time has come for you and your client to part ways:

1. **Choose Clients from the sidebar.**

2. **Choose Delete Permanently from the Action column drop-down list next to your former client's name.**

    A prompt asks whether you're sure you want to delete the client permanently.

3. **Click Yes.**

    The client is removed from your client list, and you are removed from their list of accountants. The client remains listed as a customer in your firm's accounting records. You can mark such customer records as inactive, as I discuss in Chapter 2.

Your former client can invite you back to their books if they choose, just as you can decide whether to accept said invitation.

Leveraging QuickBooks Ledger

QuickBooks Ledger is a slimmed down version of QuickBooks Online that is available exclusively to accountants. Subscriptions are $10/month/client and are billed directly to accounting firms. Each Ledger company permits one Primary Admin user and two Accountant users. Primary Admin access can be assigned to a client, who will have view-only access to the books. QuickBooks Ledger offers the following features:

» Automated bank feeds

» Bank reconciliation

» Financial statements and reports

» 1099 tracking

» Integration with tax preparation software

Ledger companies can be updated to Simple Start, Essentials, Plus, or Advanced at any time. The following types of clients are ideal candidates for this platform:

>> Users of Excel spreadsheets or paper-based books

>> Multi-entity companies with smaller business units

>> Seasonal or infrequent transaction companies

>> Trusts and estates

>> Rental property owners

>> Service businesses that do not track inventory

All the accountant tools that I discuss in Chapters 18 and 19 can be used with Ledger companies. In short, QuickBooks Ledger is intended to be a low-cost accounting solution for companies that have minimal accounting needs.

Accessing Clients' Books

The Accountant version provides single sign-on access to your clients' companies. This means that once you log in, you can access any client's books directly without re-entering credentials. You can access a client's QuickBooks company in three ways:

>> Choose a company name from the Go to QuickBooks list at the top of the screen.

>> Click the QB icon to the left of any client's name on the Your Practice screen.

>> Click the client's name to display their record, and then click the QB icon adjacent to the company name.

TIP

Hover your mouse over any QB icon to display a caption that indicates either the client's current subscription plan or their cancellation status.

Once you navigate to a client's books, the Go to QuickBooks menu lists your client's company name but remains a drop-down list. At any point, you can choose another company name from the list or click Back to Practice to return to your client list. You can also sign out of the Accountant version entirely by clicking the button with your first initial in the upper-right corner and choosing Sign Out. This button signs you out of any QuickBooks company that you're accessing as well as the Accountant version.

You and your clients have read-only access to canceled companies for one year from the subscription termination date. Terminated subscriptions can be reactivated at any time, even after the read-only period.

You can only resubscribe to or click Sign Out for companies that were terminated more than one year ago. You will then be required to sign back into the QuickBooks Online Accountant.

Transferring Admin Rights

QuickBooks Online companies have a single primary admin user who is a super-user with absolute access. As I discuss in Chapter 9, one or more additional users can be designated as company admin users. Accountant users automatically have company admin rights to a company unless they are designated as the primary admin user.

The primary admin can relinquish their role, but primary admin rights can't be changed or altered by other users, including admin users.

Accepting primary admin rights from your client

Clients who prefer for their accountant to have primary admin rights can transfer access in the following fashion:

1. **Choose Setting ⇨ Manage Users.**

2. **Click the Accounting Firms tab.**

3. **Choose Make Primary Admin from the drop-down menu in the Action column.**

4. **The equivalent of an "Are you sure?" prompt appears, from which your client clicks Make Primary Admin.**

5. **A message confirms that you've been invited to be the primary admin.**

   QuickBooks doesn't offer any indication that you've been invited, so if your client is frazzled, they might forget whether they invited you.

At this point, you can expect an email with a subject line that has your client's company name and the phrase "Account Privileges Granted." Within the email are links to accept or decline this responsibility. If you accept, you're asked to log into and verify your Intuit account; once you've done so, a screen informs you that primary account administrator privileges have been successfully transferred to you, and the previous primary account administrator has been notified by email.

Transferring primary admin rights to your client

You can return primary admin rights to any billable user within your client's company that is designated as a company admin:

1. **Access your client's books via the Accountant version.**

2. **Choose Settings ⇨ Manage Users.**

3. **Choose Make Primary Admin from the drop-down menu in the Action column next to your client's name.**

4. **Choose Make Primary Admin from the Action column.**

   A message explains that only one user can serve as the primary admin, and transferring that role downgrades your access to admin.

5. **Click Make Primary Admin to confirm the transfer; otherwise, click Cancel.**

   An automatic email invites your client to become the primary admin. When they accept the invitation, they're prompted to log in to QuickBooks. A message explains that the primary admin role has been transferred successfully and that you, the former primary admin, have been notified.

Once your client accepts the invitation, the next time you log in to the client's QuickBooks company, you no longer appear in the Manage Users section of the Manage Users screen. Your client is now the primary admin for the company, and you've become an admin user.

Setting Up Your Team

Whoever sets up the Accountant version for your firm becomes the primary administrator and can set up as many other team members as necessary. Accountant version users can be assigned prebuilt or custom roles for the firm's books in the fashion that I discuss in Chapter 13. Each team member has their own login credentials and can selectively be assigned role-based rights to clients' books as well. All team members can utilize the Accountant tools described in Chapter 18 and certain workflow tools described in Chapter 19.

Adding users

Either the primary administrator or any full-access users can set up and control user privileges in this fashion:

1. **Log in to the Accountant version as a primary admin or user with rights to add users.**

2. **Choose Team from the left menu bar to display the Team screen shown in Figure 17-3.**

3. **Click Add User.**

   The Add a New User screen opens, as shown in Figure 17-4.

4. **Fill in the name and email address of the team member you want to add.**

5. **Choose a role from the Access to Your Firm's QuickBooks field.**

   Choose Standard No Access for team members that should not have any access to the firm's books.

6. **Select one or more clients from the Access to Your Client's QuickBooks section.**

7. **Click Assign Access.**

   The Assign Access task pane opens, as shown in Figure 17-5.

8. **Select a role from the list.**

   This list contains fewer roles than the firm access list.

9. **Select a role from the list and then click Save.**

   This list contains fewer roles than the firm access list.

10. **Scroll to the bottom of the screen and click Send Invitation.**

    The new user is added to your team and assigned the status of Invited. In addition, the Status column of the Team screen indicates that an email invitation was sent to the user. After the user accepts the invitation, their status changes to Active.

Team members who already have QuickBooks Online credentials can click Accept Invitation in the invitation email; otherwise, they need to click Create Account and log in immediately after completing the sign-up process. An error prompt appears when a team member attempts to access an area they don't have access to. Users with limited rights don't see the Team or Apps commands in the Your Practice area of the sidebar.

FIGURE 17-3:
View, edit, and
add team
members.

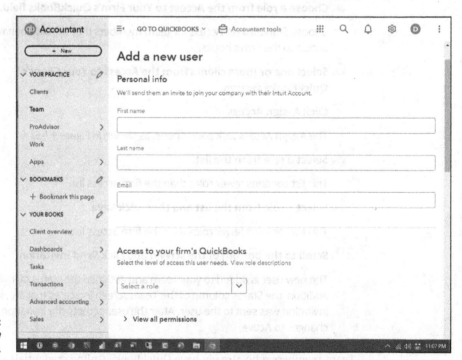

FIGURE 17-4:
The Add a New
User screen.

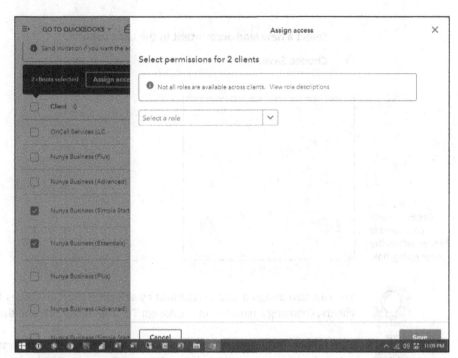

FIGURE 17-5:
The Assign
Access screen.

Assigning lead accountants

Lead accountants are the primary contact for your clients and typically have primary responsibility for overseeing the bookkeeping. Lead accountants can but don't have to be the primary admin for a QuickBooks Online company. Users are designated as lead accountants when

» **A client invites an accountant.** Accepting the invitation grants the accounting firm access to the client's books and designates the invited accountant as the lead accountant.

» **A firm member creates a client company.** The team member within the firm that creates a client company within the Accountant version becomes the lead accountant.

Primary admin or full access users can reassign lead accountants by carrying out these steps:

1. **Choose Clients, click the Filter icon, and choose Edit Leads, as shown in Figure 17-6.**

2. **Choose a client for which you want to reassign the lead accountant.**

3. Select a new lead accountant in the Lead column.

4. Choose Save.

FIGURE 17-6:
The Edit Leads
command is
hidden within the
Filter dialog box.

TIP

You can also assign a lead accountant by selecting the checkboxes for two or more clients, choosing a name from the Assign To drop-down list, and then clicking Save.

REMEMBER

You cannot inactivate a team member who is currently designated as a lead accountant for one or more clients. You must reassign the lead accountant role to another user if you want to deactivate the account of such departing team members.

Chapter **18**

Utilizing Accountant Tools and Screens

The Accountant version of QuickBooks Online adds commands to the sidebar menu and the top of the screen within your client's companies. In this chapter, I walk you through the tools and screens that empower accountants to support their clients effectively and efficiently. I also show you how to open and exit any client's set of books, as well as your firm's books.

Understanding the Dual Sidebar Menus

The sidebar menu is light gray when you're accessing the Your Practice and Your Books areas of QuickBooks Online, but it's black when you're accessing a client's books. The New button at the top of the sidebar creates new transactions in your books when the sidebar is light gray and in the QuickBooks company that you're working within when the sidebar is black.

The Your Practice section includes the following commands:

>> **Clients:** This command displays your client list, which I discuss in detail in Chapter 17.

>> **Team:** This command displays your list of team members, which I also discuss in Chapter 17.

>> **ProAdvisor:** This command connects you to your free Silver membership in the Intuit ProAdvisor program. More details on the free benefits are available at https://quickbooks.intuit.com/accountants/tools-proadvisor.

>> **Work:** This command displays practice management tools that I discuss in more detail in Chapter 19.

>> **Apps:** Click here to launch the App Center. In Chapter 7, I discuss how you can search for enhancements that can fill in gaps in QuickBooks. The App Center also shows you which apps are installed in each company, if any.

>> **Bookmarks:** Choose Add a Bookmark and then select one or more items from the Customize Your Menu window. This way, you can create one-click access to specific screens within the Your Practice and/or Your Books areas. The Your Books section appears immediately beneath the Bookmarks command and is how you use the free Advanced and Payroll Elite subscriptions that are provided for you to manage your firm's books.

Accessing Your Clients' Books

Many of your clients are likely to have a single QuickBooks subscription, but those who have two or more subscriptions can switch between companies by choosing the Gear icon ⇨ Switch Company and then choosing another company. This command is available to you as well, but it's not how you'll access your clients' companies. Instead, you'll use one of these two approaches:

>> Click the QB logo to the left of any client's name in the Client/Contact column of the Clients screen, as shown in Figure 18-1.

TIP

The status of a client's subscription appears in a caption when you hover over the QB logo in the Client/Contact column. This enables you to see the subscription level and status, as well as whether a client has a payroll subscription.

>> Click Go to QuickBooks at the top of any screen in the Accountant version and choose the name of the company you want to open.

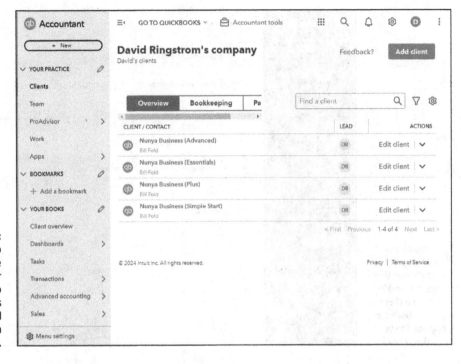

FIGURE 18-1:
Click the QB logo
to the left of the
client's name or
use the Go to
QuickBooks
command
to open a
client's company.

As shown in Figure 18-2, the client's company appears onscreen, and the sidebar menu turns black. You can carry out any task that your clients can, as well as perform additional tasks by way of the Accountant Tools that I discuss all through this chapter. Once you complete your work in a client's company, you can exit their books in three ways:

» Click the client's company name immediately to the left of the Accountant Tools button. You can choose Back to Practice to return to the practice management area or choose another client's company name from the list.

» The company name that you choose replaces the Go to QuickBooks button. Click the company name, and then choose Back to Practice to return to your Clients screen, or choose another QuickBooks company. Clicking the QB Accountant logo at the top-left corner is an even faster way to return to your Clients screen.

» Click the button in the top right that has your first initial, and then choose Sign Out. Doing so logs you out of your client's company and the Accountant version at the same time.

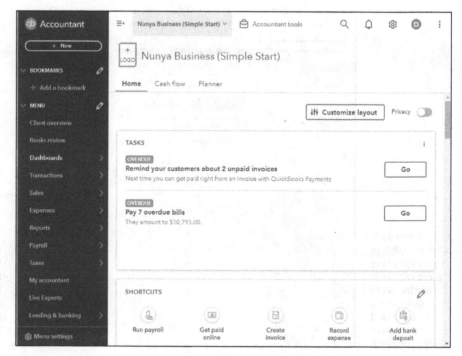

FIGURE 18-2:
A black sidebar
indicates that
you're working
within a client's
books as
opposed to your
firm's books.

WARNING Make sure that you sign out *before* closing the QuickBooks browser tab. In Google Chrome, anyone with access to your keyboard can click the three-dot menu at the top right, choose History, and then choose QuickBooks from the Recently Closed screen to return to your practice or any client's books without providing credentials.

WORKING IN MULTIPLE WINDOWS

Hands down, the easiest way to have multiple windows is to use the QuickBooks Online Advanced Desktop app for Windows, which you can access by choosing the Gear icon ⇨ Get the Desktop App. This free app allows you to access multiple QuickBooks companies at once. You can access your client's books no matter what subscription level they have. Any of your clients with Advanced subscriptions can download the Desktop App in the same fashion.

Conversely, in a web browser you can open two or more pages at the same time within a single QuickBooks Online company. To do so, click the Accountant Tools button, shown in Figure 18-2, and then choose New Window to duplicate the page you're viewing in another browser tab. Now you can use either tab to navigate to a different screen within the company.

All the major browsers let you duplicate tabs, so the New Window command is simply a convenience. In most browsers, if you right-click any tab, the shortcut menu should include a command that contains the word *Duplicate*.

If you want to access two or more QuickBooks companies at the same time, you can't simply open another browser tab. Instead, you need to use a separate browser, such as Google Chrome, Mozilla Firefox, or Microsoft Edge. In Chapter 23, I show how you can use profiles in Google Chrome to access multiple QuickBooks companies simultaneously.

Touring the Client Overview screen

When you access a client's books by way of the Accountant version, an Overview command appears at the top of the sidebar menu. This Client Overview screen differs from the Home tab that appears when you choose Dashboard from the sidebar. Your clients can't see this screen. The Client Overview command also appears within the Your Books section of the sidebar when you're not working within a client's books. The Client Overview screen includes the following sections:

>> **Company Setup:** As shown in Figure 18-3, this section shows your client's subscription level, payroll subscription status, and whether sales tax is enabled. It also has a listing of any enabled apps.

>> **Banking Activity:** Here you see a listing of the reconciliation status of any bank or credit card accounts, along with the bank balance and QuickBooks balance for each account. Click any account name or the number of unreconciled transactions to display the corresponding register.

TIP

Click your browser's Back button to return to the Client Overview screen from a register screen.

>> **Common Issues:** This listing alerts you to payments that haven't been deposited; uncategorized asset, income, and expense transactions; A/R and A/P aging amounts more than 90 days old; the opening balance equity amount; and any negative asset or liability accounts. It also includes a View Chart of Accounts link and a Reports button from which you can display the Balance Sheet or Profit and Loss report.

>> **Transaction Volume:** This section enables you to view the number of bank account transactions, sales receipts, invoices, invoice payments, bank deposits, journal entries, expenses, bills, and bill payments for any period that you choose.

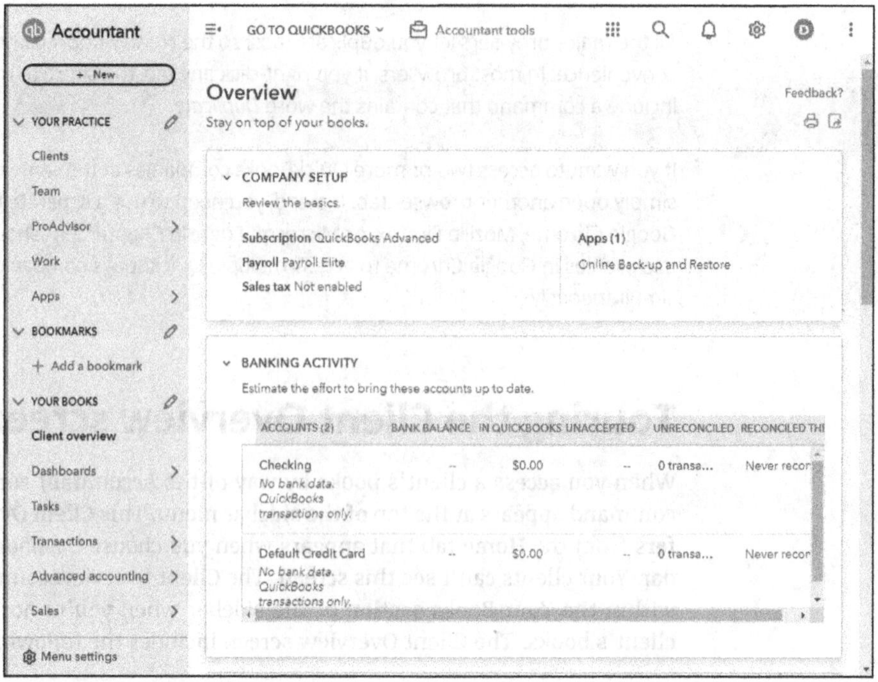
Accountant
GO TO QUICKBOOKS
Accountant tools
+ New
Overview
Stay on top of your books.
Feedback?
YOUR PRACTICE
Clients
Team
ProAdvisor
Work
Apps
BOOKMARKS
+ Add a bookmark
YOUR BOOKS
Client overview
Dashboards
Tasks
Transactions
Advanced accounting
Sales
Menu settings
COMPANY SETUP
Review the basics.
Subscription QuickBooks Advanced
Payroll Payroll Elite
Sales tax Not enabled
Apps (1)
Online Back-up and Restore
BANKING ACTIVITY
Estimate the effort to bring these accounts up to date.
ACCOUNTS (2)
BANK BALANCE
IN QUICKBOOKS
UNACCEPTED
UNRECONCILED
Checking
No bank data. QuickBooks transactions only
$0.00
0 transa...
Default Credit Card
No bank data. QuickBooks transactions only.
$0.00
0 transa...

FIGURE 18-3: The Client Overview screen that accountants can view.

Exploring the Books Review screen

A Books Review command that only you and your team can see appears on the sidebar when you're working within a client's books. This command doesn't appear within your firm's books. With the Books Review screen open, you can choose Monthly or Cleanup from the drop-down menu to the right of the screen title, as shown in Figure 18-4. Just below the screen title, click the Edit icon to specify the date range that you're reviewing. Typically, the Books Review is set to the previous month. The Cleanup and Monthly versions of Books Review are identical, except the Cleanup version has a Setup tab that's not available in the Monthly version.

REMEMBER

You can only choose from the months presented on the list. Perhaps you're setting up the books for a company as of June 1, but today's date is in the month of May. In that case, you can only select a month or months from January through April for the cleanup start dates. Once the calendar rolls around to June, you can then choose May.

TIP

You can record your progress through the Books Review process by choosing To Do, Waiting, and Done from the top-right corner of each section within the Books Review screens.

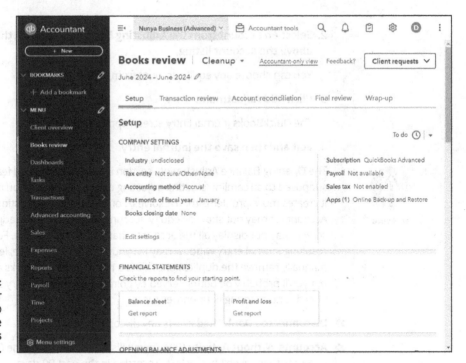

FIGURE 18-4:
The Setup tab for
the Cleanup
version of the
Books
Review screen.

Starting out with the Setup tab

You typically only use the Cleanup version of Books Review when you're bringing a new client onboard. You don't typically see the Setup tab on an ongoing basis. This tab includes the following sections:

TIP

>> **Company Settings:** This area repeats information that appears on the Client Overview screen but offers an Edit Settings link that's an alternative to choosing the Gear icon ⇨ Account and Settings.

If you don't see the Setup tab, choose Monthly to the right of the Books Review screen title and then choose Cleanup.

>> **Financial Statements:** Run a Balance Sheet or Profit and Loss report.

>> **Opening Balance Adjustments:** You can use this section to initiate adjusting journal entries and maintain documentation of said entries.

To create journal entries and maintain documentation, follow these steps:

1. **Enter an adjustment amount in the Beginning Statement Balance column, shown in Figure 18-5.**

   Enter either a positive or a negative amount, depending on your needs.

2. **Select an account from the Adjusting Equity Account list that appears above the account listing.**

    You can choose any equity account from the list.

3. **Click Add Adjustment.**

    The QuickBooks Journal Entry screen appears.

4. **Edit and then save the journal entry.**

WARNING

The Opening Balance Adjustments section is a well-intentioned feature that's supposed to streamline creating adjusting entries. However, you may find that it creates more problems than it solves. For instance, the Adjusting Equity Account list may not show all equity accounts. The body of the adjustments screen may not display all the accounts that you want to adjust. Further, the resulting journal entry window may list your journal entry twice, leaving you to manually remove the duplication. This is a nice feature if it works as expected, but you'll probably be better served by going to the journal entry screen directly and entering your entries there.

» **Disconnected Bank Feeds:** Lists any disconnected bank feeds.

» **Accounts Without Activity (90+ Days):** Lists all accounts on the Chart of Accounts that haven't had activity recorded in the past 90 days.

» **Additional Items:** Typically includes recommendations to review the Chart of Accounts for industry- and entity-specific accounts, as well as duplicate accounts. As shown in Figure 18-6, +Add enables you to add new items to the list. You can also click any item name to display detailed notes, along with links to edit or delete the task.

Examining the Transaction Review screen

The Cleanup and Monthly versions of the Books Review screen have a Transaction Review screen that displays the following:

» The number of unreviewed bank transactions.

» All uncategorized transactions for the specified period.

» All transactions without payees.

» All undeposited funds.

» All unapplied payments.

» Additional items that you want to check each month, such as personal transactions, loan payments, and recording cash transactions. You can add or delete items in this list in the same fashion as on the Setup screen.

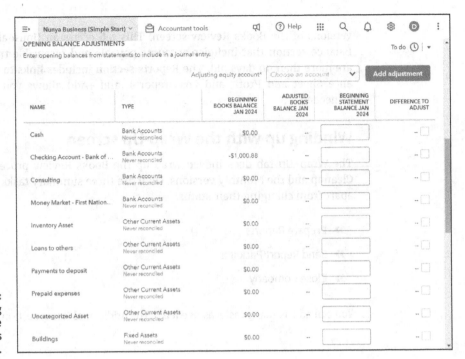

FIGURE 18-5:
The Opening
Balance
Adjustments
section.

NAME	TYPE	BEGINNING BOOKS BALANCE JAN 2024	ADJUSTED BOOKS BALANCE JAN 2024	BEGINNING STATEMENT BALANCE JAN 2024	DIFFERENCE TO ADJUST
Cash	Bank Accounts Never reconciled	$0.00	--		-- ☐
Checking Account - Bank of ...	Bank Accounts Never reconciled	-$1,000.88	--		-- ☐
Consulting	Bank Accounts Never reconciled	$0.00	--		-- ☐
Money Market - First Nation...	Bank Accounts Never reconciled	$0.00	--		-- ☐
Inventory Asset	Other Current Assets Never reconciled	$0.00	--		-- ☐
Loans to others	Other Current Assets Never reconciled	$0.00	--		-- ☐
Payments to deposit	Other Current Assets Never reconciled	$0.00	--		-- ☐
Prepaid expenses	Other Current Assets Never reconciled	$0.00	--		-- ☐
Uncategorized Asset	Other Current Assets Never reconciled	$0.00	--		-- ☐
Buildings	Fixed Assets Never reconciled	$0.00	--		-- ☐

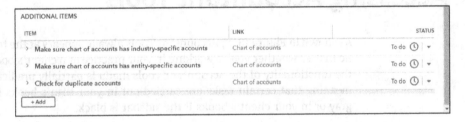

FIGURE 18-6:
Click +Add to add
new tasks to the
Additional
Items list.

ITEM	LINK	STATUS
› Make sure chart of accounts has industry-specific accounts	Chart of accounts	To do 🕐 ▾
› Make sure chart of accounts has entity-specific accounts	Chart of accounts	To do 🕐 ▾
› Check for duplicate accounts	Chart of accounts	To do 🕐 ▾

+ Add

Evaluating the Account Reconciliation screen

The next tab in both the Cleanup and the Monthly versions of Books Review enables you to keep tabs on the reconciliation status of bank and balance sheet accounts. You can see the number of unreconciled transactions by account, as well as the last reconciled date. The Outstanding Transactions list shows uncleared transactions that are more than 90 days old. As with the other screens, you can add or remove tasks from the Additional Items section.

TIP

Use Select Accounts to choose which accounts appear on the list.

Flipping through the Final Review screen

Contrary to its name, the Final Review isn't the final tab in the Books Review process. Instead, it's the next-to-last one in both the Cleanup and the Monthly versions of the Books Review screen. This tab offers an Unusual or Unexpected Balance section that includes accounts payable and receivable transactions that are more than 90 days old. The Reports section includes links to review the Balance Sheet and Profit and Loss reports, and +Add allows you to add reports as needed.

Winding up with the Wrap-Up screen

The Wrap-Up tab does indeed wrap up the Books Review process for both the Cleanup and the Monthly versions. On it are three summary tasks you can't alter, apart from changing their status:

>> Prepare Reports

>> Send Report Package

>> Close Company

You can add as many tasks as needed to the Additional Items section by way of +Add.

Accessing Accountant Tools

As shown in Figure 18-7, Accountant Tools always appears at the top of the screen, no matter whether you're working in your practice or a client's books. Like + New, the functionality of the Accountant Tools menu is partially predicated on context, meaning that certain tasks are carried out in your firm's books if the sidebar is gray or in your client's books if the sidebar is black.

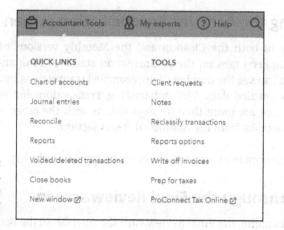

FIGURE 18-7: Accountant Tools is designed to streamline repetitive tasks.

Touring the tools list

The Accountant Tools menu includes the following commands:

>> **Chart of Accounts:** This alternative to choosing the Gear icon ⇨ Chart of Accounts displays the Chart of Accounts screen.

>> **Journal Entry:** This alternative to choosing +New ⇨ Journal Entry displays the Journal Entry transaction screen. Click the clock icon at the top-left corner to display a list of recent journal entries.

>> **Reconcile:** This alternative to choosing the Gear icon ⇨ Reconcile displays the Reconcile screen. I discussed reconciling bank and credit card accounts in Chapter 5.

>> **Reports:** This alternative to choosing Business Overview ⇨ Reports (Reports) from the sidebar menu displays the Reports screen. I discuss built-in reports in Chapter 6 and custom reports for Advanced subscriptions in Chapter 14. Later in this chapter, I discuss the Performance Center tab of the Reports screen that only accountants can access.

>> **Voided/Deleted Transactions:** This command displays the Audit Log screen filtered for deleted/voided transactions occurring in the current month.

TIP

Export to CSV enables you to create a comma-separated value file that contains any transactions displayed onscreen that you can then open in Microsoft Excel or Google Sheets.

>> **Close Books:** This command is an alternative to the Gear icon ⇨ Advanced ⇨ Accounting. Click the words Close Books and then toggle on Close the Books if needed. Specify a Closing Date and indicate whether users should be required to enter a password before recording changes in a closed period.

>> **New Window:** This command is an alternative to using a command within your browser to duplicate the current window, which I discuss earlier in this chapter in the "Working in Multiple Windows" sidebar.

>> **Client Requests:** I discuss client requests in Chapter 19, but in short, this is a feature of the Accountant version that enables you to monitor requests that you've made of clients. Note that this command only appears on the Accountant Tools menu when you're actively working within a client's set of books.

>> **Notes:** This command displays a Notes screen that you can use to record notes about a client's company. You can then specify whether the note should

be visible to your team or only to you. This command is also only available within a client's books and isn't available when working in your practice or your firm's books.

You can notify a team member of a note by typing @ in the body of a new or existing note and then selecting from the list that appears. QuickBooks displays "No match found" if you are the only person on your team with access to a given client's books.

>> **Reclassify Transactions:** This command enables you to search for balance sheet or profit and loss transactions that you want to move to different accounts, classes, or locations. I discuss this feature in more detail in the "Reclassifying transactions" section of this chapter.

>> **Reports Options:** This command displays a Report Tools button, viewable only to accountants, that allows you to specify the default date range and reporting basis for reports. It also displays the closing and reconciliation status of the books.

>> **Write Off Invoices:** Your clients inexplicably don't have access to an easy way to write off invoices, but fortunately you do. I discuss this feature in more detail in the "Writing off invoices" section later in this chapter.

>> **Prep for Taxes:** Think of this as an expanded version of the Books Review screen that I cover earlier in this chapter. The screen includes the following tabs:

- *Year-End Tasks:* A task list from which you can add or remove tasks as needed, as well as track the status of each task.

- *Documents:* A customizable document repository that is separate from any documents that your client may have uploaded to their company as attachments. Once you add a folder, you can use the drop-down menu to create a subfolder, add attachments or links, rename or delete the folder, and mark files for carrying forward to a new tax year.

I discuss the details of using attachments in Chapter 1.

- *Review and Adjust:* This screen enables you to compare the prior and current year balance sheet and profit and loss reports.

- *Grouping & Statements:* Use this screen to group related accounts to create alternate views of the financial statements.

- *Tax Mapping:* Here you can assign each account on your client's chart of accounts to the corresponding line on their tax return.

TIP

In addition, a Tools button at the top-right allows you to download all the information to a ZIP file, carry forward the previous year's tax prep, or lock the current year tax prep.

The Prep for Taxes screen allows you to transfer your client's accounting data to ProConnect Tax, Lacerte Tax, or ProSeries Tax after you select your professional software and your client's tax form from the Tax Mapping tab.

» **COA Templates:** Chart of accounts templates allow accountants to define and customize a set of accounts tailored to a specific client's industry or business needs, streamlining the setup process across multiple clients.

Reclassifying transactions

The Reclassify Transactions screen shown in Figure 18–8 allows you to change the account for any transactions for any period, regardless of the closing date, so be careful! You can also change the class or location in Plus and Advanced companies. Follow these steps to reclassify transactions:

1. **Choose Accountant Tools ⇨ Reclassify Transactions.**

   The Reclassify Transactions screen appears, as shown in Figure 18-8.

2. **Choose Profit and Loss or Balance Sheet from the Account Types list.**

3. **Choose Accrual or Cash.**

4. **Choose an account from the list to display all transactions for that account for the specified period.**

5. **Adjust the date range as needed.**

6. **Make selections from the filter lists to isolate the transactions you want to reclassify.**

7. **Click Find Transactions if you changed the date range or filters.**

8. **Choose one or more transactions from the resulting list, and then choose Reclassify.**

9. **As shown in Figure 18-9, optionally change the account, class, or location for the transactions, and then click Apply.**

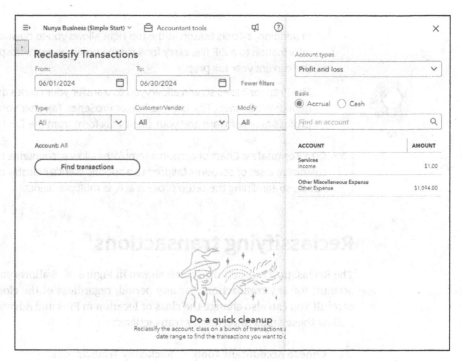

FIGURE 18-8:
The Reclassify
Transactions
screen.

Reclassify transactions

Make changes to all **2** selected transaction lines.

Change account to

Select ▼

Change class to

Select ▼

Change location to

Select ▼

Cancel   Apply

FIGURE 18-9:
The Reclassify
Transactions
dialog box.

Writing off invoices

Choose Accountant Tools ⇨ Write Off Invoices to display the Write Off Invoices screen shown in Figure 18-10, which enables you to view invoices and then write them off to an account of your choice. At the top of the screen, you set filters to display the invoices you want to review. You can view invoices more than 180 days old, more than 120 days old, in the current accounting period, or in a custom date range that you set. You can also set a balance limit. Select any invoices that you want to write off, and then click Write Off. Select an account if needed from the confirmation prompt shown in Figure 18-11, and then click Apply to write off the invoices; otherwise, click Cancel.

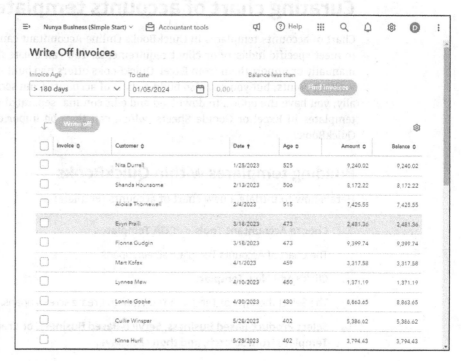

FIGURE 18-10:
The Write Off
Invoices screen.

FIGURE 18-11:
Confirm that
you want to
write off the
selected invoices.

WARNING

The Write Off Invoices feature doesn't make adjusting entries in the current period; instead, it adjusts the period in which the transaction was originally created, which can affect closed periods negatively. See the "Writing Off Bad Debt" section in Chapter 2 to see how to write off an invoice without affecting a prior period.

Curating chart of accounts templates

Chart of accounts templates in QuickBooks Online Accountant can be customized to meet specific industry or client requirements. You can create these templates manually or import them from Excel. QuickBooks offers two built-in templates as starting points, but you can also build a chart of accounts from scratch. Additionally, you have the option to download and edit comma-separated value (CSV) file templates in Excel or Google Sheets, which can then be imported directly into QuickBooks.

Building templates within QuickBooks

Here's how to initiate a new chart of accounts template:

1. **Choose Accountant Tools ⇨ COA Templates.**

   The Chart of Accounts Template screen opens.

2. **Click +Add New Template.**

   The Select the Type of Template You Want to Create screen opens.

3. **Select Product-Based Business, Service-Based Business, or Create Template from Scratch, and then click Save.**

   The Create New Template screen opens.

4. **Fill in the Template Name field.**

5. **To assign account numbers, toggle Account Numbers on.**

6. **For each account that you want to create, fill in the Account Name, Account Type, and Detail Type fields.**

7. **Click Save when the template is complete.**

   The new template appears on the Chart of Accounts Template screen.

TIP

Chart of accounts templates can be edited at any time, so you do not need to complete the work in one sitting.

The following additional commands are available when establishing chart of accounts templates:

>> **+Add New Sub Account:** Creates a blank row for a sub-account.

>> **Delete:** Removes an account from the chart of accounts.

>> **Duplicate:** Copies an account from the chart of accounts.

>> **+Add New Parent Account:** Creates a blank row for a parent account. You'll likely need to scroll to the bottom of the screen to see this new account.

Importing templates

The Chart of Accounts Templates screen contains an Import button, but as of this writing does not offer any guidance as to how the import file should be structured. You can, however, download a collection of comma-separated value (CSV) templates that you can edit to your liking within Excel or Google Sheets and then import into QuickBooks. To access the templates, visit https://www.quickbooks. com/support and then enter the search term **Import Chart of Accounts Templates.** Select the article titled "How to import Chart of Accounts templates" and look for the download link. An importable chart of accounts template has five columns:

>> Account Number

>> Account Name

>> Type

>> Detail Type

>> Description

The template examples provided by Intuit include a description column that cannot be imported into QuickBooks. The other four fields are required for the import, although you can leave the account number field blank if you do not want to incorporate account numbers into your template.

I discuss the contents of these fields in Chapter 1 where I discuss maintaining a chart of accounts within a QuickBooks company. Once you build or edit the template within your spreadsheet application, save your work as either an Excel workbook or a comma-separated value file, and then carry out these steps:

1. **Choose Accountant Tools ⇨ COA Templates.**

   The Chart of Accounts Template screen opens.

2. **Click Import.**

   An Import Your Accounts dialog box appears.

3. **Click Select File.**

   An Open dialog box appears.

4. **The Map Your Spreadsheet Fields screen opens.**

5. **Review the fields in the Your Spreadsheet column and choose the corresponding columns within your spreadsheet or CSV file if needed.**

6. **Click Save.**

   The Create New Template screen opens.

7. **Fill in the Template Name field and make any other changes you want to the template.**

8. **Click Save to add the template to the Chart of Accounts Template screen.**

Maintaining templates

An Apply button appears adjacent to each template on the Chart of Accounts Template screen. Let's first look at the commands available on the drop-down menu:

REMEMBER

» **Edit:** Opens the Edit Template screen from which you can modify the template.

  Changes made to chart of accounts templates do not impact companies where the template has been applied.

» **Delete:** Removes the template from the list.

» **Duplicate:** Adds an exact copy of the chart of accounts template to the Chart of Accounts Template screen.

Applying templates

Templates can be applied to new or existing QuickBooks companies. Existing accounts won't be affected, but new accounts will be added. Accounts that have the same name or account number will be flagged and not added.

Here's how to apply a chart of accounts template to a QuickBooks company:

1. **Choose Accountant Tools ⇨ COA Templates.**

   The Chart of Accounts Template screen opens.

2. **Click Apply adjacent to the template that you want to apply.**

   The Select a Client to Apply This Template screen opens.

3. **Make a choice from the Select a Client field.**

4. **Click Save.**

   The Chart of Accounts Template screen reopens, and a list of any accounts that were not added appears.

Undoing reconciliations

I feel like the Accountant Tools menu should include an Undo Reconciliations command, but it doesn't. Many of your clients would give their eye teeth for the ability to undo reconciliations, particularly those who previously had that ability in QuickBooks Desktop.

Even though it's not on the Accountant Tools menu, you can undo the reconciliation of certain asset, liability, and equity accounts for your clients, which includes bank and credit card accounts. Follow these steps:

1. **Choose Accounting ⇨ Reconcile.**

   The Reconcile tab of the Accounting screen appears.

   TIP

   Your clients can display a Reconcile screen that's almost identical by choosing Transactions ⇨ Reconcile.

2. **Choose History by Account.**

   The History by Account screen appears.

3. **Choose an account from the list.**

   You can reconcile certain asset, liability, and equity accounts.

4. **Click the drop-down arrow in the Action column adjacent to the most recent reconciliation and choose Undo, as shown in Figure 18-12.**

5. **Click Yes after reviewing the warning prompt; otherwise, click Go Back.**

WARNING

The Undo command doesn't appear on the Action column of the History by Account screen for your clients. Reconciliations can only be undone using the Accountant version. Additionally, undoing a reconciliation only reverses the changes made during the reconciliation process. Any transactions reconciled directly within a register or any manual actions performed outside the reconciliation will remain unaffected.

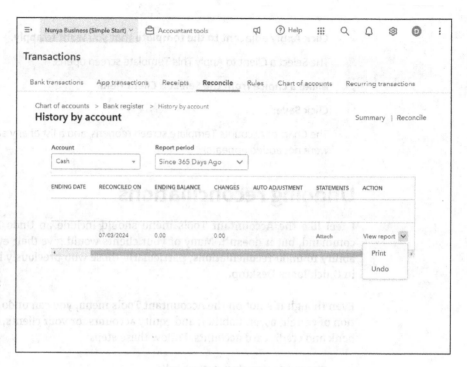

FIGURE 18-12:
Accountant version users can undo reconciliations in any QuickBooks company.

Graphing Your Clients' Financial Data

QuickBooks Simple Start, Essentials, and Plus users have a limited array of charts available to them when they choose Dashboards ⇨ Business Overview. Advanced companies have access to the Performance Center tab, which is available across all subscription levels when accountants access a client's books through the Accountant version. You can share Performance Center charts with your clients by clicking Export and choosing one or more charts to be saved in a PDF file.

Perusing the Performance Center

The Performance Center enables you to generate prebuilt and custom charts for any of your clients by way of the following steps:

1. **Choose Reports ⇨ Performance Center tab.**

   The Performance Center tab appears on the Reports screen.

   REMEMBER

   Your clients can't access this screen unless they have an Advanced subscription.

2. **The Performance Center appears and displays ten charts in most QuickBooks versions.**

   Some charts, such as the A/R and A/P aging, are as of today, but other charts allow you to choose from a selection of date ranges. These charts appear by default on the Performance Center for all subscription levels:

   - Expenses Over Time
   - Revenue Over Time
   - Gross Profit Over Time
   - Net Profit Over Time
   - Accounts Receivable
   - Accounts Payable
   - COGS Over Time
   - NPM vs. Industry Benchmarks (Net Profit Margin)
   - GPM vs. Industry Benchmarks (Gross Profit Margin)

   Advanced companies include a Net Cash Flow chart. The Gear icon enables you to specify the industry to use for charts that offer benchmarks.

   You can add up to 25 charts to any QuickBooks company.

3. **You can modify the layout of the Performance Center in the following ways:**

   - Click Customize Layout to rearrange the order of the charts and then click Done.
   - Click the three-dot menu between any chart to display a menu from which you can edit the chart by changing parameters, export the chart to a PDF file, or delete the chart from the Performance Center.

   You can restore any built-in charts that you delete by selecting from the Quick Add Charts list. Any chart on the list can be added to the Performance Center tab multiple times if you want to adjust the settings to create different perspectives.

   - Click Add a New Chart to create a customized chart.

Creating new charts

Accountants sometimes speak in shorthand, so this section relates to graphically presenting QuickBooks data, as opposed to maintaining a client's chart of accounts. (See Chapter 1 if you're looking for guidance on that.) You can add new charts based on any of the following categories:

- » Expenses
- » Revenue
- » Gross Profit
- » Net Profit
- » Accounts Receivable
- » Accounts Payable
- » COGS (Cost of Goods Sold)
- » Cash Flow
- » Current Ratio
- » Quick Ratio

Use the following steps to create a new chart, such as the one shown in Figure 18-13:

1. **Click Add a New Chart on the Performance Center tab of the Reports screen.**

2. **Choose a category from the list and then click Continue.**

3. **Specify the name for your chart.**

4. **Select the time period for the chart.**

5. **Make a Group By selection, if available.**

   You can group charts by classes, locations, items, income, or customers.

6. **Apply filtering options, if available.**

   Some charts offer the ability to filter by classes, locations, items, customers, or income. These options are predicated by a company's subscription level.

7. **Choose to compare a chart against a time period, if available.**

   You can choose to compare it to the previous period or the previous year, same period.

8. **Choose between vertical bars and trend line, if available.**

   Vertical bars is another term for a column chart, and trend line is another way of referring to a line chart.

9. **Click Add to Dashboard to save your chart, or click the X in the upper-right corner to discard the chart.**

   You can also click Back to change your chart type.

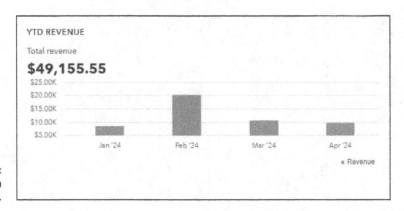

TIP

You can click the Note button below any chart to add up to 10,000 characters about the chart. The three-dot menu offers the following options:

>> **Edit Chart:** Returns you to the Add New Chart screen, where you can tweak your settings.

>> **Export Chart:** Creates a PDF file containing the chart.

>> **Delete Chart:** Removes the chart from the Performance Center dashboard.

REMEMBER

The Export button for the Performance Center gives you the option to export multiple charts to a PDF file and control the order that the charts appear in.

TIP

The Create Custom Charts link that appears to the left of the Add Quick Charts button in Advanced companies launches the Custom Report Builder feature. I discuss this feature in more detail in Chapter 14.

Chapter **19**

Orchestrating Practice Management

I n this chapter, I walk you through the practice management features that the Accountant version provides. The practice management tools are immediately available whenever you log in to the Accountant version. You can also return to them at any time by clicking on your client's company name at the top of the screen and then choosing Back to Practice.

Introducing the Work Screen

The Work command appears within the Your Practice section of the sidebar in the Accountant version. Your clients can't see the Work screen, and you decide which elements of the Work screen each of your team members can see. As shown in Figure 19-1, the Work screen tracks work to be completed for both your clients and your members of your firm by way of

» Automated notifications from your clients' QuickBooks companies

» Projects and tasks that you create

» Requests that you send to your clients

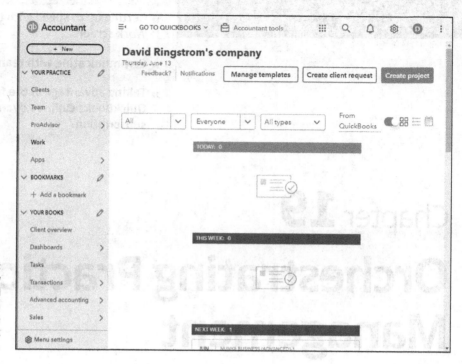

FIGURE 19-1:
A mostly
unpopulated
Work screen
within the
Accountant
version.

The Work screen in Figure 19-1 is mostly blank because I've only set up one project thus far.

TIP

I discuss adding team members in Chapter 17.

REMEMBER

The word *projects* has two different connotations in QuickBooks. Plus and Advanced users can use projects to track related transactions as a means of monitoring the profitability of certain endeavors. Conversely, in the Accountant version, projects are containers for one or more tasks to be completed.

The Work screen offers three different views — Grid, List, and Calendar — that you can filter by using three buttons and a toggle:

TIP

>> **All:** The first filter defaults to giving you a bird's-eye view of your practice. From this list, you can choose Clients Only to see only tasks related to your clients, or Firm Only to view only internal tasks. You can also choose a specific client.

   You must create a project or task for a client before they show up on this list.

>> **Everyone:** The second filter shows you tasks assigned to everyone in the firm. You can choose Me to see your personal to-do list or choose a specific team member to see that person's tasks.

>> **All types:** The third filter controls which types of items appear on screen. You can choose Projects, Tasks, or Requests from this list.

>> **From QuickBooks:** This toggle controls whether automated notifications generated by each client's QuickBooks company appear on your Work screen.

You can use all three filters in conjunction with one another so that you see as much or as little detail as you need in each moment.

The Work screen also has three buttons in the top-right corner:

>> **Manage Templates:** This button displays the Templates screen that allows you to create project templates, which are basically preconfigured to-do lists for work to be done on an ongoing basis. As shown in Figure 19-2, the Templates screen includes Quick Start templates that are prepopulated with related tasks. You can't modify the built-in templates, but you can duplicate them as starting points for your own templates.

>> **Create Client Requests:** This button displays the Create a Request task pane, shown in Figure 19-3, that you can use to document a request you're making of a client. You can optionally notify your client of the request, which saves you from having to log the request and then separately email it.

>> **Create Project:** This button displays the Create Project task pane, shown in Figure 19-4 when there is work to be completed that doesn't fit within a template you've created.

FIGURE 19-2:
The Templates screen.

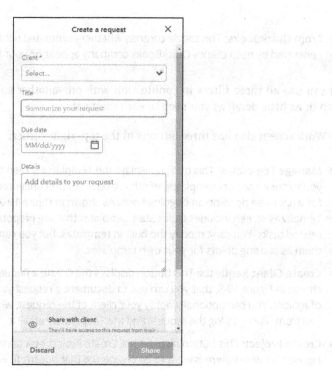

FIGURE 19-3:
The Create a
Request
task pane.

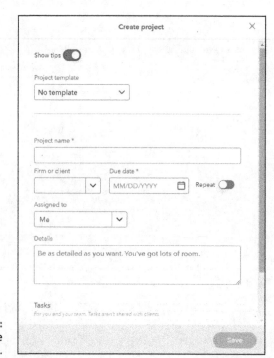

FIGURE 19-4:
The Create
Project task pane.

You can view the tasks and requests you create in three different ways on the Work screen, but the next section covers how to create templates.

Creating templates

The repetitive nature of accounting-related tasks means it's easy for items to fall off your radar or blur into the woodwork. You can counter this by creating project templates that are composed of tasks or steps to be completed. Here's how to create a template:

1. **Choose Work on the sidebar and then click Manage Templates.**

   The Templates screen opens.

2. **Click Create Template to display the task pane.**

3. **Type a name for the template, such as Month-End Tasks, in the Project Name box.**

4. **If you want to display the Due Date options shown in Figure 19-5, Enable the Repeat toggle.**

   You can set projects to recur on a weekly, biweekly, monthly, quarterly, or yearly basis on specific days of your choice. The scheduling options presented vary, based on the frequency you select.

5. **Use the Details field (see Figure 19-4) to add narrative information about the project, if desired.**

6. **Click Add a Task to display the fields shown in the Tasks Pane in Figure 19-6.**

7. **Assign a name to the task, such as** Bank Reconciliation.

8. **The Due Date field for the task lets you choose between Set Later or Offset.**

   Set Later means you need to set the due date when you create a new project based on this template. Conversely, Offset enables you to schedule the task a specified number of days prior to the project due date.

9. **Add other tasks as needed and then click Save.**

10. **Create additional templates as needed, and then click the Work link at the top-left side of the screen or choose Work from the sidebar menu.**

TIP

The Save Template button is disabled if you haven't filled in a required field in the task pane.

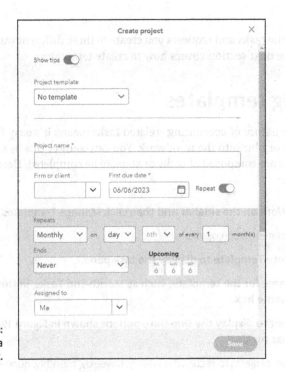

FIGURE 19-5:
Establishing a
recurring project.

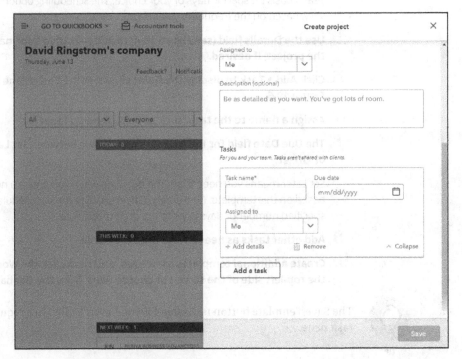

FIGURE 19-6:
Adding a task
to a project.

Creating client requests from the Work screen

A client request can be anything related to a client's QuickBooks company or your business relationship with them. Here's how to create a client request:

1. **Choose Work on the sidebar menu and then click Create Client Request.**

   The task pane shown in Figure 19-3 appears.

2. **Choose a client name from the list.**

3. **Enter a title for the request, such as** Engagement Letter.

   This is similar to crafting a subject line for an email.

4. **Specify a due date for the request.**

   The due date is a required field.

5. **Enter the details of the request, much like the body of an email.**

6. **Optional: Click Documents to upload one or more documents related to the request.**

   This is similar to adding an attachment to a QuickBooks transaction.

TIP
   The Documents button doesn't appear within the Create a Request task pane until after you choose a client from the list.

7. **The Notify Client option defaults to enabled, but you can turn it off if you don't want to notify your client of the request.**

8. **Click Share to save the request.**

   The Share button retains its label even if you toggle off the Notify Client option.

9. **The request appears on your Work screen, as shown in Figure 19-7.**

   A Sent indicator appears at the bottom of the task if you notified your client of the request. This takes the form of a gray shaded area beneath the task along with an envelope icon and the word Sent.

If you choose to notify your client, they receive an email message notifying them of the request, and then the request appears within their QuickBooks company.

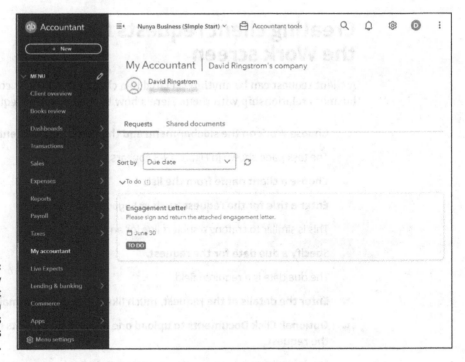

FIGURE 19-7:
The My
Accountant
screen within
a client's
QuickBooks
company.

Creating client requests from the Accountant Tools menu

You can also initiate client requests while you're working within a client's set of books:

1. Choose Accountant Tools ➪ Client Requests.

The Client Requests task pane appears.

2. Click +Add Request.

3. Enter a title for the request, such as Engagement Letter.

This is similar to crafting a subject line for an email.

4. Specify a due date for the request.

The due date is a required field.

5. Enter the details of the request, much like the body of an email.

6. Click Documents to upload one or more documents related to the request.

This is similar to adding an attachment to a QuickBooks transaction.

7. **The Notify Client option in the Share with Client section is enabled by default, but you can toggle it off if you don't want to notify your client in this fashion.**

8. **Click Share to save the request.**

   The Share button retains its label even if you toggle the Notify Client option off.

9. **The request appears in the Client Requests task pane and is also on the Work screen when you return to the Your Practice section of the Accountant version.**

Viewing requests within your clients' companies

Here's how your clients can view requests that you make of them:

1. **Choose My Accountant from the sidebar menu.**

   The My Accountant screen shown in Figure 19-7 appears. Your clients can choose Due Date or Recently Updated from the Sort By list.

TIP

   You can view the My Accountant screen in the same fashion that your clients see it by activating their company within the Accountant version and then choosing My Accountant from the sidebar menu.

2. **Click any task to display the task pane shown in Figure 19-8.**

3. **Your client can expand the Documents section to view documents you've shared or upload new documents.**

4. **Your client can expand the Comments section to view and post comments.**

WARNING

You can't edit or delete comments added to a request.

Your clients can't delete requests, but you can. Click on any request on the Work screen to display the task pane for the request, and then Click the Delete Request icon at the top right. QuickBooks asks you to confirm the deletion and reminds you that any documents attached will remain in the Documents tab. You can also change the status of a request to In Progress or Completed. Your clients cannot change the status.

FIGURE 19-8:
The To Do task pane within a client's QuickBooks company.

Engagement letter

🗓 Due June 30

TO DO

Please sign and return the attached engagement letter.

📄 Documents   **1** ›

💬 Comments   **0** ›

Managing projects and tasks

Projects typically are a collection of tasks to be completed by a specified date. Each project is assigned to a client or to your firm, and each task within a project has a due date and is assigned to a team member. Here's how to create a task-tracking project:

1. **Choose Work from the sidebar menu, and then click Create Project.**

The screen shown in Figure 19-4 appears.

2. **Choose a template from the Project Template drop-down list if desired.**

3. **Enter a name for the project, such as** Annual Budget.

4. **Choose between My Firm or a client name from the Firm or Client drop-down list.**

Use My Firm to track internal projects that aren't related to a specific client.

5. **Set a project due date.**

You must schedule the due dates for any tasks associated with this project on or before the project due date.

6. **Assign the project to a team member by using the Assigned To field.**

Assign the project to the team member responsible for the overall project. You can assign tasks to other individuals.

Click the Repeat slider to set up the time frame to use for recurring projects, such as monthly bank statement reconciliation or quarterly payroll tax filings.

TIP

7. **Enter narrative information about the project in the Details field.**

8. **Optional: Click Add a Task to add one or more tasks to the project.**

9. **Click Save to save the project.**

TIP

Projects scheduled for more than 30 days in the future don't appear on the Grid View of the Work screen but do appear in List View, as I discuss in the next section.

You can edit any project or task that you add, but you can't edit the automatic tasks that a QuickBooks company posts. Click on any project or task on the Work screen to display a task pane like what you used to create the project. You can edit the project details as well as add, remove, or update tasks. Buttons along the bottom of the task pane enable you to delete the project, convert it to a template, or duplicate it.

TIP

You can't convert a project into a task or a task into a project.

As you make progress on a task, you can update its status directly from Grid View on the Work screen. Click the arrow on a task card to change its status, as shown in Figure 19-9.

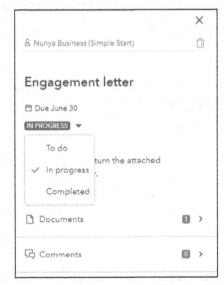

FIGURE 19-9:
Use the arrow on a task or project card to display the list of available statuses.

Tasks can have a status of To Do, In Progress, Blocked, or Done. You use Blocked status when something is stopping you from completing a task.

Looking at Work screen views

As I discussed previously, the Work screen allows you to filter your to-do list as granularly as you want. The Work screen also offers three different views:

» **Grid:** This default view uses cards that allow you to monitor requests, projects, and tasks due within the next 30 days, as shown earlier in Figure 19-1.

» **List:** The List button appears at the top-right corner of the Grid and displays all requests, projects, and tasks in list form, as shown in Figure 19-10.

» **Calendar:** The Calendar button also appears at the top-right corner of the grid and shows you the number of requests, tasks, or projects that are due on a given day, as shown in Figure 19-11. Inexplicably, the calendar is not interactive, so you can only use it to view the number of tasks due on a given day, and then use Grid or List View to see and/or edit the actual tasks.

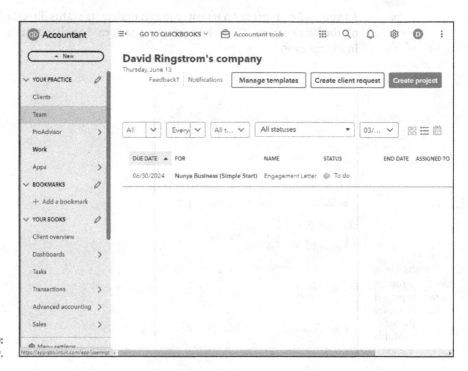

FIGURE 19-10:
The List View.

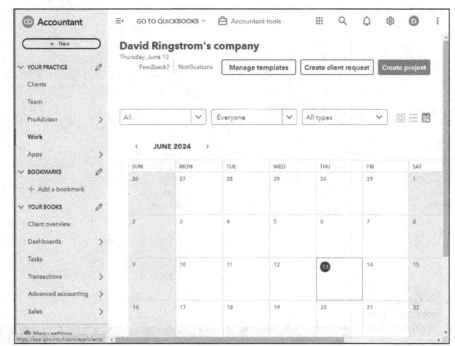

FIGURE 19-11:
The Calendar
View with one
task due
on June 13.

REMEMBER

Filters that you apply affect all three views.

Communicating with Team Members about Work

At the risk of stating the obvious, communication is paramount when you're working in a team environment. You can provide notifications by email for a variety of actions associated with the projects and tasks on the Work screen. If you want to turn notifications on or off, click the Notifications link at the top of the Work screen shown in Figures 19-10 and 19-11. Doing so displays the Notifications tab of the Company Settings task pane shown in Figure 19-12.

Click the Edit icon in the top-right corner of the Email section to turn email notifications on and off for various actions that take place on the Work screen. Click Save when you finish, and then click Done.

TIP

By default, each team member is notified of new assignments and due dates, but team members configure their notification settings within the Accountant version.

Settings

? Help ✕

Company

Notifications

QuickBooks
Checking [NEW]

Sales

Expenses

Payments

Time

Advanced

Work notifications

Email   Stay up-to-date on your work. When you get a new work assignment, or when someone   ✎
                      makes a change to your projects or tasks, we send a notification to your inbox at:

                      david@acctadv.com

                      New assignments   On
                      Due dates   On
                      Details   Off
                      Status   Off
                      Name   Off
                      Assignees   Off
                      Deletions   Off

Privacy | Security | Terms of Service

Done

FIGURE 19-12:
Set up email
notifications for
team members
regarding work.

Optimizing Your Free QuickBooks Online Advanced Subscription

The Accountant version offers one free QuickBooks Online Advanced subscription for use with an accounting firm's books, along with a free Payroll Elite subscription, which is accessed by way of the Your Books section of the sidebar menu. Accountant version users have up to 1,060 days to migrate their accounting records from QuickBooks Desktop into their firm's free Advanced company. You can import your desktop data multiple times during this window if needed; each import overwrites any existing data in the firm's Advanced company.

REMEMBER

The Your Books subscription integrates with the Accountant version and is intended to house your accounting firm's data, not a client's data or a subsidiary of your accounting firm. Every client in your client list is automatically established as a customer in the Your Books company, but team members aren't set up as employees.

6

Microsoft Excel Analysis

Chapter **20**

Analyzing QuickBooks Data in Excel

D ata within accounting programs often feels trapped under glass, particularly in QuickBooks, where users frequently face limited customization options for reports. In Chapter 6, I discuss how most users can customize reports to a certain extent, while Chapter 14 shows how Advanced users can overcome these constraints with the Custom Report Builder feature. However, in this chapter, I demonstrate how you can unlock your accounting data with Excel, regardless of your QuickBooks subscription level.

For this chapter, I used the sample Plus company for QuickBooks Online, which you can access at https://qbo.intuit.com/redir/testdrive. I chose this company to provide an easy way for you to generate reports that have actual data in them. You can also follow along with your own data. If you're new to Excel, my new book *Microsoft 365 Excel For Dummies* will help you get up to speed.

TIP

I used the Microsoft 365 version of Excel when writing this chapter. You can carry out everything I discuss in this chapter in Excel 2013 and later. You can accomplish most techniques within Google Sheets as well.

Disabling Protected View in Microsoft Excel

Microsoft Excel treats any reports downloaded from the Internet, such as any report you export from QuickBooks, as a threat and opens them in Protected View. This is a sandbox mode within Excel that enables you to safely view a report so that you can determine whether it truly is a threat.

Spoiler alert: Any reports exported from QuickBooks Online are perfectly safe, but the fact remains that Protected View can slow your work down, especially if you frequently export reports from QuickBooks to Excel. Allow me to demonstrate what I mean by exporting the Check Detail report to Excel:

1. **Choose Reports on the sidebar menu.**

   The Reports page opens.

2. **Type** Invoice List **in the Search field and then press Enter.**

   Alternatively, choose Invoice List in the Who Owes You section.

3. **To alter the period shown, select from the Report Period field.**

4. **To create more space onscreen for your report, click the Collapse Sidebar button.**

5. **Click Export/Print ⇨ Export to Excel.**

   See Chapter 6 for more information about running reports in QuickBooks.

6. **Open the report in Excel by double-clicking the report name in your Downloads folder; alternatively, you can choose File ⇨ Open ⇨ Browse in Excel and then open the workbook.**

7. **Click Enable Editing on the message bar shown in Figure 20-1 to access your report.**

Protected View is well-intentioned, but you can disable the feature if you want:

1. **Choose File ⇨ Options in Excel for Windows.**

   The Excel Options dialog box opens.
   Excel for macOS doesn't offer the Protected View feature.

REMEMBER

2. **Choose Trust Center ⇨ Trust Center Settings.**

   The Trust Center dialog box opens.

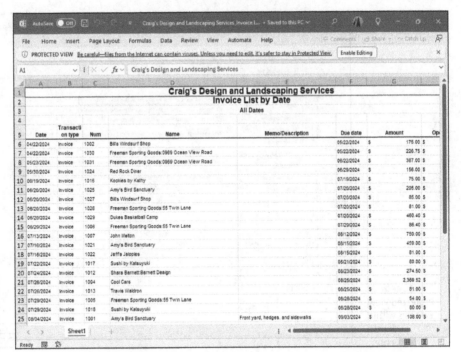

FIGURE 20-1:
You cannot edit a
workbook in a
report when
Protected View
is active.

3. **Click Protected View in the left column and clear the checkbox titled Enable Protected View for Files Originating from the Internet, as shown in Figure 20-2.**

You can clear the checkbox titled Enable Protected View for Outlook Attachments as well, if you want.

WARNING

Always leave Enable Protected View for Files Located in Potentially Unsafe Locations checkbox turned on.

4. **Click OK twice to close the Trust Center and Options dialog boxes.**

Now you will no longer need click Enable Editing whenever you open a QuickBooks report in Excel.

TIP

You can use Protected View situationally in Excel for Windows should you encounter a spreadsheet of unknown provenance. To do so, choose File ⇨ Open ⇨ Browse and click once on the workbook name. Click the arrow next to the Open button and choose Open in Protected View.

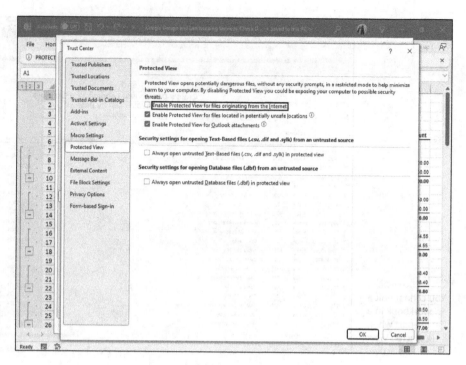

FIGURE 20-2:
Protected View
settings within
Excel's
Trust Center.

Filtering Data

The Filter feature in Excel is one of my favorites because it enables me to get a bird's-eye view of data within a report by clicking the Filter button at the top of any column or take things a step further by collapsing a report to show specific data.

Maybe you want to isolate just the overdue amounts on your accounts receivable aging schedule. The Filter feature is one way that you can accomplish this. Here's how to do so:

1. **Click any cell in the body of your report and then choose Data ⇨ Filter (or Home ⇨ Sort & Filter ⇨ Filter).**

   You can also press Ctrl+Shift+L (Cmd+Shift+L in macOS).

2. **Click the Filter button at the top of any column, such as cell H5 in Figure 20-3.**

3. **Clear the checkboxes for data that you don't want to see in this context, such as $0.00 and (Blanks), and then click OK.**

4. As shown in Figure 20-3, only rows that have a non-zero open balance are displayed.

You can filter on as many columns as you want.

5. Choose Data ⇨ Clear to remove the filter settings and see the entire report again.

Alternatively, choose Data ⇨ Filter to turn the Filter feature off, which, in turn, displays the entire report again. The Clear command keeps the filter buttons in place while clicking Filter toggles the buttons off.

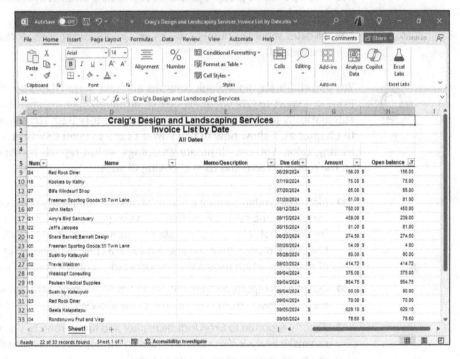

FIGURE 20-3:
A filtered Invoice
List By
Date Report.

REMEMBER

The Filter feature protects hidden rows, meaning that if you color-code, delete, or otherwise alter anything in any of the visible rows, nothing in the hidden rows is affected. However, deleting an entire column does remove any data that's within hidden rows, but only in the column that you deleted.

Sometimes the Filter feature is sufficient to help you get at what you want to see within an accounting report. In other cases, you may need to perform some data cleanup before you can achieve the desired results.

Preparing QuickBooks Reports for Analysis

Reports that you export from QuickBooks typically violate one or more of the following ground rules for analysis-ready data:

» All columns are contiguous, meaning the data set has no blank columns.

» All rows are contiguous, meaning the data set has no blank rows.

» The data set has no subtotal or total rows, which avoids double counting.

» The data has no groupings, such as segregating invoices by customer and bills by vendor.

» All dates should be numeric values, yet QuickBooks reports store dates as text instead.

TIP

You can eliminate most blank columns and text-based dates by choosing Export/ Print ➪ Export to CSV when exporting, although opening such files in Excel may automatically leading zeros, such as from inventory item IDs or certain ZIP codes. In Chapter 21, I show how to use Power Query to open CSV files while preserving leading zeros. You can eliminate groupings within reports by choosing Group By on the report screen, and then choosing Clear All.

» Blank cells within amount columns should be completely blank or contain zero, but some cells may be filled with two dashes instead. This causes Excel formulas that reference such cells to return an error such as #VALUE!, while PivotTable reports treat the entire column as being composed of text instead of numbers, which means the amounts are counted instead of summed.

» QuickBooks reports are generally limited to 40 columns, although some reports may have fewer columns while others may allow you to go beyond 40 columns.

» Reports exported to Excel include header and footer rows by default, which can make analysis more difficult. Turning the headers and footers off results in a more analysis-ready export to Excel.

I'll export the Transaction List by Date report to Excel so that you can see the steps that are necessary to overcome some of the nuances.

Exporting Modern View reports to Excel

Modern View reports have been gradually introduced in QuickBooks over the past two years, replacing what were previously known as Classic reports. Intuit aims to apply Modern View to all reports by December 2024. I'm going to trust that they follow through on this plan and assume that by the time you're reading this, Classic reports are no longer available.

Let's export the Modern View version of the Transaction List by Date report to Excel so that you can see how to transform any problematic columns:

1. **In QuickBooks, choose Reports from the sidebar menu.**

   The Reports page opens.

2. **Type** by date **in the Find a Report field, press ↓, and then press Enter.**

   Alternatively, choose Transaction List by Date in the For My Accountant section.

3. **Select This Year from the Report Period field.**

   Alternatively, choose any period you want or choose Custom from the list to set a specific date range.

4. **Click Export/Print ⇨ Export to Excel.**

5. **Click the Downloads button at the top of the Chrome window, then select the Excel workbook to open the report.**

   By default, reports that you export land from QuickBooks in your Downloads folder.

6. **Select the cells in column A that contain dates.**

   You can leave dates stored as text, but you'll have the best experience if you convert the dates to numeric values.

7. **Choose Data ⇨ Text to Columns.**

   The Convert Text to Columns wizard is displayed, as shown in Figure 20-4. Ostensibly, this feature allows you to take text in one column and split it into two or more columns, but you can also use it to transform text-based dates or amounts into numeric values.

   If you select column A on the worksheet frame, as opposed to selecting individual cells, you may encounter an error prompt that says, "We can't do that to merged cells." This arises when the header rows for a report has been exported to Excel. This is one reason to turn off the header rows in QuickBooks *before* you export to Excel. Alternatively, you can select the header rows in Excel, typically cells A1:A3, and then choose Home ⇨ Merge Cells to unmerge the cells. You'll then be able to select the entire column without issue.

   You can transform only one column at a time with the Convert Text to Columns wizard, so if you have multiple date columns, you need to clean up each one individually.

8. **Click Finish.**

   Alternatively, you can click Next twice and then click Finish if you want to see the options available within the Convert Text to Columns wizard.

9. **Select column I, which contains amounts where zeros are represented by two dashes.**

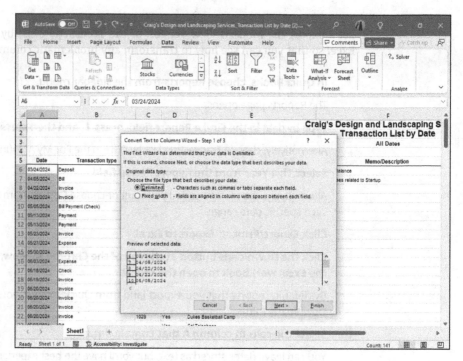

FIGURE 20-4:
Excel's Convert
Text to
Columns wizard.

10. **Choose Home ➪ Find and Select ➪ Replace or press Ctrl+H (Cmd+H in macOS).**

    Make sure that column I is still selected before you choose the Replace command; otherwise, you replace text across the entire worksheet instead of within a single column.

11. **Enter two dashes in the Find What field.**

12. **Enter a zero in the Replace With field, as shown in Figure 20-5.**

13. **Click Replace All ➪ OK ➪ Close.**

14. **Choose any cell in your data.**

    Spreadsheet users often think they must select all within a data set before carrying out an action in Excel. Selecting everything is necessary for applying formatting (such as colors, fonts, and number formats), but isn't necessary for performing data actions.

15. **Choose Insert ➪ Table ➪ OK or press Ctrl+T (Cmd+T in macOS). Then press Enter in the Table dialog box that is displayed.**

    The My Table Has Headers checkbox should be selected automatically in the Create Table dialog box, confirming that the first row of your list contains column titles.

16. Select the total row of the report, choose Home ⇨ Delete drop-down ⇨ Delete Sheet Row. Repeat this action for any footer rows that appear at the bottom of the report.

Total rows exported from QuickBooks are static in nature but can be replaced with dynamic total rows within Excel tables.

17. Choose Table Design ⇨ Total Row.

This command adds a total row to the bottom of your list, automatically summing or counting the last column, depending upon its content. Click any cell in the total row to display a menu from which you can select options such as Sum, Average, or Count. Excel adds the corresponding formula to that column's total. If you then filter or slice the table, the total row will only tally the visible rows.

18. Choose File ⇨ Save or press Ctrl+S (Cmd+S in macOS) to save the transformed report.

Saving the workbook at this point gives you the option to close without saving and reopen if you make a mistake during any of the upcoming analysis techniques.

The report is now in an analysis-ready format.

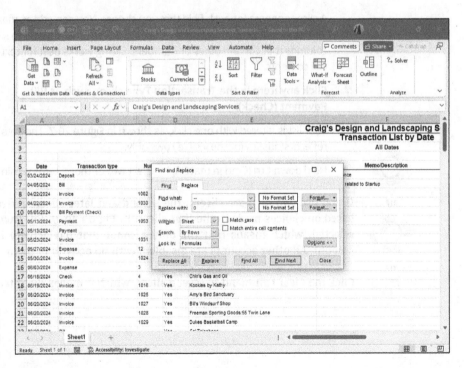

FIGURE 20-5:
Replacing two dashes with zeros.

Slicing data

The Slicer feature streamlines filtering tasks in Excel by enabling you to filter lists with a single mouse click. You can create slicers for as many columns as you want within your data, but unlike the Filter feature, your data does have to be formatted as an Excel table, which I described how to do in the previous section. Now let's add one or more slicers to your report:

1. **Click any cell in an Excel table, and then choose Table Design ⇨ Insert Slicer to display the Insert Slicers dialog box shown in Figure 20-6.**

You can use slicers to filter PivotTables as well. I show you how to create a PivotTable in the section "Summarizing Data with PivotTables," later in this chapter.

WARNING

Make sure to select a cell near the top of your table when inserting slicers. If you select a cell near the bottom of the table, your slicers may vanish off the screen when you make a selection. If this happens, choose Data ⇨ Clear to redisplay all hidden rows.

2. **Choose one or more fields, such as Transaction Type and Account, and then click OK.**

A slicer appears for each field that you choose. You can add as many slicers as you want, but keep in mind that it usually doesn't make sense to slice on columns that contain dates or numbers. Slicing works best for text-based cell contents.

3. **Click any item in the Transaction Type slicer, such as Bill Payment (Check).**

Your list is filtered with one click, as shown in Figure 20-7. The Total Row now reflects statistics for the visible rows only.

TIP

Hold down Ctrl (Cmd in macOS) to select two or more items within a slicer.

TIP

If you use two or more slicers, the second and later slicers reflect any matches based on choices made in the first slicer. In Figure 20-7, Bill Payment (Check) is selected, which means that the only account that has activity is the Checking account. All other accounts are disabled, with no activity in them.

Click the Clear command to reset a slicer, which removes the filter.

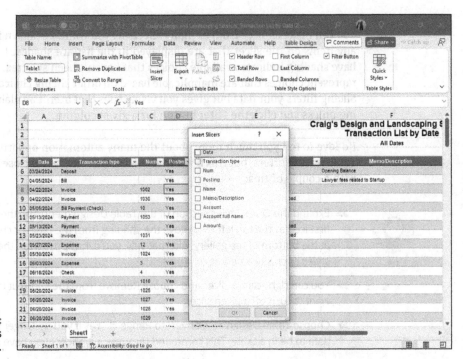

FIGURE 20-6:
Insert Slicers
dialog box.

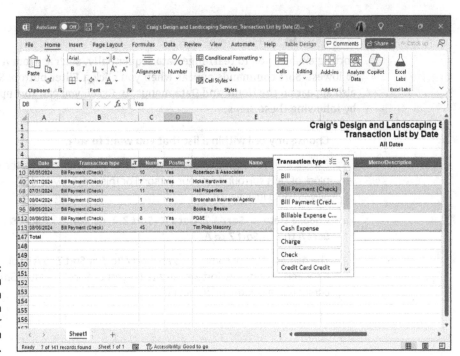

FIGURE 20-7:
Slicers allow you
to filter data
formatted as a
table or
PivotTable with a
single click.

You can make choices from as many slicers as you want. As shown in Figure 20-9, any items on the slicer that are displayed in the list are shaded. Items that don't have shading indicate available choices that haven't been selected. Disabled items represent choices that are inapplicable based on other slicing choices you've made. Slicing filters your data but gives you visual cues that aren't available when filtering unless you click the Filter button for a given column.

I'd love to tell you much more about the many automation opportunities that the Table feature offers, but this book is about QuickBooks, so I'll close this discussion with a couple of tips:

TIP

» Expand the Quick Styles section of the Table Design menu and then click the first icon at the top left to remove the shading from the table or choose Clear at the bottom of the gallery. Alternatively, you can choose from the prebuilt styles or create a new style.

» You can right-click a slicer and choose Remove from the shortcut menu if you want to turn off a given slicer.

» Choose Table Design ⇨ Convert to Range ⇨ Yes if you no longer want the data to be in a table. This command removes any slicers you have in place.

Sorting data

Sorting enables you to rearrange data sequentially, such as from A to Z or highest to lowest. Sort commands appear when you click a Filter button. Sort commands also appear on the Home and Data menus. In Excel, you can sort up to 64 columns by following these steps:

1. **Choose any cell within a list that you want to sort.**

   Excel is always tracking what's referred to as the *current region,* the contiguous block of cells surrounding your cursor. For this reason, you don't need to select all your data in advance.

2. **Choose Data ⇨ Sort A-Z, Data ⇨ Sort Z-A, or Home ⇨ Sort & Filter ⇨ Sort A to Z or Sort Z to A.**

   The names of these commands are Sort A to Z or Sort Z to A if your cursor is in a column of text, and Sort Smallest to Largest or Sort Largest to Smallest if your cursor is in a column of numbers.

3. **If you want to sort based on two or more columns, click the Sort button to display the Sort task pane.**

You can also use the Sort task pane to sort based on color or conditional formatting. If you dig deep enough, you can sort on custom lists or even sort lists sideways, meaning sorting columns from left to right or right to left versus sorting rows up and down the spreadsheet.

Summarizing Data with PivotTables

The PivotTable feature in Excel enables you to transform lists of data into meaningful summary reports simply by clicking or dragging fields within the PivotTable Fields task pane. Even better, nothing you do in a PivotTable affects the original data. Although it can seem intimidating, I want to assure you that this feature is one of Excel's easiest features to master.

Understanding PivotTable requirements

Be sure that your data conforms to all the data analysis ground rules that I listed in the "Preparing QuickBooks Reports for Analysis" section earlier in this chapter, and then convert your dataset into an Excel table. The Table feature enables a PivotTable to "see" any data that you append to the bottom of your current report, such as if you were to copy and paste data for a new month; otherwise, the new data you add to your list might be left off your PivotTable report.

Follow these steps to create a PivotTable:

1. **Select any cell in your list.**

2. **If necessary, choose Insert ⇨ Table ⇨ OK.**

3. **Choose Table Design ⇨ Summarize with PivotTable (or Insert ⇨ PivotTable).**

The Create PivotTable task pane opens.

4. **Accept the default settings by clicking OK.**

A blank PivotTable canvas opens on a new worksheet in your workbook, along with a PivotTable Fields task pane. You also see two new tabs in the Excel ribbon: PivotTable Analyze and Design.

REMEMBER

The PivotTable Analyze and Design tabs, as well as the PivotTable Fields task pane, are context sensitive. If you move your cursor to any cell outside the Pivot-Table canvas, the menus and task pane disappear; they reappear when you click inside the PivotTable canvas again. This behavior can be a bit disconcerting if you're new to the feature.

Adding fields to PivotTables

At this point, you're ready to add fields to your PivotTable:

1. **In Windows, click the checkbox for Account from the PivotTable Fields task pane. In macOS, drag the Account field into the Rows area.**

   When you click the checkbox for a given field, Excel for Windows places text or date-based fields in the Rows area. Excel for macOS places all fields in the Values area when you click a field's checkbox.

TIP

   You can drag fields into other areas at any time. You can only place fields in the Filters or Columns area by dragging the field name or right-clicking the field name and choosing an area.

2. **Drag the Date field into the Columns area.**

   If your dates are numeric values, Excel 2019 and later automatically group the transactions by month and then day. Otherwise, you will see a column for each date. This situation also arises if your dates are stored as text, which is the default format in QuickBooks. Refer to the Text to Columns discussion in the "Exporting Modern View Reports to Excel" section earlier in this chapter to convert the text-based data into dates that Excel recognizes.

3. **Click the checkbox for the Amount field to position it in the Values area.**

   I didn't apply any number formatting to the numbers within the PivotTable in Figure 20-8, so that you can see the raw format that first appears. You can change the formatting in a PivotTable in the same fashion as any other cells in Excel.

TIP

Double-clicking any number within a PivotTable drills down into the underlying transactions, like drilling down into a QuickBooks report. A new worksheet displays that shows you the data that the number you double-clicked is based upon.

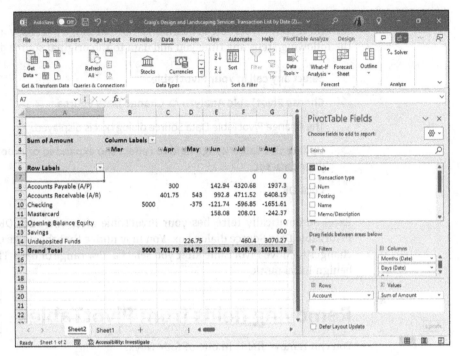

The table in the figure shows:

Sum of Amount	Column Labels					
	Mar	Apr	May	Jun	Jul	Aug
Row Labels				0		0
Accounts Payable (A/P)		300		142.94	4320.68	1937.3
Accounts Receivable (A/R)		401.75	543	992.8	4711.52	6408.19
Checking	5000		-375	-121.74	-596.85	-1651.61
Mastercard				158.08	208.01	-242.37
Opening Balance Equity						0
Savings						600
Undeposited Funds			226.75		460.4	3070.27
Grand Total	5000	701.75	394.75	1172.08	9103.76	10121.78

FIGURE 20-8: PivotTables allow you to create instant summaries of your data by dragging and dropping fields.

Refreshing and resizing PivotTables

PivotTables display a snapshot in time of your data. This is different from formulas, which recalculate automatically. You can refresh a PivotTable in three ways:

REMEMBER

» Right-click on the PivotTable and choose Refresh.

» Choose PivotTable Analyze ➪ Refresh.

The PivotTable Analyze tab is present only when your cursor is inside a PivotTable.

» Choose Data ➪ Refresh All.

The Refresh command refreshes only a single PivotTable, whereas Refresh All refreshes all PivotTables within a given workbook. Keep in mind that refreshing only includes data that the PivotTable can "see." If your PivotTable is based on a table, then your PivotTable automatically considers any new data when you refresh. If your PivotTable is based on a normal range of cells, you must carry out the following steps any time you add data to the original source data:

1. **Select any cell in your PivotTable.**

2. **Choose PivotTable Analyze ⇨ Change Data Source.**

   The Change PivotTable Data Source dialog box is displayed.

3. **Update the Table/Range field to reflect the expanded cell coordinates of your data set.**

4. **Click OK.**

Excel automatically refreshes your PivotTable after you click OK in the Change PivotTable Data Source dialog box. You may notice that the name of the dialog box changes to Move PivotTable after you select a new range of data. This is an odd but benign Excel quirk.

Removing fields from PivotTables

You can remove fields in one of four ways:

» Clear the checkbox for a field in the main area of the PivotTable Fields task pane.

» Drag any field within an area off the PivotTable Fields task pane and release your left mouse button.

» Click the arrow on the right side of any field in an area and choose Remove Field from the drop-down menu.

» Right-click the field within the PivotTable and choose Remove from the shortcut menu.

TIP

I could go on and on about PivotTables, but I'll limit myself to a couple of closing tips:

» Plus and minus buttons appear within PivotTables when you have two or more fields in the Rows or Columns area. For instance, drag Name into the Rows area to view activity by account and then name. Use these buttons to expand or collapse individual segments of reports or choose PivotTable Analyze ⇨ Collapse Field to collapse all segments, or PivotTable Analyze ⇨ Expand Field to expand all segments. Your cursor must be within the contents of a row field to use these commands.

» Choose PivotTable Analyze ⇨ Insert Timeline to select a date-based field and then click OK. As shown in Figure 20-9, timelines are like slicers but are used to filter PivotTables for specific date ranges.

» See *Microsoft Data Analysis for Dummies* by Paul McFedries if you want to delve more deeply into PivotTables.

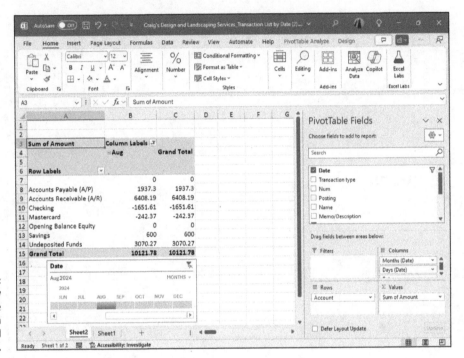

FIGURE 20-9:
Timelines allow you to control the contents of a PivotTable based on date ranges.

Chapter **21**

Automating QuickBooks Analysis with Power Query

I n Chapter 20, I explain how you can export QuickBooks reports for analysis in Microsoft Excel. I also explain how you can manually create a PivotTable report from your data. In this chapter, I show you how to automate the steps by using Power Query to create set-and-forget connections to reports. You still need to export reports to Excel from QuickBooks, but if you save over an exported report that's linked to Power Query, the rest of the linking and transformation process is mostly automated. If you read to the end of the chapter, you can find out how to make the process completely automated.

Power Query can automate all various report clean-up steps. This makes reports much easier to work with. It also enables features like PivotTables and filtering that may be challenging or impossible in the report's native format.

Introducing Power Query

As you may surmise by the name, Power Query enables you to connect to data sources, such as reports that you export from QuickBooks. The connections are refreshable, so you can save new copies over your previous exports to have a set-and-forget approach to reporting. You can instruct Excel to refresh the data connections automatically, as well as refresh any PivotTables or PivotCharts that are tied to the data when you open the workbook. In short, it's a means of automating repetitive tasks without writing programming code.

For this chapter, I used the sample Plus company for QuickBooks Online, which you can access at https://qbo.intuit.com/redir/testdrive. I chose this company to provide an easy way for you to generate reports that have actual data in them. You can also follow along with your own data.

Checking out Power Query

Let's export the Chart of Accounts Report from QuickBooks to a CSV file so that you can get an initial lay of the land with Power Query:

1. **In QuickBooks choose Settings ⇨ Chart of Accounts.**

   The Chart of Accounts list is displayed.

2. **Click Run Report.**

   The Account List report opens.

3. **Click Export/Print ⇨ Export as CSV.**

   By default, reports that you export from QuickBooks are saved to your Downloads folder.

4. **Launch Microsoft Excel and press Ctrl+N (or Cmd+N in macOS) if a blank workbook doesn't appear on the screen.**

5. **Choose Data ⇨ Get Data ⇨ From File ⇨ From Text/CSV.**

6. **Select the CSV file from your Downloads folder and then click Import.**

   A dialog box opens and displays a preview of the CSV file.

7. **Click Transform Data to launch the Power Query Editor.**

   Alternatively, you can click Load, which bypasses the Power Query Editor and imports data directly into a new worksheet.

At this point the Power Query Editor opens on your screen.

Touring the Power Query Editor

The Power Query Editor enables you to transform data that you have imported into your workbook. As you'll see in the "Transforming reports" section later in this chapter, Power Query can make it easy to transform QuickBooks reports into analysis-ready data formats. Let's look at some of the major features of the Power Query Editor:

>> **Ribbon interface:** Power Query has a tabbed interface much like Excel's.

>> **Queries pane:** This pane along the left side lists all available queries in each workbook. In this case, the name of the CSV file that you imported into the Power Query Editor appears here.

>> **Current view:** A worksheet-like grid offers a live preview of your data, in this case you're seeing the contents of the CSV file that you imported.

>> **Query settings:** A task pane on the right side of the screen enables you to rename a query and shows as a list of transformation steps that have been applied to your data. In this case, only two steps should appear:

- *Source:* This step links Power Query to the data source you specified — in this case a CSV file. In this example, you could click the Settings button to display a dialog box from which you can click Browse, select a different CSV file with the same layout, and then click OK. Doing so replaces the current data that appears in the Power Query Window, and is then returned to Excel.

- Every Power Query connection has a Source step, which means you can swap a newer version of your data into your workbook at any time rather than repeating the Power Query steps again.

TIP

- *Changed Type:* This step signifies that Power Query has automatically changed the data type for one or more columns. You can manually change the data type for a given column in the Current View by clicking the icon at the left side of the column heading.

>> **Status bar:** A row of information appears along the bottom of the screen to give you various information about your query.

You can't work in Excel and Power Query at the same time. This means that if you're working in the Power Query Editor, the only way you can access your spreadsheet is to choose Close and Load on the Home tab of Power Query's ribbon or close Power Query and discard any changes.

REMEMBER

Let's now carry out a couple of transformation steps:

1. Choose Home ⇨ Use First Row as Headers.

This moves the data from the first row of the Current View grid up into the frame, thereby replacing the generic headers, meaning Column1, Column2, and so on.

2. Choose Home ⇨ Choose Columns.

The Choose Columns dialog box opens.

3. Deselect all fields except for Account Name and Account Type and then click OK.

The Current View grid should now only have two columns.

4. Click the Filter button in the Account Type column heading, clear Select All, select Income and Expense, and then click OK.

The Current View grid should now only display Income and Expense accounts.

5. Choose Close & Load.

The Power Query Editor closes, and the data you saw in the Current View grid now appears in a new Excel worksheet.

The preceding steps may feel rather pedestrian, meaning you're probably thinking, "Well, I could have just done the same thing in Excel." That's true, but the difference with Power Query is that you can save a new version of the CSV file over the original, and then right-click the Account List table in the Excel worksheet and choose Refresh to import the new data without redoing the transformation steps. You can even automate the refresh process, which I discuss in the "Keeping Power Query Results Current" section later in this chapter.

Automating QuickBooks Report Analysis

In Chapter 20, I discuss how to export reports from QuickBooks. Reports that are exported to Excel from QuickBooks tend to store dates and sometimes amounts as text, which can result in repetitive clean-up work. You may also find yourself copying and pasting data from QuickBooks exports into other workbooks. Power Query eliminates the copying and pasting and also provides a set-and-forget approach for cleaning up QuickBooks reports automatically.

Transforming reports

Reports that you export to Excel from QuickBooks Online have a couple of potential snags:

» Date columns are formatted as text, which means certain Excel features don't recognize the data as being date-based.

» Zero amounts and blank fields are represented by two dashes instead of a zero or blank cells. Formulas that refer to such cells often return #VALUE!.

Connecting to a report

You can use Power Query to manually clean reports once and then have the transformation applied automatically again if you save over the original Quick-Books export:

1. **In QuickBooks, choose Reports from the sidebar.**

The Reports page is displayed.

2. **Start typing** Transaction List by Date **in the Search field, and then choose that report title in the search results.**

The Search field makes it easy to locate reports without scrolling through the entire list.

3. **Click General Options, clear all checkboxes in the Header and Footer sections, and then close the General Options task pane.**

Turning off headers and footers on reports streamlines the data transformation process in Power Query by eliminating the need to remove extraneous rows.

4. **Select a date range, such as This Year, from the Report Period field.**

Many QuickBooks reports default to the current month, but you can designate any period.

Click Save As to add a customized report to the Custom Reports tab of the Reports screen. In the future, you can run the customized version to eliminate carrying out repetitive actions.

TIP

5. **Choose Export/Print ⇨ Export to Excel.**

See Chapter 6 for more information about running reports in QuickBooks.

6. **Click the Downloads button at the top of the Chrome window, then select the Excel workbook to open the report.**

   By default, reports that you export from QuickBooks are saved to your Downloads folder.

7. **In Excel choose File ⇨ Save As ⇨ Browse, choose a permanent location for the workbook, optionally change the file name, and then click Save.**

   Specifying a more permanent location than your Downloads folder enables you to save new versions of reports over the existing workbook, eliminating the need to transform the data repeatedly.

8. **Press Ctrl+W (Cmd+W in macOS) or choose File ⇨ Close to close the Excel workbook.**

9. **Press Ctrl+N (Cmd+N in macOS) or choose File ⇨ New ⇨ Blank Workbook in Excel to create a blank workbook.**

   You can also select any worksheet within an existing workbook. Power Query will return the results to a new worksheet, so there's no risk of overwriting existing data.

10. **Choose Data ⇨ Get Data ⇨ From File ⇨ From Workbook.**

11. **Browse for and select the file that you saved in Step 7, and then click the Import button in Excel for Windows (or Transform Data in Excel for macOS).**

    A Navigator dialog box is displayed, as shown in Figure 21-1.

12. **Choose the worksheet containing the data you want to access, typically Sheet1, and then click Transform Data.**

WARNING

In Chapter 20, I discuss how Protected View in Excel for Windows sometimes prevents data from appearing onscreen, meaning reports show all zeroes instead of amounts. Protected View can affect Power Query as well. If you see only zeros instead of amounts in the data preview, click Cancel in the Navigator window. Open your QuickBooks report in Excel, click Enable Content if needed, and then save the QuickBooks report with a new filename and close it. You should then be able to carry out Steps 1 through 10 again without issue.

Transforming a report

The Applied Steps list in Figure 21-2 shows that the Applied Steps window has four steps. Depending on your version of Excel, your Applied Steps window may only have two steps. In older versions of Excel, the third and fourth steps — Promoted Headers and Changed Type — are sometimes added automatically. These steps are intended to help by jump-starting your data transformation, but they can sometimes cause conflicts, especially if the first row of your data contains a report title rather than column headings.

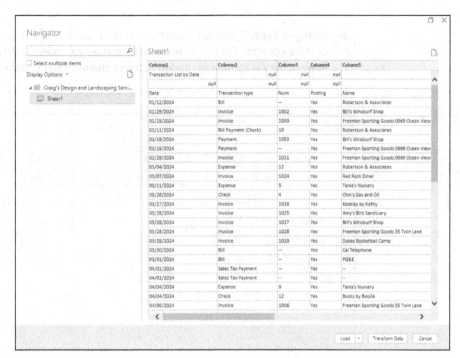

FIGURE 21-1:
The Power Query
Navigator
window.

Here's an overview of the steps you may encounter when initiating a Power Query transformation:

>> **Source:** This step ties Power Query to your data source — whatever it may be. You can click Settings and select a different data source with the same layout. You can change the source to point to a newer version of your file.

>> **Navigation:** This step populates the Current View with your data. If needed, you can click Settings and choose a different worksheet within your workbook.

WARNING

Be cautious not to delete the Navigation step, as doing so will prevent you from viewing your data. If this happens, the easiest way to restore viewability is to choose File ⇨ Discard and Close and then restart your import.

>> **Promoted headers:** This step moves the data from the first row of your file into the column headings of the Active View. If your actual headings are further down on the report, you may need to remove this step by clicking Promoted Headers and then clicking the X that appears.

WARNING

When removing items from the Applied Steps list, be careful. If you remove Promoted Headers, the subsequent Changed Type step might trigger an error because it can no longer reference one or more columns by name. If this occurs, click on Changed Type and then click the X that appears. You can then add new transformation steps as needed.

>> **Changed Type:** This step means that the data type has been changed for one or more columns. For instance, a column containing dates stored as text, but Power Query automatically added a step to change the text into dates.

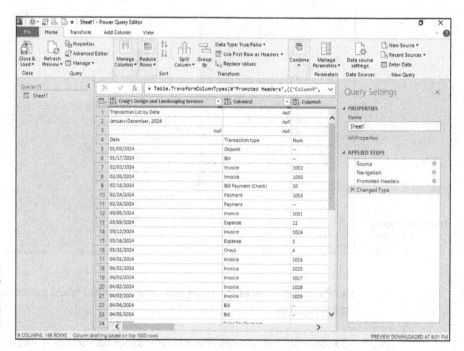

FIGURE 21-2:
The Power Query Editor shows the QuickBooks report you just imported.

Since some Excel users will start out with two items in the Applied Steps list and others will have four, let's get everyone on the same footing.

1. **If Promoted Headers is present in the Applied Steps list, right-click on the step, choose Delete Until End, and then click Delete.**

2. **If the column headings, such as Date, Transaction Type, Num, and so on are not in row 1, carry out the following steps. Otherwise, proceed with Step 3.**

   a. *Choose Home ⇨ Remove Rows ⇨ Remove Top Rows. The Remove Top Rows dialog box opens.*

   b. *Specify the number of extraneous rows to remove, and then click OK. If the column titles appear on row 5, then enter **4** in the Number of Rows field. A Removed Top Rows step appears in the Applied Steps list.*

c. *Right-click the Removed Top Rows step, choose Rename, and change the name to Removed Top 5 Rows. Renaming steps in Power Query makes it much easier to understand the purpose of each transformation.*

3. Choose Home ⇨ Use First Row as Headers.

The column headings move into the header row of the Current View section, and a Promoted Headers step appears in the Applied Steps list.

4. Click the Data Type button in the Date column, represented by ABC123, and then select Date from the menu.

The ABC123 data type is like the General number format in Excel, and often results in dates being presented in serial number form rather than as dates. Setting the data type in Power Query eliminates the need to manually format the dates once you return the data to your workbook.

TIP

For optimal results, always change the data type for non-text columns to the appropriate format.

5. Click on the Amount column heading to select the entire column, as shown in Figure 21-3.

6. Choose Home ⇨ Replace Values.

The Replace Values dialog box shown in Figure 21-4 is displayed.

7. Type two dashes (--) in the Value to Find field.

REMEMBER

If an exclamation mark appears next to the Value to Find field then the column that you are attempting to transform is comprised entirely of numeric values. In such cases, click Cancel because there is nothing to replace, and the OK button will be disabled.

8. Type a zero (0) in the Replace With field, and then click OK.

A Replaced Value step appears on the Applied Steps list.

9. Right-click the Replaced Value step, choose Rename, and change the name to Replaced Double Dashes with 0.

Renaming steps in Power Query makes it much easier to understand what a transformation is doing.

10. Change the data type for the Amount column to Currency, as shown in Figure 21-5.

Figure 21-5 shows the data types that you can assign to any column within your query. The Using Locale option allows you to apply international settings to a column.

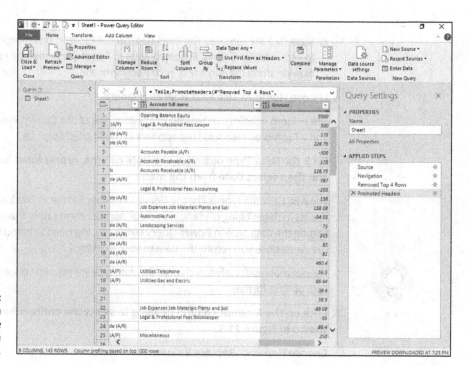

FIGURE 21-3:
You must select a column before carrying out a transformation.

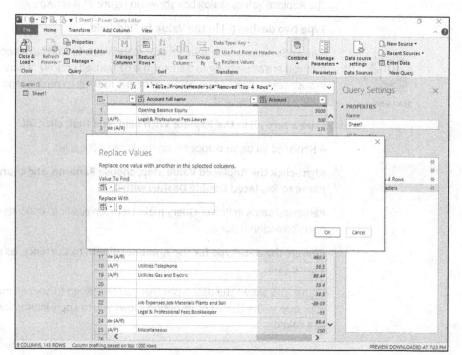

FIGURE 21-4:
The Replace Values dialog box in Power Query.

TIP

Some rows in the Amount column would have reported `Error` if we hadn't replaced the dashes with zeros. It's important to remove text like this from a column *before* changing the data type, as described in these steps.

11. **Choose Home ⇨ Choose Columns.**

    The Choose Columns dialog box opens, as shown in Figure 21-6.

TIP

The Choose Columns dialog box provides an easy way to remove unwanted columns from a report.

12. **Clear the Num, Posting, and Account Full Name checkboxes and then click OK.**

    The fields are presented in the order in which they appear in the report, but you can click the AZ button to alphabetize them or use the Search field to shorten the list.

13. **Click the settings button next to the Removed Other Columns step in the Applied Steps pane, as shown in Figure 21-7.**

    You can revise a step that you've added to a Power Query transformation if a settings icon appears.

14. **You can now remove additional columns, such as the Memo/Description field, and click OK.**

    At this point, the report should have five columns — specifically Date, Transaction Type, Name, Account, and Amount. You've cleaned up the anomalies that QuickBooks introduces into the reports, so you can return the data to Excel.

15. **Choose Home ⇨ Close and Load.**

    Make sure to click the icon for Close and Load, versus the words. If you click on the Close and Load drop-down, you'll then need to click Close and Load a second time.

At this point your cleaned up QuickBooks report appears in a new worksheet in Microsoft Excel, as shown in Figure 21-8.

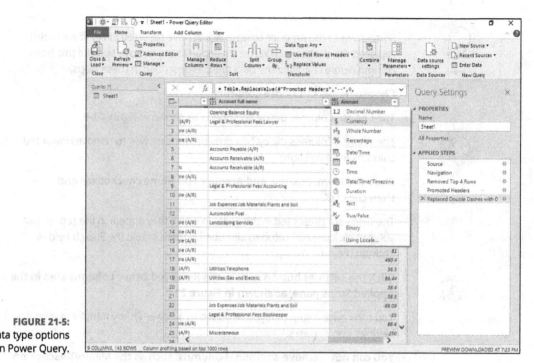

FIGURE 21-5:
Data type options
in Power Query.

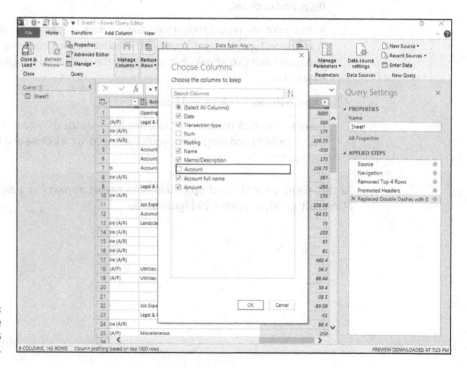

FIGURE 21-6:
The Choose
Columns
dialog box.

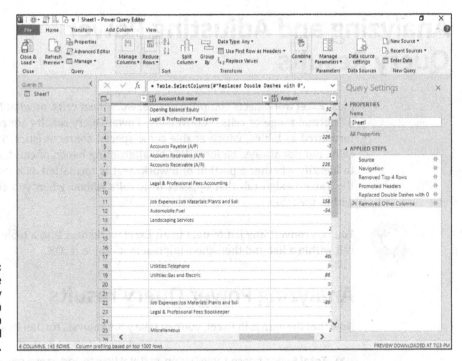

FIGURE 21-7:
You can revise any Power Query step that has a Settings button in the Applied steps list.

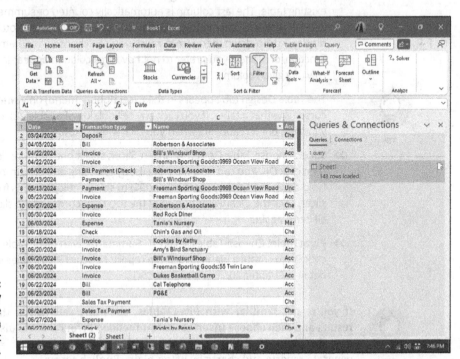

FIGURE 21-8:
Power Query results are returned to a new worksheet by default.

Analyzing and Adjusting Power Query Results

Most Excel worksheets comprise normal worksheet cells, or what Microsoft terms a "normal range of cells." Conversely, Power Query results are returned to cells formatted as tables, which enable some special characteristics. Tables can typically, but not always, be identified by alternating bands of color. A sure-fire way to identify whether a portion of a worksheet is formatted as a table is by way of the Table Design tab that appears in Excel's ribbon when you click on any cell within the table.

TIP

You can convert any list of data in an Excel worksheet into a table by clicking any cell within a list and then choosing Insert ⇨ Table ⇨ OK.

Analyzing Power Query results

Now that the data is in Excel, you can take your analysis further in a couple of ways:

>> **Total Row:** Choose Table Design ⇨ Total Row to add a total row to any existing table. The last column is automatically counted or summed, depending on the type of data in the column. Click any cell within the total row to display a drop-down menu from which you can choose a mathematical function, or None if you prefer to not have a calculation appear in the total row of a given column.

TIP

The Table Design tab appears in the Excel ribbon (menu) only when your cursor is within a table. If you click any cell outside of a table, the ribbon tab vanishes, but it reappears when you click within a table again.

>> **Slicer:** Choose Table Design ⇨ Insert Slicer, select one or more fields, and then click OK. You can now filter the list by choosing any item from the slicer. Hold down the Ctrl key (Cmd in macOS) to select multiple items from the slicer. Click the Clear Filter button at the top-right corner of the slicer to view all items again.

>> **PivotTable:** Choose Table Design ⇨ Summarize with Pivot Table and then click OK to create a blank PivotTable report. I discuss PivotTables in more detail in Chapter 20.

TIP

If you're not familiar with PivotTables, click any cell within the Power Query results and then choose Insert ⇨ Recommended PivotTables to display some suggested reports. If you're using Microsoft 365, choose Home ⇨ Analyze Data to generate reports and charts by using plain-English terms.

Editing Power Query results

You may invariably discover that you missed some details in transforming your report or that you filtered data or hid a column that you want to see. You can return to the Power Query Editor at any point by using any of these methods:

» Click any cell within a list generated by Power Query and then choose Query ⇨ Edit.

» Right-click any cell within a list generated by Power Query and then choose Table ⇨ Edit Query.

» Right-click any connection in the Queries & Connections task pane and choose Edit.

TIP

The Queries & Connections task pane appears automatically whenever you return results to Excel from Power Query. You can display the task pane at any time by choosing Data ⇨ Queries & Connections.

Click Close and Load within the Power Query Editor to save your changes and return to Microsoft Excel.

Keeping Power Query Results Current

Data that you return to Excel from Power Query is a snapshot in time rather than a real-time feed. A major benefit of Power Query is that you have to perform the transformation steps only once. Going forward, you can save new versions of your QuickBooks reports and other data sources over the original files that you connected to Power Query and then refresh the results manually. You can also instruct Excel to refresh results from Power Query automatically when you open the workbook that contains the Power Query results that you returned to Excel.

Updating Power Query results manually

When you want to transform a newer version of a report, such as the Transaction List by Date or Profit and Loss by Customer reports, use the following steps:

1. **Follow the usual steps in QuickBooks to export the report to Excel.**

2. **Open the report in Excel, and then choose File ⇨ Save As and save the report over the original file that you selected with Power Query.**

3. **Open the workbook where you created the Power Query transformation, and then choose Data ⇨ Refresh All.**

Although Power Query establishes a connection to data sources, such as reports that you export from QuickBooks, it doesn't create a live feed. The latest version of your data appears in your workbooks only after you refresh the data.

Refreshing Power Query results automatically

You can instruct Power Query to refresh automatically when you open a workbook that contains one or more queries:

1. **Click any cell within a list of data generated by Power Query.**

   The Query menu appears in the Excel ribbon only when you click a cell within data that has been brought into Excel from Power Query.

2. **Choose Query ⇨ Properties or choose Data ⇨ Properties to open the External Data Range Properties dialog box, and then click the Query Properties button to the right of the Name field.**

3. **Clear the Enable Background Refresh checkbox, select the Refresh Data When Opening the File checkbox, and (if available) select the Enable Fast Data Load checkbox, as shown in Figure 21-9.**

   Enable Background Refresh enables you to keep working in your spreadsheet while data from an external source is being refreshed. However, it tends to create confusion because the refresh happens more slowly — to the point that you may think nothing is happening.

   The Refresh Data When Opening the File option instructs Excel to reach out to the external workbook automatically and grab the latest version of the data, thereby creating a self-updating reporting tool.

   Fast Data Load speeds the refresh process by directing all of Excel's resources to the refresh process, which in turn means you can't carry out any work in Excel while the refresh occurs. However, the refreshing happens faster, so it's a minor tradeoff.

   You can change these options at any time. For example, you might turn off Refresh Data When Opening the File if you want to archive a snapshot of a data set for a particular point in time.

4. **Click OK to close the Query Properties dialog box.**

Query properties that you set are unique to each Power Query connection, so you must carry out the preceding steps every time you establish a new data connection via Power Query.

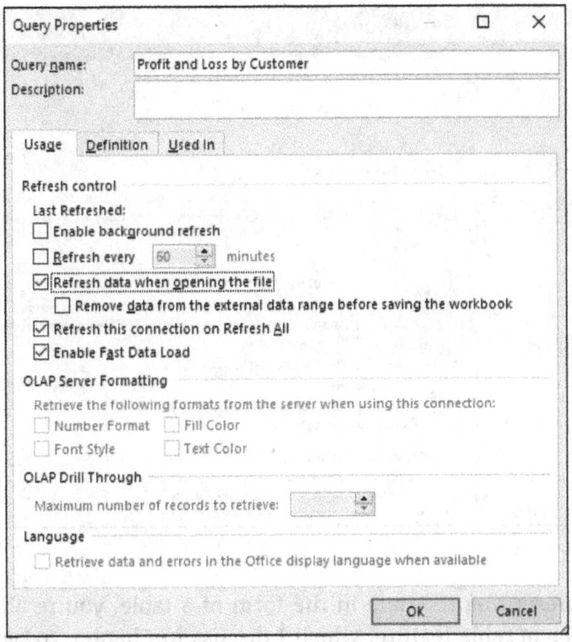

FIGURE 21-9:
Adjusting query
properties
enables you
to have a self-
updating report.

Now that you've set the query properties for your Power Query connection, you need to eliminate one other speed bump to streamline the update process. Follow these steps to disable the Enable Content security prompt that otherwise appears every time you open your workbook:

1. **Save and close the workbook that contains a Power Query connection.**

2. **Reopen your workbook.**

    Resist the urge to click the Enable Content prompt so that you can suppress it permanently for this workbook. If you did click Enable Content, close your workbook, reopen it, and proceed to Step 3.

3. **Choose File ⇨ Info ⇨ Enable Content ⇨ Enable Content to suppress the security prompt.**

    As shown in Figure 21-10, the Enable Content option makes the document a trusted document. When you mark a document as such, Excel no longer requires you to choose Enable Content before you refresh the workbook.

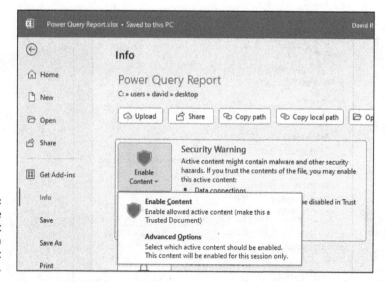

FIGURE 21-10:
Suppressing the
Enable Content
prompt for a
specific
workbook.

If you're presenting the data in the form of a table, you're all set. But if you're using the PivotTable feature, which I discuss in Chapter 20, you need to change one more setting to ensure that your report is completely self-updating. Follow these steps:

1. **Select any cell within a PivotTable and choose the PivotTable Analyze menu.**

The PivotTable menus are context-sensitive, so the PivotTable Analyze and Design menus vanish when your cursor isn't within a PivotTable.

2. **Choose PivotTable Analyze ⇨ Options.**

The PivotTable Options dialog box opens, as shown in Figure 21-11.

3. **Click the Data tab, select the Refresh Data When Opening the File checkbox, and then click OK.**

This option instructs Excel to refresh your PivotTable when you open the workbook.

WARNING

Make sure that you set both your Power Query connection and any PivotTables based on Power Query data to refresh automatically when you open the file; otherwise, you might find yourself reviewing stale information. Choose Data ⇨ Refresh All in Excel to be certain that everything in your workbook is updated.

TIP

If you want to learn more about Power Query, see *Excel Power Pivot & Power Query For Dummies* by Michael Alexander.

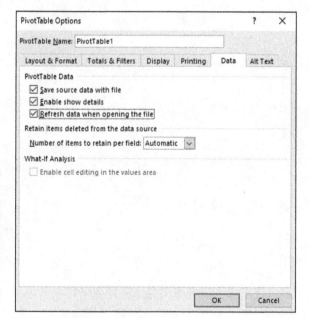

FIGURE 21-11:
You must also
click Refresh Data
When Opening
the File to enable
a PivotTable
that's tied to
Power Query to
update itself
automatically.

7

The Part of Tens

IN THIS PART . . .

Master ten common journal entries.

Improve efficiency with ten Chrome shortcuts.

IN THIS CHAPTER

» **Adjusting asset and liability accounts**

» **Recording recurring fees, petty cash expenditures, and payroll**

» **Recording and applying prepaid expenses**

» **Allowing for and writing off bad debt**

» **Posting depreciation**

Chapter **22**

Ten Common Journal Entries

Q uickBooks goes to great lengths to shield users from as much accounting as possible, but in this chapter you roll up your sleeves and do some old-school accounting in the form of journal entries. The good news is that journal entries are typically a tiny percentage of the transactions you enter into QuickBooks — if you even have to do it at all. I start by showing you how to get to the journal entry screen and record a journal entry in general terms. Then you work through ten common journal entries.

TIP

You may be surprised to learn that behind the scenes *every* transaction you input into QuickBooks is transformed into a journal entry. Look for the More button at the bottom of most transaction screens and then choose Transaction Journal to view the underlying journal entry for any transaction you have entered. Remember, the More button doesn't appear until you have saved the transaction at least once.

Understanding Debits and Credits

Regardless of whether you see it, every accounting transaction is composed of debits and credits. The sum of the total debits must always match the sum of the total credits. A transaction can have any number of debits and credits as long as the sum of each matches. The Balance Sheet report in QuickBooks Online offers a great way to understand debits and credits because certain accounts have natural debit balances, whereas others have natural credit balances. At a high level, your balance sheet is broken down into three categories:

>> **Assets:** This section reflects what your business owns or is owed. Asset accounts typically have a debit balance but may sometimes have a credit balance, such as if you overdraw a bank account.

>> **Liabilities:** This section reflects records monies that your business owes to others and typically has a credit balance. You might encounter liability accounts that have a debit balance when you pay more payroll taxes than are due, for instance.

>> **Equity:** This section reflects the net worth of the business, meaning assets minus liabilities. Equity accounts typically have a credit balance, but they can have a debit balance. This might happen, for example, if an owner is taking more money out of the business than they should.

It's time to move the high-level discussion of debits and credits to the Profit and Loss statement. This statement can have several categories, but I collapse it down to two:

>> **Revenues:** This section reflects income that your business has earned. Behind-the-scenes revenue or income accounts typically have credit balances.

>> **Expenses:** This section reflects costs that your business has incurred, which means that expense accounts typically have debit balances.

With that explanation in hand, allow me to explain why your bank is making it difficult for you to comprehend the concept of journal entries. Perhaps you run a transaction journal for a $1,000 Sales Receipt transaction that looks something like this.

Account	Debits	Credits	Description
Cash	$1,000.00		Revenue from sales receipt
Revenue		$1,000.00	Revenue from sales receipt

In this scenario, you're increasing both cash and revenue, and the journal entry is in balance. Where things get confusing is when your bank reports activity on your account from *their* perspective. You see, they're holding onto your money for you and must return it to you upon demand. To *them*, your money is a *liability*, whereas to *you*, it's an *asset*. You just increased your asset by $1,000 with the previous journal entry. Here's what the bank's journal entry looks like.

Account	Debits	Credits	Description
Cash	$1,000.00		Record customer deposit
Liabilities		$1,000.00	Record customer deposit

Both of these are also increases. Their asset, cash, is increased by $1,000, but because they're just holding the money for you, their liabilities also increase. Conversely, you earned $1,000, so your asset, cash, is increased, and your revenue is increased. Maybe that amount makes up your only earnings for the year, and you had no expenses. At the end of the fiscal year, QuickBooks automatically records a journal entry that debits income by $1,000 and credits retained earnings by $1,000, like this.

Account	Debits	Credits	Description
Revenue	$1,000.00		Close fiscal year
Retained earnings		$1,000.00	Close fiscal year

In this case, revenue is decreased by $1,000, so your revenue starts over at zero for the new year. Retained earnings is increased by $1,000 and represents money that has been earned but has not yet distributed to the company's owners. This is a grossly oversimplified example because a normal closing entry zeroes out all income and expense accounts by debiting or crediting as needed to bring the account balances to zero, with the net remaining amount being offset to retained earnings.

Creating Journal Entries

Most transactions are easily entered through the corresponding transaction screens in QuickBooks, but certain adjustments can be made only by way of a journal entry or are most easily recorded in that fashion. Here's how to create a journal entry:

1. **Choose +New ⇨ Journal Entry.**

   The journal entry screen appears, as shown in Figure 22-1.

2. **Input a date into the Journal Date field.**

Enter the date that you want the transaction to affect your books. Many journal entries are known as adjusting entries, such as those that record depreciation or recognize prepaid expense, and are typically recorded on the last day of a month. There's no hard and fast rule, though.

REMEMBER

Journal entries that affect a bank or credit card account should always reflect the actual transaction date so that the activity shows up properly when you go to reconcile your account.

3. **Optional: Change the Journal Number.**

QuickBooks increments this number automatically, but you can enter up to 21 characters in this field.

4. **Choose an account from the first row of the journal entry in the Account column.**

On most other transaction screens, QuickBooks refers to accounts as categories. In this case, you're choosing an account from your chart of accounts.

I discuss reviewing and customizing your chart of accounts in Chapter 1.

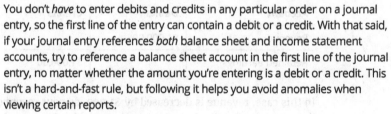

TIP

You don't *have* to enter debits and credits in any particular order on a journal entry, so the first line of the entry can contain a debit or a credit. With that said, if your journal entry references *both* balance sheet and income statement accounts, try to reference a balance sheet account in the first line of the journal entry, no matter whether the amount you're entering is a debit or a credit. This isn't a hard-and-fast rule, but following it helps you avoid anomalies when viewing certain reports.

REMEMBER

5. **Enter a debit or credit amount as a positive amount.**

You can't enter a debit and a credit on the same line. If you enter a debit amount and a credit amount in the same row, the second amount you enter is kept, and the first amount is erased.

WARNING

You can, but you shouldn't, enter negative amounts in the Debits and Credits fields. For one, it's difficult to ensure that your journal entry balances. For another, the minus sign instructs QuickBooks to record the negative credit that you entered as a debit and a negative debit as a credit, so your entry posts in the opposite fashion than you're expecting.

6. **Enter a description for the journal entry row.**

I provide some descriptions in the journal entries that I discuss later in this chapter.

7. **Optional: Choose a name from the list, meaning a customer or vendor.**

Be particularly careful about choosing names on journal entries because doing so can circumvent the checks and balances that the transaction screens in

QuickBooks put in place for you. For instance, if you incorrectly tag a customer on a journal entry, you can end up in a situation where the ending balance on your aged accounts receivable report no longer matches the accounts receivable balance on your balance sheet.

8. **Repeat Steps 2 through 7 on the second row of the journal entry.**

   You can enter as many rows as you like and leave unneeded rows blank.

TIP

   It's always best to consult an accountant if you have uncertainties about recording a journal entry.

9. **Click Save to save your transaction.**

   A Make Recurring button appears once you save the transaction. I discuss recurring transactions in Chapter 9.

10. **Run a balance sheet or Profit and Loss report in QuickBooks to ensure that your journal entry had the desired effect.**

   It's easy to enter debits and credits in the wrong places, so check to see if the account balances changed as you expected. If you entered the amounts incorrectly, use the Search command at the top of the screen to access your journal entry, move the debit and credit amounts into the proper columns, and then save your journal entry again.

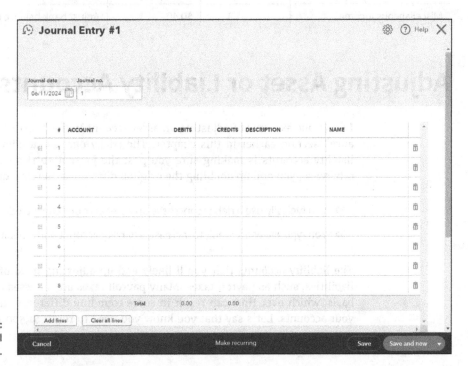

FIGURE 22-1:
The Journal
Entry screen.

Correcting a Bank Balance

Maybe you're reconciling your bank account, which I discuss in Chapter 5, and find that your account balance is off by a minor amount, say 40 cents. You might choose to scour your books to find the transaction that was incorrectly entered, or you might decide to just adjust your bank balance.

If your bank balance is 40 cents higher than the bank thinks it should be, you can enter a journal entry along these lines.

Account	Debits	Credits	Description
Miscellaneous expense	$0.40		Adjust bank balance to actual
Cash		$0.40	Adjust bank balance to actual

Conversely, if the bank thinks you have more money than you believe you have and you want to go with their number, your journal entry might look something like this.

Account	Debits	Credits	Description
Cash	$0.40		Adjust bank balance to actual
Miscellaneous income		$0.40	Adjust bank balance to actual

Adjusting Asset or Liability Accounts

I cover one example of adjusting an asset account in the "Correcting a Bank Balance" section earlier in this chapter. The tricky part about adjusting asset and liability accounts is making sure you post the journal entries correctly because otherwise, you end up doubling the original difference. Here's a quick refresher:

>> You typically use a debit to increase an asset account and a credit to reduce it.

>> You typically use a credit to increase a liability account and a debit to reduce it.

The liability accounts that you'll likely end up adjusting most often are payroll liabilities, such as payroll taxes. Many payroll taxes are assessed on a percentage basis, which over time can result in some rounding differences accumulating in your accounts. Let's say that you know you need to remit $1,500 in payroll taxes for December. The sum of your payroll tax accounts should be $1,500, but it could be $1,500.10, with the extra 10 cents reflecting rounding. Here's how to enter a journal entry to correct the balance.

Account	Debits	Credits	Description
Payroll Taxes Payable	$0.10		Adjust balance to actual
Payroll Tax Expense		$0.10	Adjust balance to actual

Assuming that you haven't paid the payroll tax amount yet, your balance sheet should reflect a balance of $1,500.00. If it reflects $1,500.20, you recorded the entry backward. Use the Search button to retrieve your journal entry, flip the debits and credits between columns, and then save your journal entry again.

Recording a Recurring Fee

Let's say that your bank charges an ongoing fee of $15 per month. A journal entry to record such a fee looks like this.

Account	Debits	Credits	Description
Bank charges	$15.00		Record monthly bank charge
Cash		$15.00	Record monthly bank charge

Once you enter the journal entry, you can click Make Recurring and then carry out the following steps:

1. **Assign a template name, such as** Monthly bank fee.

2. **Leave the type set to Scheduled, which is the default.**

3. **Enter 0 (zero) in the Create Days in Advance field.**

4. **Leave the interval set to Monthly on Day. Choose the day of the month that the fee typically is assessed, such as the 15th, and leave Every Months set to 1 (one).**

5. **Choose a starting date for the journal entry from the Start Date field.**

6. **Leave the End Date field set to None if you expect the fee to continue in perpetuity, or set an end date for the transaction.**

I cover more of the ins-and-outs of recurring transactions in Chapter 9.

Entering Petty Cash Expenditures

Petty cash is a small amount of physical currency that you might keep in a drawer to fund coffee runs, tips for the DoorDash driver, a quick run to the office supply store, and other sorts of small expenditures. To fund the petty cash drawer, you can write a check in QuickBooks to Cash that you take to the bank to convert to cash, or you can use an ATM card and enter the transaction as an expense, but rather than choosing an expense account, you choose Petty Cash as the category (account). The purpose of a journal entry is to record the expenditures from the petty cash fund so that your books reflect the amount of cash you physically have on hand.

Here's the behind-the-scenes journal entry to fund the petty cash account.

Account	Debits	Credits	Description
Petty Cash	$100.00		Fund petty cash
Checking		$100.00	Fund petty cash

This entry reduces your checking account by $100 and increases petty cash, another asset account, by $100. Here, then, is what an expenditure journal entry might look like.

Account	Debits	Credits	Description
Meals/Entertainment	$23.48		Starbucks run for Client Z
Office Supplies	$3.74		Emergency purchase of paper clips
Postage	$8.89		Certified mail postage
Petty Cash		$36.11	Record petty cash expenditures

At this point, you hopefully still have $63.89 in your drawer to put toward future petty cash expenditures. If there's a difference, you can adjust the petty cash account in the same fashion as you do a bank account.

Recording a Prepaid Expense

Prepaid expenses apply a similar matching principal to depreciation but typically over a shorter time span. For instance, let's say that you purchase a business owner's insurance policy on January 1, 2025. Your behind-the-scenes journal entry might look like this.

Account	Debits	Credits	Description
Insurance Expense	$1,200.00		Annual insurance premium
Cash		$1,200.00	Annual insurance premium

There's nothing particularly wrong with recognizing all the insurance expense in one month, but it can skew budgeting, and it doesn't match the expense with the associated income from the other 11 months of the year. You might record the entry like this instead.

Account	Debits	Credits	Description
Prepaid Expenses	$1,200.00		Annual insurance premium
Cash		$1,200.00	Annual insurance premium

This entry has no impact on your profit and loss statement, and although it reduces your cash account by $1,200, it also increases an asset account by $1,200. This doesn't mean you need to record such expenses with a journal entry. You can instead use a Check or Expense transaction and then choose Prepaid Expenses instead of Insurance Expense for the category or account. From there, you need to set up a recurring entry to amortize the prepaid expense.

Amortizing a Prepaid Expense

If you've been reading through the other journal entries in this chapter, you probably have a sense of what this entry looks like.

Account	Debits	Credits	Description
Insurance Expense	$100.00		Recognize prepaid insurance
Prepaid Expenses		$100.00	Recognize prepaid insurance

You can set this up as a recurring journal entry in the same way I described the recurring bank fee earlier in this chapter. You do, however, set an end date for such a journal entry so that you start recognizing an expense as an asset that has been fully amortized. Doing so results in a negative asset on your balance sheet and might overstate your monthly expenses.

Maintaining an Allowance for Doubtful Accounts

An allowance for doubtful accounts is an accounting construct by which a business recognizes that some percentage of customers will renege or refuse to pay their invoices due, also known as accounts receivable. Recording an allowance for doubtful accounts can reflect a business reality, but it can also have income tax benefits because the journal entry results in a Bad Debt expense that reduces taxable income. As with accumulated depreciation, the allowance isn't recorded directly against the asset account — in this case, accounts receivable — but rather against a contra account (an offset to another account), such as Allowance for Doubtful Accounts.

The business has $100,000 in accounts receivable, and based on past experience, 5 percent of these unpaid invoices are expected to be written off. A journal entry recognizing this eventual expense looks like this.

Account	Debits	Credits	Description
Bad Debt Expense	$5,000.00		Bad debt allowance
Allowance for Doubtful Accounts		$5,000.00	Bad debt allowance

Just as Accumulated Depreciation is a contra account to any fixed asset accounts you may have, Allowance for Doubtful Accounts is a contra account to Accounts Receivable. If later in the year you decide that conditions have improved and that a 3 percent allowance is sufficient, you can reflect that change with the following journal entry.

Account	Debits	Credits	Description
Allowance for Doubtful Accounts	$2,000.00		Adjust bad debt allowance
Bad Debt Expense		$2,000.00	Adjust bad debt allowance

In this case, the journal entry reduces Allowance for Doubtful Accounts by $2,000, to a new balance of $3,000. Bad Debt Expense is reduced in the same fashion.

Writing Off Bad Debt

Maybe you have a customer who goes out of business before paying your $500 invoice. You can record the following journal entry.

Account	Debits	Credits	Description	Name
Bad Debt Expense	$500.00		Write off invoice	
Accounts Receivable		$500.00	Write off invoice	Defunct Co.

The end result of this entry is that a $500 credit is applied to the customer's account because you can't associate a journal entry with a specific invoice. Thus, this journal entry falls into the arena of "not that you would, but you could." See Chapter 2 for a forms-based approach to writing off bad debt that applies the credit against the invoice that will never be collected.

Posting Depreciation

Depreciation is an accounting concept designed to spread the cost of an asset (such as the cost of a warehouse) over its usual life rather than recognizing it all in one period. Maybe the asset costs $480,000 and has a 40-year useful life. A number of different *generally accepted accounting principles* (often referred to as GAAP) are available for computing depreciation, but in this case, I'm keeping it simple with straight-line depreciation, with which you divide the cost of the asset by its useful life, less any salvage value, which for this example is assumed to be zero. $480,000 divided by 40 years is $12,000 of depreciation per year, or $1,000 of depreciation per month.

The behind-the-scenes journal entry to purchase the building might look like this.

Account	Debits	Credits	Description
Buildings	$480,000.00		Warehouse purchase
Cash		$480,000.00	Warehouse purchase

If you purchased the building on January 1, 2025, you need to record $12,000 of depreciation in calendar 2025. A typical monthly depreciation entry might look something like this.

Account	Debits	Credits	Description
Depreciation Expense	$1,000.00		Record monthly depreciation
Accumulated Depreciation		$1,000.00	Record monthly depreciation

Notice that the offset to the depreciation is an account called Accumulated Depreciation. Because Accumulated Depreciation has a credit balance, on the balance sheet it offsets the Building account. The net difference is known as the *book value of the asset*.

REMEMBER

Book value is an accounting construct that reflects the unamortized value of the asset. Conversely, market value is what you can get if you sell the warehouse to someone else. Your books don't typically reflect the market value of assets you hold. This is a great conversation to have with your accountant if you have questions because numerous theories and strategies can be applied to valuing assets.

TIP

In Chapter 15, I describe how to simplify depreciation expense calculations in Advanced subscribers by way of the Fixed Assets feature.

Chapter 23

Ten Cool Chrome Shortcuts

Keyboard shortcuts can help you fight back against the repetitive and transactional nature of accounting work. In this chapter, I get you started with ten Google Chrome keyboard shortcuts. Chances are pretty good that these shortcuts work in other browsers as well.

TIP

If you're looking for QuickBooks Online keyboard shortcuts, I have you covered at www.dummies.com. Search for *QuickBooks Online For Dummies* to find this book's Cheat Sheet.

TIP

Throughout this chapter, I mention supplemental shortcuts that complement the ten primary shortcuts I've chosen. You can access a complete list of keyboard shortcuts for Chrome at https://support.google.com/chrome/answer/157179.

Speeding Up Surfing

Working on the Internet, and QuickBooks Online specifically, can result in a number of repetitive tasks. Even small tweaks in your browsing habits can have a cumulative effect that results in reclaiming some of your day and minimizing wear and tear on your wrists. In this section, I show you how to save a few keystrokes when typing in web page addresses, and how to see more of your screen when you get to your destination.

Navigating to websites faster

Type a site name, such as **intuit**, in the address bar and then press Ctrl+Enter to automatically add www. and .com to the beginning and end, respectively, and navigate to that site.

REMEMBER

This technique works only for primary domains, like www.intuit.com. You can't navigate to https://qbo.intuit.com in this manner because the site's address is qbo.intuit.com versus www.qbo.intuit.com.

Toggling full-screen mode

Chrome's full-screen mode means two different things depending on which operating system you're using:

>> **Windows:** Press F11 to toggle the tabs, address bar, and bookmarks bar on or off.

>> **macOS:** Press Ctrl+Cmd+F to expand or contract the size of a Chrome window. This action does not affect tabs, the address bar, or bookmarks bar.

REMEMBER

QuickBooks Online Advanced and Accountant users can download and install the QuickBooks Online desktop app, which also enables you to log in to multiple companies at once if all are associated with the same Intuit account. See Chapter 13 for more details.

Accessing Downloads and History

You can access reports and files that you download via the Downloads button in the toolbar to the right of the address bar. A card appears on screen for a brief period after each download. In this section, you find out how to easily access your downloads and history.

Displaying the Downloads page

Press Ctrl+J (or Cmd+Shift+J in macOS) to display the Downloads page in a new tab. This provides easy access to reports that you've recently exported to Microsoft Excel from QuickBooks Online.

TIP

Press the Tab key twice to navigate to the first download. You can then use the Down Arrow key to navigate through the Downloads list. Press Enter in Windows to open a download or use your mouse to click Show in Folder. In macOS, press Enter to download the file again or click Show in Finder with your mouse to open the corresponding folder.

All reports that you export from QuickBooks will appear in your Downloads folder unless you carry out the following steps:

1. **Choose the Chrome menu ⇨ Settings ⇨ Downloads.**

2. **Toggle the Ask Where to Save Each File Before Downloading setting on.**

3. **Press Ctrl+W (or Cmd+W in macOS) to close the Settings page or close the browser tab.**

   Going forward, a Save As dialog box will enable you to choose the location and name for the file that you are saving.

Displaying the History page

Press Ctrl+H (or Cmd+Y in macOS) to display the History page. Press the Tab key four times to navigate to the first link in the list. You can use the Down Arrow key to move through the list. When you get to the page you want to open, press Enter to open the link in the current tab, which replaces the History page.

Working with Tabs

Every bit of information you consume on the Internet appears in tabs within your browser. In this section, I show you several ways to maximize your use of tabs.

Opening and activating a new tab

Press Ctrl+T (or Cmd+T in macOS) to create and activate a new browser tab. Your cursor is placed in the address bar, ready for you to type a web address, often referred to as an URL (uniform resource locator).

REMEMBER

Press Ctrl+N (or Cmd+N in macOS) to create a new tab in a separate window. You can press Ctrl+Shift+Tab (or Cmd+Option+Left Arrow in macOS) to activate another tab in the current window, but you need to press Ctrl+Tab (or Cmd+` in macOS) to switch between windows. (That backward apostrophe is known as the *grave* symbol and shares space with the ~ key just below the Esc key on your keyboard.)

Closing the current tab

Press Ctrl+W (or Cmd+W in macOS) to close the current tab. If you have only a single tab open, your Chrome window closes as well. When you have multiple tabs open in the window, only the active tab closes. Use Ctrl+Shift+W (or Cmd+Shift+W in macOS) to close the current window, which will close all open tabs.

TIP

If you bump yourself out of QuickBooks by closing the wrong browser tab, simply display the History page and then choose the first QuickBooks link on the list to pick up immediately where you left off.

Saving open tabs as a bookmark group

Press Ctrl+Shift+D (or Cmd+Shift+D in macOS) to create a new folder with bookmarks to your current set of open tabs. This is a great way to remember your place when carrying out a research project that involves multiple web pages. You can also press Ctrl+D (or Cmd+D in macOS) to create a bookmark for the currently open tab.

Opening your home page in the current tab

Press Alt+Home (or Cmd+Shift+H in macOS) to open your home page in the current tab. If this doesn't work when you first try it, you may need to enable the Home Page feature by using these steps:

1. **Choose Chrome Menu ⇨ Settings ⇨ Appearance.**

2. **Toggle the Show Home Button on and then specify a home page, such as `https://qbo.intuit.com`, to display the login page for QuickBooks Online.**

Activating a specific tab

Press Ctrl+1 (or Cmd+1 in macOS) to activate the first tab in your Chrome window. You can use 1 through 8 to access the first eight tabs. Ctrl+9 (or Cmd+9 in macOS) activates the last open tab, so if you have ten open tabs, you can't jump directly to the ninth tab.

REMEMBER

You can press Alt+Left Arrow (or Cmd+Option+Left Arrow in macOS) to navigate one tab to the left or use Alt+Right Arrow (or Cmd+Option+Right Arrow in macOS) to move one tab to the right.

Creating a tab in a new profile

Press Ctrl+Shift+M (or Cmd+Shift+M in macOS) to choose a different profile and create a new Chrome window, which in turn enables you to log in to an additional QuickBooks Online company at the same time.

TIP

Press Alt+Tab (or Ctrl+Left Arrow/Ctrl+Right Arrow in macOS) to switch between windows. Speaking of Windows, Ctrl+Tab allows you to switch between open windows *within* applications like Microsoft Excel. In macOS, Ctrl+Tab switches you between open applications.

Index

About the Author

David Ringstrom, CPA, is the president of Accounting Advisors, Inc., an Atlanta-based spreadsheet consulting and training firm he started in 1991. David helps his clients streamline repetitive business processes and teaches scores of live webinars each year. He also owns Students Excel, an online service that helps accounting professors teach Excel more effectively. Over his career, David has written hundreds of freelance articles about spreadsheets and accounting software, some of which have been published internationally. He has served as the technical editor for more than three dozen books, including *QuickBooks Desktop For Dummies*, *Quicken For Dummies*, and *Peachtree For Dummies*, and he's the author or coauthor of seven books, including *Idiot's Guide to Introductory Accounting* and *Exploring Microsoft Excel's Hidden Treasures*. David's next book will be *Microsoft 365 Excel for Dummies*.

He resides in in Atlanta, Georgia with his children, Rachel and Lucas.

Author's Acknowledgments

I want to thank Jamie Lloyd for his invaluable support with technical aspects of this book, as well as Debra Kahraman for her steadfast encouragement during the writing process itself. As always, I extend my gratitude to the entire Wiley team for their efforts in bringing this book to life. Special thanks to Dan DeLong, the extraordinary technical editor whose suggestions have made all five of my editions of *QuickBooks Online For Dummies* better. Thanks also to Kezia Endsley, who served as the project editor for this edition.

Publisher's Acknowledgments

Executive Editor: Lindsay Lefevere

Project/Copy Editor: Kezia Endsley

Technical Editor: Dan DeLong

Production Editor: Saikarthick Kumarasamy

Cover Image: © mavo/Shutterstock